Theodore Roosevelt

THE WAYFARER'S LIBRARY

The PILLARS OF SOCIETY

A. G. Gardiner

LONDON & TORONTO: J. M. DENT & SONS, LTD.
NEW YORK: E. P. DUTTON & Co.

TO

MY WIFE

A

PREFACE TO POPULAR EDITION

This volume is the second in order of three dealing with personality in public affairs. The first, *Prophets, Priests, and Kings,* approached the subject from the point of view of events after the memorable election of 1906; the second dealt with it in the light of the great struggle which began with the Budget of 1909 and culminated in the battle for Home Rule in 1914; the third, *The War Lords,* discussed it in relation to the European catastrophe. Three of the subjects touched in this book appeared also in *Prophets, Priests, and Kings,* but the author felt justified in returning to them in view of the large part they had played in affairs in the interval. The book was first published before the outbreak of the European war. That event has brought many of the personalities dealt with in these pages into a fiercer light and into new relations with the public. Lord Kitchener has found the task which is to test the "Kitchener legend"; Lord Fisher no longer walks the greensward in front of the figure-head of the old *Calcutta,* but is once more on the ship in the midst of the greatest storm that has ever beat upon our coasts; Mr. Asquith faces the hosts of Germany instead of those of Ulster; Mr. Churchill has "written his name in blood" in the Dardanelles, and is now on the battlefield himself; Mr. Lloyd George is turning the nation into a munitions factory instead of financing social reform; Mr. Belloc has temporarily forgotten the misdemeanours of Jew and Puritan in his brilliant elucidation of the strategy of the war; Sir John Simon has left the primrose path and gone out into the wilderness; Mr. Bonar Law has risen to the great argument of the war with a simplicity and a devotion that have blotted out the memory of "the new style"; Sir F. E. Smith, "galloper" no longer, fills the solemn office of Attorney-General—indeed, hardly any one mentioned in this book has escaped some part in the convulsion that has changed the outlook, the hopes, and, in some measure, the opinions of all of us. To reshape the sketches in the light of the great catastrophe that has befallen the world would have been to falsify the point of view. They are left, therefore, practically in their original state, and must be read as estimates of men made before the ordeal of the war had subjected them to the most searching test of character and capacity that has been applied to statesmen and soldiers since the Napoleonic wars. Two of the subjects dealt with—Mr. Joseph Chamberlain and Lord Strathcona—have died since the book originally appeared.

March 1916.

CONTENTS

PILLARS OF SOCIETY

KING GEORGE V

THE governing fact about King George is that he is a sailor. He was trained not for a throne, but for the quarter-deck of a battleship. During those formative years, when most boys are playing cricket and conjugating *amo* ashore, he was tossing about the Seven Seas, swarming up the yardarm or stoking the fire, calling at strange ports in far-off lands, learning the rough lessons of the sea, and sharing the wholesome comradeship of plain men. It was a hard school; but no king ever had a better. It brought him face to face with realities. He saw the meaning of duty and discipline, learned to respect those who labour with their hands, and entered into the life of the common people.

He owes this advantage to the fact that he had the good fortune not to be born the heir to the throne. He escaped the artificial training of monarchs in the making. His father's childhood had been a torture. He was surrounded by "influences" and by ponderous and learned souls. He received long written explanations from his father and mother on the minutest matters of conduct. He was watched day and night, haunted by guardians and tutors, was not allowed to read novels—not even Sir Walter—and did not play, for he had no play-fellows. His father held that the heir-apparent must be kept aloof from his future subjects, and must be preserved " from the contaminating influence of boys less carefully trained " than himself. Throughout his boyhood and youth the young Prince's life was darkened by a tyrannical affection which confined him in a gilded cage, chafed him with a thousand fatuous restraints, and deafened him with lessons and exhortations. His whole pleasure-loving career was a comment on that mistaken training.

In the same way, King George's tastes are a comment on the more wholesome atmosphere which surrounded his childhood and youth. He is not the first English King to belong to the middle classes. George III. was entirely middle class. But he is the first English King to belong to the working classes by the bond of a common experience. He moves among them not as a stranger from some starry social sphere, but as one to the manner born. He has reefed the sail and swabbed the deck and fed the fire. He has stood at the helm through the tempest and the night. He knows what it is to be grimy and perspiring, to have blistered hands and tired feet. In short, he knows what it is to be a working man. It is his unique merit as a king. When he goes down to Cornwall he dons the overalls of the miner, descends the pit, and explores the workings of the mine. When he is in Lancashire he goes through the mills and the foundries, looking at the machinery with the eye of a mechanic and rubbing shoulders with the operatives in the spirit of a fellow-workman. He visits the racecourse perfunctorily. It is a part of the traditional business of his calling, and he is not the man to shirk what he conceives to be a duty. But when he wants a really enjoyable day he spends it among the people, at some place like the General Post Office, or the British Museum, or the Radium Institute, or the Garden Suburb.

There is no affectation in this. It is true that he is anxious to win the goodwill of the people, and that he knows he has not his father's genial road to their hearts. But his comradeship with the common people is not an elaborate pretence to gain an end. It springs from a genuine fellow-feeling. It is the heritage of his long apprenticeship to the sea. And it carries with it the thirst of the practical artificer to know "how it is done." He has the mechanic's interest in the machinery of things, and one learns without surprise that his presents to his children are largely mechanical toys.

There is another phase of his character which is the product of his upbringing. He is the first King of Greater Britain. His father's orbit was the Continent, and the foci of his orbit were the courts of Europe. High politics, ceremonies, and acts of grace were the things that filled his official life. He knew Paris as intimately as a Cook's guide, talked German better than he talked English, fled to the Continent whenever he wanted amusement. King George is "All British." We boast of the Empire on which the sun never sets, but until now we have never had a King who had seen the Empire. King George knows it probably as well as any man of his time. It is not a splash of colour on the map, but a reality translated into terms of city and plain, mountain, veldt, and prairie, with the heaving seas between. Here he opened a Parliament, there he commanded a ship, every place he associates with some vital memory of men and things. This knowledge colours his whole outlook. Just as surely as his father found his interest on the Continent, so King George is fascinated by the vision of the Britain that he has seen growing up overseas. King Edward belonged to the old world; King George to the new.

There is loss as well as gain in this. King Edward was singularly free from the vice of insularity. He was cosmopolitan in the best sense of that unpleasant word. He had no narrow racial prejudices, was equally at home in all company, had that note of human freemasonry which makes one indifferent to whether men are Latin or Teuton, Slav or Celt, Jew or Gentile. Perhaps, indeed, his circle was a little too heterogeneous. Certainly it was more than a little too much confined to wealthy men of a certain race.

In all this King George is the antithesis of his father. At a recent exhibition of Max Beerbohm's caricatures there was one delightful drawing that never failed to evoke a gust of laughter. It pictured a group of four distinguished friends of King Edward, men of vast wealth and influence, marching in Indian file, with doubtful and expectant faces. Underneath was the legend, " Are we as welcome as we were? " There is no doubt about the answer. They are not. King George's tastes are simple and commonplace. His father was Sybaritic; he is almost Spartan. He is constitutionally a man of plain and moderate appetites, and his life at sea emphasised his constitutional tendency. He is neither *gourmand* nor *gourmet*. The cruel slander about over-indulgence in drink was singularly wide of the mark in regard to one who is physically as well as temperamentally inclined to asceticism. His father belonged to the *ancien régime*—to the tradition of the " good livers " and three-bottle men. King George in this, as in so many other respects, is more akin to the modern man who drinks Apollinaris and puts soda-water in his claret.

But King Edward's cosmopolitanism saved him from one peril which besets those whose thoughts dwell exclusively on the Empire. He was never a Jingo. The presence of " foreigners " on the earth offered no puzzle to his understanding. They were a fact to be accepted, not a nuisance to be suppressed. He was proud of the Empire with a wholesome pride; but one could not conceive him declaiming with Mr. Kipling, " What do they know of England who only England know? " In a word, he was big enough to be a Little Englander, by which I mean that he knew that if England was sound at the heart it would be sound at the extremities, and that freedom was the talisman of empire. King George's training threatened to lead him astray here. He was captured by the tawdry Imperialism of the nineties. The Jameson Raid was a misfortune because "we had gone off at half-cock; next time we would make surer work." We did, at an infinite cost of blood and treasure. But the result was not quite what was expected, and when King George came to the throne General Botha, the commander of the foe in the Boer War, was present at the Coronation as the Premier of a loyal and free South Africa. The lesson of that great episode, coupled with the teaching of his father and the collapse of Imperial Preference, has not been lost on King George. His enthusiasm for the overseas dominions remains; but it is purged of its youthful crudeness. He sees that an enduring Empire is not an artificial, but a natural growth, springing out of the soil of free institutions; that true Imperialism is a spiritual sympathy more than a material bondage. George III. threw away the greatest jewel of the Empire at the bidding of a false and harsh Imperialism. It is for George V. to make amends, and, under the advice of his Ministers, to consolidate the splendid fabric of the Empire on the principle of an unfettered confederation of free peoples, held together by common ties of blood, religion, speech, literature, tradition, and love of liberty.

That he is capable of penetrating the crust of officialism and probing to the heart of central truths was shown when, on his return from India in 1906, he used these significant words in a speech at the Guildhall:

> "I cannot help thinking, from all I have heard and seen, that the task of governing India will be made all the easier if, on our part, we infuse into it a wider element of sympathy. I predict that to such sympathy there will be an ever-abundant and genuine response."

The speeches of kings are ordinarily so swathed in the cotton-wool of conventional phrases that when a plain word like this leaps out it has the effect of a blow. It was a blow that was and is needed. The disease of an arrogant contempt for the Indian had entered into our public-school administration of that country. The King saw it, as everybody with open eyes saw it, and he said so in unmistakable words. And the effect was instantaneous. I have been told by a distinguished Indian member of the Viceroy's council that as the result of that speech a marked and happy change came over the attitude of the Anglo-Indian towards the Indian. So powerful still is the plain truth spoken from a high place.

The King has, indeed, the frankness of the sailor much more than the restraint of the monarch. His father was all diplomacy. People rarely spoke of him without using the word " tact "—that last refuge of verbal bankruptcy. Let us rejoice that it has now been decently buried. No one accuses King George of " tact." Like Mr. Biglow's candidate, he is naturally

> " A plain-spoken kind o' creetur
> Thet blurts right out wut's in his head."

One might even continue the parallel further, and say that

> " Ef he's one pecoolar feetur
> It is a nose that wunt be led."

For he is as firm in his opinions as he is emphatic in their expression. His father was little burdened with political prejudices. His temperament was that of the diplomatist rather than that of the politician. He was the smoother of differences, and sought to create an atmosphere in which all disagreements were reconciled, and black and white were merged in grey. King George has a simpler, less equivocal mind. He sees black and white in sharp contrast, and it is not easy for him to conceal his views under the mask of neutrality. He feels keenly, and wears a mask with difficulty. But, like most frank natures, he is responsive to eager and forceful personalities, and Mr. Chamberlain and Mr. Lloyd George have in turn made a deep impression upon him. He has the love of the direct mind for the man who is forging straight ahead for a definite port. He is disposed to think that the port must be right if the captain is driving there confidently under a full head of steam.

There is, in short, no subtlety or cunning in his intellectual composition. It is the mind of the seaman, whose problems are the problems of facts and not of psychology or casuistry or compromise. And his tastes and pleasures are the seaman's too. He loves his home with an antiquated passion that would fill Mr. Bernard Shaw's soul with loathing. Courts are not commonly the scene of happy domesticities. Family life, which needs fresh air and freedom, struggles vainly in that hot-house atmosphere of ceremonies, formalities, and official friendships, where intrigues and back-stair influences flourish luxuriantly. But King George in this matter, as in so many others, including personal appearance, strongly resembles his cousin, the Tsar of Russia. And he has been singularly happy in his marriage.

The Queen, like her husband, has the middle-class seriousness and sense of duty. She is almost the only woman in society who cannot be called "a society woman." Her manner is entirely free from the assertiveness which is the note of modern breeding. She speaks little, and without persiflage, irony, or any of the qualities most cultivated in drawing-rooms. The mother who, hearing the King speak, regretted that she had sent her daughter to an expensive boarding-school to catch the authentic note of the aristocracy when, after all, the King himself spoke "just like an ordinary man," would have suffered a double measure of regret if she had heard the quiet, unaffected speech of the Queen. She was trained in an old tradition of womanhood, and has the air and interests of the mid-Victorian time rather than those of to-day. When with the present Bishop of Birmingham I had the duty of showing her round the Sweated Industries Exhibition held at the Queen's Hall, I was impressed by the quiet thoroughness of her inquiry. She had obviously not come to see or to be seen, but to learn a lesson, and one could not fail to notice her plain sincerity, and her avoidance of those futile affectations of sympathy which are at once so banal and so popular. She left a clear impression of a real woman, with a grave bearing and no false sentiment. When she pats an orphan on the head or gives sixpence to a beggar I do not think she would want half a column of laudation in the newspapers to commemorate the fact that she shares the common sympathies of humanity.

The influence of her steady, prosic personality upon the King has been eminently good, and the happiness of their home life is a commonplace. Perhaps the Court is less gay than it used to be, for the Queen prefers knitting to ceremony, and the King likes a book better than bridge, and his children better than either. When one of the boys was asked whether he loved his mother or father the more he replied, "Well, dada spoils me most." But what the Court has lost in gaiety it has gained in many more substantial ways, not least in the matter of public respect. It was the home life of George III. which made him possible in spite of his mischievous policy. There was a certain truth in the saying of the wit that "the people would never desert him so long as he went to church every Sunday and was faithful to the plainest woman in the kingdom." King George's attachment to his home is not the least of his assets in his account with his people.

It is not surprising that he felt with such bitterness the slander on that home. For years it had been said that as a youth he had contracted a marriage at Malta. At first the lady was a daughter of an Admiral Tryon, and when it was discovered that Admiral Tryon hadn't a daughter she became the daughter of an Admiral Seymour. The story was a wicked invention, but that did not prevent its being widely believed. The backwoods and the bush knew all about it, and the American papers could even show you the "marriage lines." Everywhere you met people who knew the lady, or had an aunt who knew her aunt, or had lunched with someone who lived in the same street and saw her pass every day with a pale face and a poodle. The slander was denied, but what of that? Virtue can be soiled with a breath; but scandal is a tougher growth. As Falstaff said of the camomile, the more it is trodden on the better it grows. King Edward would have taken it all in the day's work. Scandal ran off him like water off a duck's back. "They say! What say they? Let them say." He would have lit another cigar, cocked his hat at a sporting angle, and passed on his way beaming. He took the comedy view of life. King George is a man of different mettle—serious in mind and combative in spirit, one who does not take things lying down. He leapt at the throat of the slander. Defiant of advice and of the headshakings of the public, he dragged the thing into court, and like all lies, it fell dead in the light. There was never a more complete exposure, and the incident gave the public the first real glimpse of the man. It liked the glimpse. And those who had believed or half-believed the tale felt ashamed of their credulity. The dragon will give King George a wide berth in future.

Æsthetically, as in all else, he belongs to the common people. Apart from shooting, in which he excels, he has few sporting passions. Games of chance make no appeal to him, and his hobby of stamp-collecting is eminently middle class. Music and drama touch him only on the recreative side, and he prefers them both in old-fashioned and obvious forms. The modern problem-play leaves him cold, and Wagner bores him. He is not what Johnson would call "a clubbable man," and his friendships are few but firm. It is said that when he was asked to be president of a new service club in contemplation some years ago he replied, "Oh yes, but don't you think the Army and Navy could get on without another club?" And the question, with its blunt rebuke, struck the idea dead.

A plain, direct, straight-speaking man, taking his office seriously, hating display and flummery, governed by a strong sense of duty, thoroughly obedient to the constitutional tradition of the monarchy, King George V. has the prospect of a long and happy association with his people. He is neither a brilliant man, nor an eccentric. He represents the average intelligence, the traditional view, and the plain man's respect for authority, whether in morals or statecraft. His limitations are his merits, for the virtues of a modern monarch should be negative and official. The Vicar of Wakefield tells us that he "chose his wife, as she did her wedding gown, not for a fine glossy surface, but for such qualities as wear well." We may say the same of the King. The surface is unpretentious; but the material is made for wear.

LORD KITCHENER

It was at a reception to Mr. Roosevelt that I met Lord Kitchener. No stranger contrast of personality could be conceived than that furnished by these two famous men—the one shaking hands with everybody, at home with everybody; the other stiff, silent, formidable. He came into the room like the Day of Judgment, searching, implacable. His face wore the burnished livery of the Indian sun, his eyes beneath the straight, heavy eyebrows roved with cold, slow scrutiny over the crowd of fashionable people who ceased their chattering and made way for him. One eager lady stepped forward. "Oh, may I have the honour of shaking hands with Lord Kitchener?" He looked down upon her from his great height in stony silence, shook hands, and passed on. A distinguished novelist barred the way. "May I have the pleasure? I am So and So," mentioning a name as familiar as Lord Kitchener's own. The soldier looked at him as though he had never heard of such a person, took the offered hand, and again passed on.

If, as Emerson says, manners are invented to keep fools at a distance, Lord Kitchener is in a class of manners by himself; but he is not a cheerful figure in a drawing-room. A pillar of ice could not lower the temperature more completely. At his coming the idle chatter is silenced as the birds are silenced at the oncoming of a storm. Tried by the test of O'Connell, he might on a superficial survey be taken as the most representative Englishman of his time—for though he was born not far from O'Connell's own birthplace he is entirely English by race and upbringing. "The

Englishman," said O'Connell, " has all the qualities of the poker, except its occasional warmth." There are those who know that Lord Kitchener has his moments of warmth and laughter, and one person has been at pains to collect good stories about him. They are not very mirthful stories. The nearest approach to humour in them was his reply to a request to talk on the telephone to a notoriously hard-swearing general in South Africa—" I will not talk to him on the telephone; he would fuse the wire." It is not much on which to build a reputation for gaiety. I speak, of course, of Lord Kitchener as he appears to a public view. In private he is genial and even talkative, and at the dinner-table he is an excellent companion, and never more at home than when, as I have seen him, he has a Frenchman on either hand, for he talks French with unusual ease and fluency.

His gift of silence in public is one of the secrets of his power over the crowd. Lord Charles Beresford was taken seriously as a sailor until he took himself seriously as a prophet. The public forgives loquacity in a politician; but it likes its men of action to talk in monosyllables. It believes that stillness is the mark of strength. Skilfully used, silence will make dullness itself seem learned. Irving had that gift in a marked degree. When the conversation travelled beyond the narrow limits of his knowledge he fell into an eloquent silence, which seemed charged with the most shattering criticisms that he left chivalrously unspoken. Lord Kitchener's silence is not designed for effect: it springs from a solitary and self-reliant mind, indifferent alike to attack or applause, fixed only on the task in hand. He offers neither explanations nor defences, and he does not argue, which is a tiresome business: he tells you. What he has done he has done. If you like it, well; if you don't like it, that is your affair. He would think as little of placating public opinion as Coriolanus thought of flattering the mob. Even if he is found out he does not trouble. When on resigning his command in India he made a farewell speech, it was discovered that it was a flagrant plagiarism of the farewell speech delivered four years before by Lord Curzon, altered to suit the new circumstances and spoiled in the stealing. He had, no doubt, been the victim of an idle underling, who thought he could not improve on Lord Curzon's prose style, and forgot, as Disraeli once forgot in similar circumstances, that men have memories. Lord Kitchener neither apologised nor explained. And no one thought the worse of him. I am not sure that they did not think better of him, as a blunt soldier who took the idle rubbish of speech from any heap that was handy.

He lives in deeds, not words. No one of his time has at once said so little and done so much. Nor has anyone of his time gone farther with more entire reliance on his own merits and more complete scorn of the arts of advertisement. It cannot even be said that he owes his success to an electric personality or to an indisputable genius. It is true that his presence gives the sense of security and power. There is about him something of the quality of General Kléber, of whom it was said that it made men brave to look at him. If he does not make you feel brave at least he makes you feel strong. But he has not the magic that Napoleon exercised over the minds of men, nor the apocalyptic fervour with which Cromwell fired them, nor the swift instinct by which Charles XII. assured them of victory. His mind is slow and ponderous; but it gives the impression of moving with the mass and the certainty of the Nasmyth hammer. Perhaps the man of genius would crack the nut without the hammer. But at all events Kitchener does crack the nut. He belongs to the school of Wellington or Grant more than to the school of Napoleon or Lee. He will "fight it out on that line if it takes all summer." He has the patience of Torres Vedras rather than the swift inspiration of Austerlitz. His merit, in short, is for organisation rather than for battle. He is not a great warrior, but, like Carnot or Moltke, a great organiser of victory, and he belongs therefore to the new rather than the old tradition of warfare. Both in Egypt and in South Africa his record was that of the engineer, slowly sapping and mining the fastnesses of the enemy, here building a railway to penetrate the desert, there carrying out a vast scheme of block-houses to round up the Boers—striking only when his schemes were complete and the hour had struck. It is not by his battles that he will take high rank among commanders. Neither Omdurman nor Paardeberg was a military exploit of high quality. It is as the business man of war—cold, calculating, merciless, moving without pity or passion to his goal—that he will have an enduring place in history.

Some men say that he is cruel. But he is only cruel in the sense that he is engaged in a cruel game which has no place for the humanities. You cannot afford to have a kind heart when you go out to kill men. He believes in Lord Fisher's "Three R's of War"—Ruthless, Relentless, Remorseless. Roberts' failure after Paardeberg was due to his horror at the sacrifice of life, and his determination to wait for surrender rather than shed more blood. Kitchener has no such qualms, and there have been many incidents which show his indifference to sacrifice when he thinks the sacrifice necessary. His message to poor Hannay at Paardeberg is a case in point. It had the same quality of ruthlessness that Stonewall Jackson displayed when one of his officers pointed out that a certain instruction meant the total annihilation of his men, and he replied, "Colonel, I always make it a rule to attend to my wounded and bury my dead. You have heard the instruction. Go!" With Grant at the Bloody Angle he would have lit another cigar and poured more men into that pit of carnage. If he could not have beaten Lee by generalship he would have beaten him, as Grant beat him, by sheer destruction of life. He is not cruel, but he is without compassion. He keeps his eye on the end, and steels his heart against the tugs of pity. To him soldiering is not a profession; it is a religion. Solitary, without home ties, living his life in strange lands, he wears himself the hair shirt, not of the mystic but of the martinet. And he insists on the same hard regimen for others. He would have no married officers with him in the Soudan, nor would he allow his staff to go to Cairo for the dissipations of the season. So in South Africa, he refused to let any of his officers be joined by their wives in Pretoria. Is it not enough to be a soldier? What have you to do with wife or kindred? He has no tenderness for the tainted wethers of the flock. If a man falls ill once, he is suspect; twice, he is condemned. He is told that someone has sunstroke. "Sunstroke! What the devil does he mean by having sunstroke?" He is a harsh taskmaster; but he is obeyed. "How long will this take you?" he asks one to whom he has given a military operation. "Twelve days." "You must do it in six." It is done in five. It is easy to over-praise this hardness and to attribute a god-like magic to it. Even soldiers are human, and the greatest generals have been those who, among their other qualities, included the normal sympathies of the normal man. The blots on his name are the blots of a merciless purpose. He burned the farms of the Boers and poured the women and children into the deadly concentration camps. He desecrated the grave of the Mahdi and threw the head of the "prophet" into the river lest his grave should become a shrine and the seed of future rebellion. It is the iron hand without the velvet glove.

His probity is splendid. No army ever had such a cleansing fire. Corruption, jobbery, intrigue flee before him. While he was in South Africa the contractor was held in an iron grasp. It was only when he left for India that the infamous tale of plunder, exposed by the War Stores Commission, began. In India he found the Army overrun with the friends of the friends of some powerful personage—not infrequently a lady. He swept the stables clean. It used to be said that the home-coming ships were filled with the rubbish that he had ruthlessly discarded. His fidelity to the public interest has made him the most economical general of his time. After his conquest of the Soudan, Lord Salisbury said of him that he was the only general who had fought a campaign for less—£300,000 less—than he promised to fight it for. And Lord Cromer declared that if he had not been one of the first generals of the world he would have been one of the first Chancellors of the Exchequer.

He has never exploited himself, never appealed to the mob, or uttered a word that bore on politics. When he returned from India, after his tour of the world, the Tory Press hailed him as the deliverer. He was to be the scourge of a miserable Government. Never was there a greater disappointment. He came silent, enigmatic, and so remained. He is not the man to be made the catspaw of parties. But within his own sphere his will is iron. On that will he broke Lord Curzon. There have been few personal conflicts in our time so dramatic as that in which the masterful purpose of Kitchener and the pride of Curzon came to grips before the judgment-seat of Lord Midleton. On the issue itself I still think that Lord Curzon was right. He stood for the civil control of the Army, and was fundamentally right. Rarely has a timid judge been called upon to decide between such foes. Lord Midleton's mind swayed to and fro between the fear of incurring the wrath of the one or the resignation of the other. Finally, he decided for the soldier. Lord Curzon resigned, and came back with the bitterness, not of having been beaten by a foeman worthy of his steel, but of having been sentenced by such a judge. " God may forgive him," he is said to have exclaimed, " but I never will."

Not less significant of the man was that memorable scene at Fashoda, when he met Major Marchand, and war between England and France seemed imminent. Marchand has recorded the dialogue — one of the great dialogues of history, so polite, so diplomatic, so fraught with immense consequences. The French flag floated over the fort; but the Egyptian flag must fly in its place. So said the Sirdar. The Major was firm; the Sirdar firm also. Beneath the politeness was the clash of two nations, and war trembled in the balance. The conversation ended with a whisky and soda—and the Egyptian flag floats over the fort of Fashoda.

Egypt, that land of mysteries over which the Sphinx looks out with inscrutable and immemorial calm, is the proper home of this silent, sphinx-like man. It was there that he got his foot on the ladder. He left Palestine, where he had been working for the Exploration Fund, and offered himself for the new Egyptian cavalry. It is one of the little ironies of history that he was nearly rejected because he rode so badly. But for a complacent examiner he would have remained in the backwater of the Engineers, waiting for a pension and a green old age. It is a comment on the futility of little tests. And it is in Egypt that his most enduring work has been done. He found the Egyptian troops " splendid soldiers if only they would not run away." He taught them not to run away. With them he won back the Soudan and brought peace and the railway into the desert. And now, a soldier no more, he rules the land of the Pharaohs and awaits his next task. Let us hope it will not be a task involving the shedding of blood, but his much more proper task of reorganising the Army at home as he reorganised the Army in India. Whatever it be, "the Kitchener legend" will stand him in good stead. There is no doubt a good deal of falsity about that legend. It is built on an Oriental foundation and out of an exercise of autocratic power which, however admirable when applied to subject peoples, might be found a little less admirable when applied nearer home. But in an emergency it would have its value, even if we had to smash the legend afterwards. For in war, the first essential is confidence, and Lord Kitchener communicates that quality in rare measure. When his task, whatever it be, is done, he will be able to pass from the stage to his Canterbury home and his blue and white china, leaving behind him a tradition of duty and of faithfulness not easily paralleled.

MR. ROOSEVELT

Mr. Roosevelt has made more noise in the world than any man of his time. He is a megaphone whose very whisper sounds like hoarse thunder, and when he shouts, which not frequently happens, he is heard all round the seven seas. We know him as we know Punch and Judy—by the thwack of his blows, the crack in his voice, the gleam of his teeth. His smile has become a legend, like the fatness of Falstaff or the squint of Wilkes. His huge laughter comes to us like a gale from the West; his jokes, his insults, his platitudes are as familiar as the latest jingle from the Gaiety. He is the lion comique on the world's stage, and when he roars we hold our sides and revel in his quips. "We've beaten them to a frazzle," he shouts when he is backing Mr. Taft, and the word delights two worlds. "My hat's in the ring," he cries when he comes out to destroy his old friend, and the hemispheres prepare to enjoy the spectacle of the Two Macs chasing each other round the ropes with shouts and blows. He is the Playboy of the Western World, rough, boisterous, rollicking, sending his barbaric yawp over the roof of the world.

No man ever carried the arts of the demagogue so far or achieved so much by them. The newspapers may rage against him, the Machine may work to overthrow him. He shouts them all down, and wins by sheer high spirits and effrontery. "Boys, I have had a bully time," he says to the reporters who crowd around him, and the great heart of America throbs to that note of democracy. "Good old Teddy," shouts the crowd as his train comes to a standstill on his whirlwind campaigns. "Bully for you," replies "Teddy," and the victory is won. What can William H. Taft or William J. Bryan do against a man who is known from the Bowery to the Golden Horn as Teddy? The first essential of a politician is that he shall have a sobriquet —" Pam " or Dizzy," the " Grand Old Man," or " Joe." If you cannot be translated into term of familiarity you have missed your vocation; you are not a man, but a shadow of a name. Mr. Lloyd George is almost the only example of a great popular figure who has never achieved a nickname, and even he would have done better if he had been known as " Little David " or " The Bantam."

> " Then you can call me ' Timbertoes '—thet's wut the people likes,"

said Mr. Birdofredum Sawin when putting up for Congress, and I cannot doubt that " Old Timbertoes " got in. Mr. Roosevelt has the Timbertoes trick to perfection. " By George! I am dee-lighted," is his universal welcome, and the expletive, prim enough for New England and jovial enough for the West, establishes him as the man of the people—frank, cordial, honest as the day, and not " too bright and good for human nature's daily food." He is the man

> " Who hails you Tom or Jack,
> And proves by thumping on your back
> How he esteems your merit."

And if, on the other hand, he calls men liars, and invents the " Ananias Club," to which he consigns Senator Tillman and anyone who happens to stand in his way—well, that only shows what a blunt straight-spoken fellow he is, and how thoroughly he may be trusted. And there is a breezy good-humour even about his brutalities that almost redeems them. " The editor of your paper," he said to a reporter who called to interview him, " is an infamous scoundrel and an unmitigated liar. Yes, sir, that's what he is; but I know you can't help it. All heaven and earth couldn't keep him from being what he is. Be good enough to tell him I said this. Now blaze away and I'll do the best I can for you."

In all this ebullience there is not only the candour of a singularly crude mind, but the astuteness of the most skilful electioneerer America has produced. "There," said President Cleveland long ago, pointing to Civil Service Commissioner Roosevelt as he was leaving the White House—"there goes the best politician in Washington." He is the best politician because he is the best exploiter of himself. The game of politics is a crude business anywhere. It requires a certain coarseness of fibre, a hardness of integument, that make it no fit affair for a man of sensitive mind. No saint would ever succeed in politics. In America they require the qualities of the intellectual "bruiser." The politician must emerge, as Mr. Frank Slavin or Mr. Jack Johnson emerged, by "laying out" his opponents with ruthless blows. In that vast land, with its enormous vitality, its unassimilated millions of alien peoples, its lack of tradition, its unexampled wealth, its political freedom, and its economic slavery, politics are raw, violent, emotional. Beneath the thin crust of an effete constitution there boils a mighty lake of lava that will one day submerge the land. It is a people crying out for a deliverer. And its ear is caught by the stentorian tones, the great laugh, and the bluff blows of Theodore Roosevelt. It hears him denounce the Trusts that oppress it, it sees him defy the caucus that controls its politics, it listens to his denunciation of the "Wealthy Criminal Class," and it turns to him as its Moses. It is true that he has had two terms at the White House and has done nothing to redeem his promises. But what of that? He tunes his key to a higher pitch, and crashes into the fight with his bare fists, confident that the mob will follow the noisiest lead. If he cannot make noise enough with his jokes and his insults then he does not scorn the singing of hymns and the language of the camp meeting. It was so in the great crisis of the autumn of 1912. The Republican party had finally thrown him over in favour of Mr. Taft. Was he down-hearted? No; he was, in his own phrase, "as bully as a bull moose." He organised a new party to promote his candidature, and what name so fitting as the "Bull Moose party"? It was the "old Timbertoes" trick; but he did not rely on that simply. He joined to it an appeal to the great evangelical heart of America, talked of Armageddon and "battling for the Lord," and, at the convention called to endorse his candidature, gave out the hymn "Onward, Christian soldiers," and led the singing with waving arms and stentorian voice.

"The most successful politician," I heard him once say, "is he who says what everybody is thinking most often and in the loudest voice." In that utterance he stated his own political methods. His ear is always to the ground to catch the direction of the march of the million-footed, and then he goes forward to the conflict with his big drum and his breezy war-cries, sure of his big battalions. Is war the mood of the moment? Colonel Roosevelt leaps into the saddle, calls on his Rough-riders to follow him, and spurs to the front chanting:

> "Rough, tough, we're the stuff;
> We want to fight and can't get enough."

Is the oppression of the Trusts the theme? Mr. Roosevelt is the Ajax who defies the lightnings of the "wealthy criminals." Does the popular breeze blow against the judiciary? His voice rises loudest in the demand for the "recall" of corrupt judges. Wherever the crowd is, he is always there to lead it and to give it battle-cries.

Without any high oratorical quality, without depth

of thought or originality of utterance, his power of popular appeal is nevertheless irresistible. He brims over with animal spirits; he cracks jokes; he utters platitudes; he coins phrases; he talks slang. He hits hard and laughs all the time, like Jack Johnson in the ring. His eyes gleam behind his glasses, his teeth gleam in his wide mouth. He talks slowly—in a kind of—droll — staccato, — with — nasal — inflection — and —at the—critical word—his voice—EX-PLODES—in a quaint—falsetto note—that would make—his fortune —on the—music-hall stage. He loves to preach, and he preaches at inordinate length and to everybody. "If I had been a Methodist I should have applied for a licence as a lay preacher," he once said. Dr. Lyman Abbott records that when he was reading one of his presidential addresses to some friends he wheeled round at the end of a paragraph of an ethical character and said: "I suppose my critics will call that preaching; but I have got such a bully pulpit."

But he needs neither licence nor a bully pulpit. When after "a perfectly corking time" as President he went lion-hunting in Africa, he returned through Egypt and Europe, preaching and lecturing wherever he went. No consideration of etiquette or propriety could muzzle him. At Cairo he was advised not to refer to the murder of the Prime Minister. "No," he said, "that is just what I want to say. If you don't care about it, let's call the engagement off." At the Guildhall, as the guest of the City—and in the presence of the Foreign Secretary —he told us how we were mismanaging Egypt, where he had spent about a week, and suggested that if we did not do the business on his lines we ought to get out. "You have erred," he said, "and it is—for you (falsetto) to make good—your—error." We took the impertinence with meekness, and then, chastened and reflective, went to lunch with him at the Mansion House. At the Sorbonne he told France a few things necessary to its salvation: at Berlin he explained to Europe that Rome fell because the Roman citizens would not fight: at Budapest he delivered an oration on Hungary, before the fervour and inaccuracy of which the most glowing utterances of the most extreme Magyar deputies paled into impartiality.

His courage is superb, and he is never so happy as when he is fighting. His battles are as famous as Tom Sayers', and they have the same quality of physical violence. If he cannot prick his foe with an argument, he will knock him down with the butt end of abuse—say that he is corrupt, has made his money out of speculation, is a liar or a rogue, and put him on his list of "undesirable citizens." It needed such a man to break the tyranny of the party machine, and that so far is his most conspicuous service to America. "I do not number party loyalty among the ten commandments," he says, and his war on the "bosses" has opened a new era in the unsavoury story of American politics. The Vatican made a gross mistake when it sought to muzzle the Roughrider. He would be received by the Pope, he was told, but he must not address the American Methodist Church in Rome. Mr. Roosevelt replied that it would be a pleasure to him to be received by the Pope, but he must decline to submit to any conditions which limited his freedom of action. He never had a more complete or worthy victory over intolerance. And to this quality of high courage must be attributed his fine attitude on the colour question, which culminated in his championship of Dr. Crum, the negro, for the Collectorship of Charleston. No less illustrative of his courage was his firm handling of the Venezuelan episode, when he took his stand on the Monroe Doctrine with a decisiveness that gave him a memorable victory over Germany and incidentally over this country also.

But with all his boisterous courage and frank hilarity,

he cannot be acquitted of sharp practice of the most flagrant sort. Take the incident of Panama. His complicity in the plot is recorded by his own impatient telegram. To wrest the Isthmus from Colombia for the purposes of the canal scheme, it was necessary to engineer a rising. His war vessels were ready to take advantage of it. Unhappily he sent an official telegram inquiring for news of the rebellion, *hours before it occurred*. No repudiation of complicity can stand against that fact. Or take his appeal to Harriman, the railway magnate, for campaign funds in 1904. He took the help and won the election. Later, when he was attacking the Trusts, Judge Parker charged him with having received Corporation contributions in 1904, and Mr. Roosevelt denounced him as mendacious. Yet the facts were on record.

But the most familiar and amazing illustration of the elasticity of his public conscience is furnished by his relations with Mr. Taft and his candidature of a third term as President. It was he who made Mr. Taft President in 1908. He himself had solemnly announced on his election for a second term in 1904 that he would abide by " the wise custom which limits the President to two terms." " Under no circumstances," he wrote, " will I be a candidate for or accept another nomination." Towards the end of his second term he repeated that statement, adding, " I have not changed and shall not change the decision thus announced." Attempts have been made to explain away these declarations. One might as well try to explain away the Pyramids. Mr. Roosevelt said he would respect the wise custom which denied him a third nomination—and he broke his word. And to justify the act he turned and rent his old colleague, recanted his views on arbitration, and appealed to the Senate to amend the treaties that he himself had favoured. If it did not do so, it would be guilty of " arrant, unctuous, and odious hypocrisy."

The Senate followed his advice, and the treaties which had seemed at that famous Guildhall meeting at which Sir Edward Grey, Mr. Asquith, and Mr. Balfour spoke, to herald the dawn of a new world-gospel, were turned into waste paper. It is clear, as Kent in *King Lear* declared long ago, that a bluff manner is not inconsistent with subtle purposes. One may talk much of " a square deal " without dealing squarely.

With all his volubility, few men of distinction have less to say. His mind is a storehouse of conventional knowledge and copybook maxims. You will search his speeches and his books in vain for one true vision, one flight of imaginative sympathy or insight, one note from that elemental string of humanity that " Old Abe " used to touch with such thrilling power. It is all sounding brass and tinkling cymbals. It is as though Martin Tupper has come to life and taken to politics. He moralises, but he does not spiritualise. There is no veil of mystery in that matter-of-fact temple. When I think of him I think of a remark I once heard Lord Morley make when he was challenged on some question of loyalty to his principles. " In the Irish cabin," he said, " you will find the cupboard of emblems. It represents to them the sacred mysteries that envelop their poor lives." Then after a pause, he added with a wistful smile: " I, too, have my cupboard of emblems." In Mr. Roosevelt's cupboard of emblems at Oyster Bay you will find no mystic symbols, but a big drum, a big stick, and shooting irons.

He is the high priest of the modern cult of the " strenuous " life. There are no moments of " wise passiveness " in that career of violent action. When he takes a rest you may hear the crack of his rifle and the roar of his voice from the heart of Darkest Africa. If he cannot be playing the part of Cromwell he writes Cromwell's life. If he cannot be dictator of America then he will be censor to Europe. It is all a furious whirl of primal energy. And yet it is probable that history will appraise highly his service to America. We may distrust his " big stick " Imperialism, and dislike his brazen demagogy and his coarse egotism. But he was the first to face the plutocratic tyranny under which the American democracy is sinking into an economic servitude as gross as any on record. He has shaken the domination of Wall Street. He has exposed the infamous oligarchy that has riveted its chains upon the Titan of the West. When the Titan shakes himself free he will turn to more constructive minds to shape his destinies. But for the rough work of awakening Mr. Roosevelt has great qualities. He will be remembered as the man who broke the idols.

SARAH BERNHARDT

THE other afternoon I went to a music hall, one of those wonderful palaces that have sprung up in such abundance in the last twenty years, places where for a shilling or so you may sit on velvet, and pass through purple hangings, and be shown to your seat by magnificent persons in gold lace, and have tea brought to you between the turns by maidens, whose manners are as spotless as their caps. The music hall of our youth was a thing of tinsel and orange-peel, reeking with smoke and obscenity. There are people who affect to deplore its disappearance. They exalt its freedom, its carelessness, its honest mirth. What they fail to recall is the fact of its filth. It was a noisome sewer, and one of the best signs of the times is that the sewer has been cleansed. You may go into any music hall to-day without being insulted from the stage. The fact is due to many things —education, the growing sense of public decency, Mrs. Ormiston Chant, and the L.C.C. from without; most of all Mr. Albert Chevalier from within. I am not sure that the appearance of Chevalier, a quarter of a century ago, was not a revolutionary event. It certainly marked the beginning of the modern music hall. He touched a new and richer note. He showed that the music-hall audience was hungry for something better than the *double entente,* that its tastes and its demands had been grossly depreciated by ignorant or base-minded managers. He gave his hearers wholesome laughter and honest tears, and his success purged the music hall. It has never looked back since. To-day you will find there not merely plush-covered seats and gold-laced attendants, but the art of Barrie and Bernard Shaw. You may find, too, as I found on this afternoon visit, the genius of Sarah Bernhardt.

The latter phenomenon is the measure of the change

which has come over the democracy. But it is the measure also of the fascination of the extraordinary woman whose sixty-ninth year finds her still queen of the stage. What is the secret of that fascination which holds alike the cultured and the uncultured, and ignores the barriers of speech? Partly, no doubt, it is the hypnotism of a legend. Madame Bernhardt has passed out of the region of criticism: she has become a law. The commandments of the critic have no application to her. It would be absurd for him to utter his "Thou shalt" and his "Thou shalt not" to one who has queened it for nearly half a century, and whose supremacy has something of the authority of a natural element. You might as well criticise the equator, or express your disapproval of the North Pole. You feel that they would not be more indifferent to your censure or your praise.

Her dominion over the mind has nothing in common with the dominion of Ellen Terry, whose course has run parallel with hers. Ellen Terry has won the world by the charm of a winsome personality. She carries with her the sunshine and the south wind and the breath of flowers. With her, no matter what her rôle, it is always May. The world is young and good and sweet, the dew is on the grass, the lark is carolling above. She may play what she likes; she may forget what she likes; she may throw her hands up and say, half gaily, half sadly, "Good people, I really can't remember, for I am getting old." What does it matter whether she remembers or forgets?

> "And if thou wilt, remember;
> And if thou wilt, forget,"

you say. All that you ask is that she shall be just herself. It is not an illusion you want from her, but a reality, an embodiment of a certain humanity and grace and womanliness which is her contribution to the stage. Her portrait at the Tate Gallery is one of the great things of English portraiture; but it is a mistake. She should not go down to posterity with "the damnèd spot" upon her hand, but as Olivia or Beatrice or Rosalind or Ophelia, or some other happy maiden without a "past." Her triumph, in short, is not that of an actress, but of a woman—not of an art, but of a personality. It is the affection she has captured not the imagination.

It is the contrary with Sarah Bernhardt. No one, I suppose, ever felt any such homely feeling as affection for Madame Bernhardt. It would be like offering a bunch of primroses as homage to a thunder-cloud. You would expect a flash of lightning to leap out in response. Antony, probably, would have made the venture, but Antony was born to scorch his wings in baleful fires. No doubt in her private life she is as human as most of us. "I am a mother, a grandmother, and a great-grandmother," she once said, as a sufficient answer to the story that she was going to marry again, and doubtless she has the wealth of domestic affection that such a triple rôle implies. Moreover, did not the newspaper photographer, with that delicate regard for the reticences of life which he always displays, give us the other day a picture of the great actress paying a visit at the hospital to the dying Richard Temple? But I am speaking not of her private benevolence, but of the emotions awakened by her genius on the stage. And personal affection is not one of them. She does not suggest domesticity. One does not feel that the kettle is singing on the hob or the cat purring on the hearth-rug when she is about. It is true that she is fond of animals, but they are animals of sinister import, strange and recondite creatures, suggestive of magic and the moonlight and the hot mystery of Nilotic swamps—cheetahs and chameleons, snakes and crocodiles. And the world of shapes she conjures up is as remote from our experience as her animals are from our affections. It is not merely that she plays high tragedy—"I die terribly twice a day," she once said—and that our lives happily have little great drama in them. It is that she charges her parts with a certain romantic unreality of her own. She belongs to that world of nightmares that the Germans invented and Mrs. Radcliffe imitated. It is a world where anything may happen so long as it is terrible, where flashes of lightning are more frequent than sunlight, and where if you are not poisoned with a magic potion in the second act you will probably be stabbed with a jewelled dagger in the third. It is a world, in fact, that never was on sea or land, that has no more relation to life or the human heart than the visions of the opium-eater—a world of ungoverned passions and hisses and swoons. Its appeal is to the imagination, to the thirst for wild adventures, and for a momentary escape from the familiar and the commonplace into a realm where laws and morals are consumed in a blaze of passion.

In this realm Sarah Bernhardt is the supreme high-priestess. It is her native atmosphere. She has never obeyed anybody or anything except her own imperious will. She inherits her neurotic tendencies from her mother—a beautiful Dutch woman, with a passion for music and travel—of whose fits of rage Sarah Bernhardt has given an appalling picture. "As for me," she says, "I had inherited this tendency to fits of rage from her. I am active, and always ready for fight, and what I want I want immediately." Her career has been a succession of battles with managers, with actors, with playwrights, with anybody and everybody. She broke with the Comédie Française nearly fifty years ago because she slapped the face of a lady who had shouldered her little sister aside. She has been slapping faces, metaphorically, ever since.

And her affection is as passionate as her hate. She remained in Paris during the siege, when all of her class had fled, and performed prodigies of heroism that laid the foundation of the popular idolatry with which she is regarded by her own people. She is the incomparable artist who must be obeyed. Whoever crosses her path is, *ipso facto*, in the wrong. *Quand même* is her motto; has been her motto since, as a child of nine, she broke her arm in attempting an impossible jump, and told her mother "she would do it again, *quand même*, if anyone dared her." And Aunt Faure murmured, "What a terrible child." "In spite of all"—that has been her battle-cry all through her tempestuous life; in spite of all she will have her way, win her victories, beat down her foes. In spite of all, she will not grow old. "One must know how to will—always, and in spite of all," she says. "I have fought with Time and been stronger than Time; I have striven with illness and conquered it. I have battled with death and repulsed it—requesting it to come back later. That is the secret of my youth." That and work, tireless, unceasing work—acting, writing, painting, sculpturing. In the two months' vacation she takes at Belle Isle she plays with as fierce an intensity as she works all the rest of the year. She is out from six in the morning until eight at night, hunting, fishing, playing tennis three hours at a stretch. "I don't propose to die before I am a hundred and three. Just think how that will annoy my enemies." For she always has her enemies in mind, is always living through one of her own dramas. Nearly forty years ago she fled a second time from the Comédie, she fled from Paris, from France, from her friends and her enemies. She came to London, and took it by storm. She went to America, and took that continent captive. She returned matured, victorious. She saw bigger horizons opening out before her. "I resolved to live—to be the great artist I longed to be. And that gave me a great, mischievous delight whenever I thought of the infernal displeasure of my enemies." A terrible child, indeed, Aunt Faure!

And out of this fierce temperament comes the incomparable artist. Perhaps it is only out of such a reality that such an unreality could come, for indeed they are one—must always be one. It is true that, judging from Goldsmith's epigram, Garrick was an exception:

> " On the stage he was natural, simple, affecting,
> 'Twas only that when he was off he was acting."

Sarah Bernhardt is natural both on and off the stage, for she is always acting. She is no more real and no less real when she is fighting her enemies outside than when she is dying one of numerous deaths on the stage. Her art and her life are not separate, but one. She surrenders herself to an emotion and lets it gallop itself to exhaustion, no matter whether it is a scene of Sardou's, or a scene with her manager. This emotional intensity is equipped with a wonderful vehicle of utterance and a splendid authority of gesture. She has a look that slays, a bearing that, in its dark and fearful import, summons to the mind the dread shades of the Clytemnestras and Borgias. Her voice moves in large sinuous curves, in a sort of chant that seems charged with menace. It sinks to a whisper that freezes the blood. It bursts into a torrent: it changes and hammers out the words like the strokes of doom. It was said of another French actress, Mdlle. Duchenois, " qu'elle avait des larmes dans la voix." Sarah Bernhardt has no tears in her voice, but she has swoons and deliriums, nightmares and the tortures of the damned. In all these swift mutations she is living her own life, for she has no life apart from the emotions. Hence the power that enables her to hold men of all tongues in a spell that transcends speech, by the sheer passion and momentum of her feelings. The stage has no triumph like it.

But I agree with Aunt Faure.

MR. JOSEPH CHAMBERLAIN

"It is time," said Victor Hugo, with that colossal vanity that was characteristic of him—"It is time that my name ceased to fill the world." Mr. Chamberlain might echo the saying with not less truth. He has filled the world with the rumour of his name, and shaken it with the thunder of his tread. He has made parties and broken parties, fashioned policies and wrecked them, crashed his way alike to peace and war, been the idol of the democracy and the last refuge of the aristocracy. Judged by his achievements, no man of his political eminence has been so vast a failure; judged by the disintegrating effects of his career, no man has done so much. No great legislative triumph is associated with his name; no great constructive work came from his hand; his ambition and his power were never rewarded by supreme office; he led a rebellion which failed and made him the instrument of his enemies; he made a war which he claimed as "a feather in his cap" but which the judgment of time repudiated; he invented a policy which denied his past and which he has outlived.

Yet, barren though his record is of creative statesmanship, he has done much to change the face of society. He has been the great disturber of the modern world. He burst into the rather smug Victorian parlour and smashed its idols, and politics have never been the same since. He was the first of the modern Radicals, gave Liberalism a new meaning, opened out a new order of political ideals. He made the rich tremble, and even Mr. Gladstone more than a little uncomfortable. He was less concerned about political rights

Joseph Chamberlain

than he was about social wrongs, and in that respect he has been the greatest political pioneer in this country since Cobden. He has been ever a fighter, and has given the world battle-cries and banners—never opiates or anodynes. With him the barometer has always stood at "stormy." Long ago, Lord Salisbury hit off his part in politics in one of his happy similes. "The Cabinet," he said, "is like an old Dutch weather-clock. When it is going to be fine Lord Hartington appears, and when Mr. Joseph Chamberlain is seen you may look out for squalls." Sometimes he has been on this side, sometimes on that, but always he has been on the gallop, sabre in hand, reckless of odds, reckless of consequences, bent only on victory. "Make no mistake," wrote Mr. Arthur Chamberlain in reply to a suggestion that his brother had not taken up Tariff Reform seriously—"Make no mistake. Rupert never rides but to conquer or to fall." It was a fine tribute and a just one. He has never asked for quarter, and he has never given it. "My terms are unconditional surrender"—that or his life.

It is the tragedy of Mr. Chamberlain's career that his haughty pride clashed with the masterful spirit of Gladstone. You cannot have two Cæsars in the camp, and Joseph Chamberlain is Cæsar or nothing. It is easy now to see that no terms were possible between two such men—the one governed by the principles of a great tradition, rich with the culture of the ages, full of reverence for the past, living always "as in the great Taskmaster's eye"; the other hard, direct, material, who had learned the lessons of life on the shoemaker's bench and in the counting-house of his father's business at Milk Street, in the City of London, who had given his young manhood to building up the famous screw business in Birmingham, and had served his apprenticeship to the art of government in carrying out those splendid schemes that made Birmingham for a generation the municipal model of the world. With all his great gifts, Gladstone had little sympathy with the new spirit that was abroad, of which Joseph Chamberlain was the first conspicuous expression. Gladstone's roots were in the past, and only his passion for liberty had enabled him to outgrow the limitations of his inherited and instinctive Toryism. The idea of social reconstruction did not, in his view, come within the scope of political effort. Pensions, insurance, housing, small holdings, land reform, minimum wages —all the things that are the staple of politics to-day— were outside his conception of the tasks of Parliament, and he distrusted this energetic business man from Birmingham who talked of Republicanism and went about the country raising the standard of social, as distinct from political, unrest. Disraeli, watching the new member advance to take the oath, could view the advent of Citizen Chamberlain, the terrible Republican Mayor of Birmingham, with detachment and without alarm, for he, too, had been the great adventurer— he, too, had sown wild Radical oats in the days of his youth. "At least," he said, with his sardonic smile— "at least he wears his eyeglass like a gentleman." And in that eyeglass and the orchid he doubtless saw the portents of a later revelation.

But Gladstone never trusted the man, or approved his message. He would not have admitted him to the Cabinet of 1880 but for the insistence of Sir William Harcourt, and when Mr. Chamberlain launched out on his great Radical crusade against the Lords, the Church, and the land monopoly, Gladstone reminded him of the restraints of Cabinet rank. It was not the Irish question which was the real cause of the severance. Mr. Chamberlain was a Home Ruler before Mr. Glad stone. "There can be no settlement of the Irish question without a Parliament in Dublin," he had said as far back as 1881, "but nothing can be done until we get rid of that impossible Tory, Gladstone." When the impossible Tory himself became a Home Ruler, the personal antagonism remained, and the two flew apart on the very issue that should have brought them together. The conflict was personal; the political incident only served as the occasion of a rupture that was inevitable. And when it came it was accompanied by a scene the like of which the House has not witnessed in our time. "The Prime Minister calls 'black,' and they say 'It is good,'" cried Mr. Chamberlain, referring to his late colleagues and his old leader. "The Prime Minister calls 'white,' and they say 'It is better.' It is always the voice of a god. Never since the time of Herod has there been such slavish adulation." In the midst of the storm that followed the voice of Mr. T. P. O'Connor was heard crying "Judas," and the scene culminated in tumult and blows on the floor of the House.

The current of the world is diverted by small things, and the collision between those imperious men changed the course of history. The new doctrine of social reform, of which Mr. Chamberlain was the apostle, was checked at its source, and Liberalism was doomed to twenty years of sterile wandering in the wilderness, while Toryism culminating in Jingoism ran riot under his masterful sway. I once said to Mr. Lloyd George that the reason why the Limehouse speech created such unexampled enthusiasm on the one side, and such anger on the other, was because for the first time a Cabinet Minister had told the naked facts about the land monopoly and the social wrongs it involved. "No," came the swift reply, "not for the first time. It was done once before, by Chamberlain, and if he had not been driven out of the Liberal party there would have been little for us to do to-day."

The charge which history will make against Mr. Chamberlain is not that he broke with his party, but his passion for mastery has been the governing motive of his career. He believed that he could make Toryism the instrument of his purposes. He recreated it, and gave it its motive power, and then it used him for its own ends. It found in him the ally it needed—an ally that could give it the hands of Esau to gain the inheritance. The Toryism of the Cecils, the Toryism of privilege and class ascendency, must always wear a Radical mask to win a free people. If it goes unveiled, it goes to defeat. Once that mask was supplied by Disraeli, once by Randolph Churchill, finally by Mr. Chamberlain. And in the case of Mr. Chamberlain it was most triumphant, because it was most sincere. For in spite of all the tragic repudiations of himself, he has always been a democrat. "I boast," he said long ago, "a descent of which I am as proud as any baron may be of a title which he owes to the smile of a king, or to the favour of a king's mistress, for I claim descent from one of the two thousand ejected Ministers who, in the time of the Stuarts, left home and work and profit rather than accept the State-made creed which it was sought to force upon them." He would, I think, say the same to-day. It is true that he has thrown his triple shield over the barons and the dukes; but he has thrown it over them with a certain haughty scorn. He has never been their flunkey. They have crowded his platforms and hung upon his words; but his life has been aloof from them, coldly, almost disdainfully aloof. When some one asked Beethoven if his "van" was a patent of nobility, the composer replied, striking his heart and his head, "My patent of nobility is here—and here." Mr. Chamberlain would say the same. He has a pride which would take dignities as an insult. They would suggest that he needed them—could be ennobled by them.

He has what Lord Morley has called "a genius for friendship." He does not squander that friendship;

he cultivates it intensively. The circle is narrow, but it is bound together with hoops of steel. His lifelong devotion to his old Birmingham friends, notably to Mr. Jesse Collings, is a pleasant phase of his character, and his personal friendships in politics have withstood the test of the bitterest hostilities. There are few finer episodes in friendship than his loyalty to Sir Charles Dilke in the darkest hour of his ordeal. Dilke had led the way in loyalty by insisting in 1880 that, since seats in the Cabinet were not possible for both himself and Mr. Chamberlain, his friend should have the preference. When the first Dilke trial was over, Mr. Chamberlain went to Sir Charles, pleaded with him to let the case drop, and added, "There is only one wise course to pursue. Take a tour round the world for three years. Then come back and resume your career. And I will tell you what I will do. I will resign my seat for West Birmingham and go with you." It was sound advice, and a noble expression of great friendship. If it had been followed the political history of this country would have run into other channels. It was rejected, and the great Radical partnership that seemed destined to mould the new England was broken for ever.

But if he has a genius for friendship, he has also a genius for scorn. No man ever brushed a foe out of the path with a more merciless and icy contempt, and the venom of his retorts has made them historic. "Ah," he said of Mr. Dillon, "the hon. gentleman is a good judge of traitors." And even more cruel was the reference to Mr. Healy at the time of the Parnell case—"I have noticed that whenever it is desirable to exhibit personal discourtesy to any man—*or any woman*—the hon. and learned gentleman always presents himself to accomplish it." Even so kindly and courteous a man as Campbell-Bannerman did not escape his shafts. "If he cannot be a statesman, he might at least try to be a gentleman," he said in the last speech I heard him deliver.

These things did not leap out, as the gay railleries of Mr. Lloyd George leap out, in debonair laughter. They were cold, studied, deadly. Mr. Chamberlain has always had himself and his tongue under restraint. He can preserve a silence as sphinx-like and obscure as that of Disraeli. When he returned from South Africa he remained for months buried in a strange privacy. The world said that he had played his last card, and that his day was done. Then, almost from the blue, came the bolt of Protection, and the whole political sky was changed in the twinkling of an eye. "You may burn all your leaflets and literature," said he to Mr. Herbert Gladstone, then the Chief Liberal Whip. "I am going to start you on a new trail." The same self-control and detachment marked him during all the tremendous time of the Boer war. Mr. William Watson has told me how in the blackest days of the struggle he went one evening into the smoking-room of the Devonshire Club, of which Mr. Chamberlain was a member. In a corner seat, smoking a cigar and reading a book, sat the Colonial Secretary, indifferent to all around him. Mr. Watson left, and went to dinner. Re-entering later he found Mr. Chamberlain in the same place, still smoking, still reading. Returning to the club late at night from an engagement, he entered the smoking-room. The figure in the corner seat was unmoved, still smoking, still absorbed in his book.

It is the stillness of a man who never doubts himself, takes his own reading of the public pulse and then acts with a swiftness and momentum that blind the reason. His view of the public is of a mob charged with electricity; waiting for a man to fuse it and direct the lightnings. The one fatal defect in a leader is indecision. To hesitate is to be lost—to doubt is to fail. Mr. Balfour, lost in the perplexities of this incalculable world, seeing all sides, doubting all things, convinced of the futility of action, stands at the helm nerveless and abstracted, involved in a debate that has no end. Mr. Chamberlain leaps to the wheel and crashes full steam ahead through the storm, sometimes to reach the Happy Isles, sometimes to find the gulfs have washed him down. His philosophy is simple—give the people a confident lead and they will follow, a catchword and they will adopt it as a creed, a personality and they will not bother about the argument. "What I have said I have said. Do I contradict myself? Very well, then I contradict myself. I give no explanations, offer no apologies. I have no yesterdays, carry no old clothes. I am not a slave to other men's theories or to my own past."

This energy of mind and absoluteness of opinion have been the source of his influence over the public. He has never left his hearers in doubt as to what was in his mind, and his speech is as clear and emphatic as a time-table. His power of popular appeal has perhaps never been eclipsed. It is not on a high plane, has none of the spaciousness of Gladstone or of the moral passion of Bright, little poetry and that little trite, less sentiment, and no imagination. It is governed by antipathies rather than by sympathies, and plays quite frankly upon the prejudices and fears of men—now envy of the rich who "toil not neither do they spin," now dislike of the foreigner, in another phase scorn of the Irish, always contempt for opponents.

But its energy and directness are irresistible, and the habit of his mind is so completely in tune with the average thought that he rarely misses his target. It might be said of him as Anatole France says of Napoleon: "Il pensait ce que pensait tout grenadier de son armée; mais il le pensait avec une force inouïe." And he says what he thinks with unequalled strength.

Not that his voice is loud. It is smooth and sibilant, and most silky when its matter is most deadly.

An autocratic masterfulness has always been his governing principle. Long years ago, when he was Mayor of Birmingham, he told a friend of mine his theory of action. "On every committee of thirteen," he said, "there are twelve men who go to the meetings having given no thought to the subject, and prepared to accept some one else's lead. One goes having made up his mind what he means shall be done. I always make it my business to be that one." I told that illuminating story to a distinguished political hostess. "That is interesting to me," she said, "for I have just seen one of the Senate of the Birmingham University, and he tells me that Mr. Chamberlain came to the last meeting, and said, 'I have come to the conclusion that what we want is a Siena tower.' The Senate looked up in astonishment. 'What we want is a chair for this, and a chair for that.' 'What we want is a Siena tower,' said Mr. Chamberlain implacably, 'and in order to lose no time I have got a plan here.' And he drew from his pocket a sketch of his proposed tower. 'And,' added my informant, 'we found ourselves outside an hour later, having agreed to the erection of a tower which we didn't want, at the cost of money we hadn't got, and which if we had got we needed for other things.'" If you go to Birmingham you will see that tower to-day—the enduring monument of an iron will.

This pride of will and this scorn of men have been the source of his power, but they are the key also to his failure. They have led him into grave miscalculations of other men and other forces. Gifts of strategy and popular appeal are not enough to win the enduring victories of statesmanship, and, however much allowance we make for the share that Gladstone's hostility had in turning his steps astray, a just estimate of his career will doubtless declare that the principal factor in his failure has been his own lack of large purpose and sustained motive. He has dominated the moment because he has lived in the moment and has had no vision outside the immediate reality, and no purpose beyond the immediate victory. He has always been winning the trick and losing the game. It was this temporary habit of mind, this insensibility to the deeper issues of politics that betrayed him into his mistakes. He deserted the cause of Home Rule not because he did not believe in it, but because he believed that the moment had come to challenge his leader. He did not see that the issues that were raised were greater and more enduring than any personal question, and that his revolt would only lead to a life of servitude in the interests of a party that he detested. He drifted into a war that he did not want, because he believed, as he told Campbell-Bannerman in the famous interview, that he and Kruger were only engaged in a game of bluff. He did not understand that there are some things that are outside the realm of tactics. He invented a policy that repudiated all his past and met his Waterloo because he did not realise that in the end principles do count in the affairs of men. All the journey is marked by the mighty débris of pride.

There is no story of our time so full of significance—a story of broken purposes, of great powers diverted from their true end, of a tyrannic will at war with natural sympathies. It is a tale for tears. One likes to think of him in those early days when he was the great citizen fashioning a model city, and when his clear, undazzled eye saw the vision of a new and juster England and he set out to cleave his way to it. The vision faded—the way was lost. But it is by the vision that we will judge him in the days of his silence and defeat.

LORD FISHER

One day far back in the fifties of last century a sailing-ship came round from Portsmouth into Plymouth Sound, where the fleet lay. Among the passengers was a little midshipman fresh from his apprenticeship in the *Victory*. He scrambled aboard the Admiral's ship, and with the assurance of thirteen marched up to a splendid figure in blue and gold, and said, handing him a letter: "Here, my man, give this to the Admiral." The man in blue and gold smiled, took the letter, and opened it. "Are you the Admiral?" said the boy. "Yes, I'm the Admiral." He read the letter, and patting the boy on the head, said: "You must stay and have dinner with me." "I think," said the boy, "I should like to be getting on to my ship." He spoke as though the British Navy had fallen to his charge. The Admiral laughed, and took him down to dinner. That night the boy slept aboard the *Calcutta*, a vessel of 84 guns, given to the British Navy by an Indian merchant at a cost of £84,000. It was the day of small things and of sailing-ships. The era of the ironclad and the *Dreadnought* had not dawned.

. . . . . .

A mile or two outside sleepy Thetford in Norfolk, famous as the birthplace of Tom Paine, you will come upon a pleasant country house set in a spacious park. Pass the house and follow a broad grass path and you will see the figure-head of an old, wooden battleship, inscribed with the one word *Calcutta*. It is the figure-head of the vessel that the boy went aboard that night, nearly sixty years ago, when he joined the British Navy.

It has been placed there by the boy himself. He and his old ship have retired together to his son's estate in the sandy solitude of Norfolk. The roar of the sea is far away, the long battle with the elements is over, the day's work is done. "Calm after stormy seas" has come. Together they may take their ease.

It is a little difficult to associate ease with Lord Fisher. It was certainly impossible to enjoy ease under his iron rule. When he was in command of the Mediterranean Fleet, he one day went aboard a certain vessel and walked up and down the deck with the captain. "What is that?" he said suddenly, pointing to a bell-pull which communicated with the engine-room. "That," said the captain, with prompt invention, "is the bilge-pump." "Pull it," said Sir John. The captain pulled it and the bell rang. "What is the bell for?" "To indicate the state of the bilge," replied the captain, still relying on a fertile invention. Next day the captain was removed from his command, and doubtless joined the innumerable host of those who demanded Sir John Fisher's head on a charger, or the equivalent of that offering, as the one thing necessary to maintain our naval supremacy.

The incident is characteristic of the man. He is sudden and sardonic. He whips off your head with a joke in the midst of a genial torrent of talk. He suspected that this man was inefficient. He did not set on foot elaborate inquiries: he just paid him a call, engaged him in pleasant talk, and from the quiet sky sent out a sudden flash of lightning that ended his career on the spot. That is his way. If he suspects you he does not write to you. He takes you by the arm and pours out that stream of astonishing talk, and then, just when you, good easy man, think how well you stand with the Admiral, there leaps out a sudden sword and you are pinned past escape. For he believes that the truth comes out in talking. Set a man before a sheet of paper, he says in his epigrammatic way, and he has time to tell lies.

It follows that he is not loved. The world respects the martinet, but it reserves its affection for those who give it affection. It prefers those who do not expect much from it. It admits the need of efficiency, but it hates the efficient, for he is a constant rebuke to its own love of slack and slipshod ways, a constant menace to its comfortable rut of routine and custom. It clings to its traditions, and dislikes all change because it is change. Theoretically it will admit that stagnation is decay, and that the decline of every institution in history, from an empire to a blacking business, was due to undue attachment to " creeds outworn." But its own case is always different. Its own case is always one in which " whatever is, is best," and in which the hand of the reformer is the hand of the Vandal.

Now the Navy was an institution that had run in a rut for a century. Steam had superseded the sailing-ship, the ironclad had superseded the wooden walls of the old three-decker, the whole science governing naval warfare had changed. Nelson lashed the *Victory* to the *Redoubtable:* if he met it to-day in battle he would shatter it to pieces at five miles range—or be shattered. Naval history, as Lord Fisher will tell you, is a record of exploded maxims. It was the most doubtful phase of war: it has become the most absolute—so absolute, so mathematically precise, that Admiral Fisher and Admiral Tirpitz might meet over a map and settle it without firing a shot, as you settle a game of chess by adjudicating upon the power, the number, and the disposition of the pieces. But with all this material change there had been no change of tradition. The spirit of the service remained unaltered. There was no scientific adjustment of needs to ends, no application of plain business principles to the task. The single idea was to have ships and more ships and still more ships. Beyond that elementary policy the thought of the Navy did not go.

Then there emerged slowly to the front a man of ideas, who had made a reputation by a book which had revolutionised the theories of gunnery. He had no social backing and no exceptional attractions of personality. But he had the energy of a steam-engine, the pertinacity of a debt collector, and no reverence for the past or for anything but facts. It was as "Radical Jack" that Lord Ripon first heard of John Fisher and gave him his chance as Chief of the Ordnance, and a Radical he remains to the end—one who brushes aside all forms and conventions and lays bare the root, fearless of consequences. "I am told you are a Socialist," King Edward is reported to have said to him on one occasion. "Well," he replied, "I never believed that all the brains went with a white shirt." "But you are so violent." "The Kingdom of Heaven suffereth violence," he replied—he quotes Scripture like a Puritan divine—"and the violent man takes it by force." "But you don't look at all sides." "Why should I waste my time looking at all sides when I know my side is the right side? The cleverest man we ever had at the Admiralty was Goschen, and he was the worst failure of all. He was always looking at all sides, and we never got anything done." There was no such complaint when Sir John became the professional head of the Navy. It was as though the Admiralty Board was swept by a tornado. In five years he revolutionised the Navy. There was hardly a stone that was left unturned. There was hardly an idea that had not been reversed. Ships, guns and gunnery, strategy and tactics, instruction and training, diet and rewards—all suffered a literal "sea change."

No wonder that he was not loved, that the Navy writhed like the frog under the harrow when "ilka tooth gies it a tig," that the naval clubs rang with the outraged sentiments of half-pay officers, and that ancient admirals grew purple at the unspeakable name, and fired broadsides at the iconoclast through the port-holes of the *Times*.

Fortunately for him he has a tough integument. No shaft can pierce this armour-plated man. He probably had feelings once, but he has been so long exposed to the weather that they have become indurated. The singular face, at once inscrutable and mobile, gives no key to any human emotion. The full eye, with its curiously small pupil, the wide, full-lipped mouth, drooping mercilessly at the corners, the jaw jutting out a good-humoured challenge to the world, all proclaim a man who neither asks nor gives quarter. He laughs, he cracks jokes, he talks with voluminous geniality, but behind all these breezy externals of the seaman are his "three R's of war"—"Ruthless, Relentless, Remorseless,"—and his "three H's of gunnery"—"Hit first, hit hard, keep on hitting."

For he talks in crisp phrases. "Life is phrases" is a favourite saying of his. He coins his phrases out of the ore of his own quarrying. They are his condensed comments on the experience of a lifetime, and he uses them as Mr. Chamberlain used them, to drill an idea into the mind of the public. The public is a dull dog. Dr. Dale was accustomed to say that it took ten years to get a new idea really rooted in the mind of his congregation. And Sir John Fisher would probably say the same of the Navy. He uses the art of "damnable iteration" deliberately. "Armour is vision" is one of his favourite sayings. And behind that saying is his theory of naval construction. In the old days the bigger the ship the less relatively was the spread of canvas, and hence the less speed. So the light frigate was the vision of the Navy. "But look at the Dreadnought cruisers. They travel twenty-seven knots. They are at once the vision and the power of the Navy. I would have none other."

I have said that he is as pertinacious as a debt

collector. You cannot shake him and his phrases off. They both stick. When, before he was First Sea Lord, he wanted to get a new type of ship adopted, he sent round to his colleagues punctually every Monday a memorandum on the subject. It was always the same memorandum, and it always had to be considered. And at last in sheer weariness the Admiralty adopted the idea. It was the only way of getting rid of it, and so, out of the pertinacity of this irrepressible man, was born the "all-big gun" ship that convulsed the naval world and made every ship afloat obsolete. If you accuse him of having done the world a disservice, and tell him that he ought to have been hanged at the yardarm of the first *Dreadnought*, he will reply in his allusive way, "Le Verrier and Adams did not invent Neptune; they only discovered it. The calculations of science had made the discovery inevitable. It was only a question of who would reach the goal first, and Le Verrier won. So with the *Dreadnought*. All the developments of science and of naval necessity made its discovery inevitable. I happened to be Le Verrier—that is all. England got the lead, instead of having to follow. You talk of commotion. Think of the commotion if Germany had forestalled us. You talk of cost. The *Dreadnought* is the cheapest ship afloat. It has got rid of the wastefulness that put your seamen in ships that would be worthless in war. It has not only given you efficiency of material, but the maximum efficiency of men." Whether right or wrong, the impetus of the man overwhelms opposition. You cannot go on fighting one who never hauls down his flag. You cannot overcome the man who never knows when he is beaten.

And he rarely is beaten. I am told that when he conceived the idea of having wireless telegraphy installed on the cupola of the Admiralty in Whitehall, he found that the Post Office was an insuperable barrier to the scheme. So one day half a dozen seamen swarmed up the cupola and ran up the " wireless " in the face of outraged authority. " How's this? " asked the Post Office. " By whose authority? " And the official breast swelled with official indignation. " Oh," said the Admiral, " it's only run up tentatively to see how it will work in case permission is given." I fancy permission has never been given; but if you go down Whitehall you will see the " wireless " still audaciously challenging the Post Office proprieties. He is, you see, true to the Nelsonian tradition of the " blind eye." And that is natural. He has, as I have said, reverence for nothing but facts; but Nelson's genius is a subject on which he will grow eloquent at the least excuse; and his talk is garnished with illuminating references to that great man. " History," he says, " is the record of exploded maxims, but Nelson is greater than ever. Some people think his greatest saying was 'England expects, etc.,' some that it was 'Numbers alone annihilate,' which Napoleon stole and converted into 'God is on the side of the big battalions.' One of his best was 'Your battle-ground should be your drill-ground.' I've been assailed for putting that into effect by reorganising the fleet in home waters. What was the good of the old system of drilling and manœuvring in the Mediterranean under blue skies and in smooth waters when if war ever comes you'll have to fight among the fogs and shallows of the North Sea? But in my opinion the greatest saying of Nelson was this: 'He would be a — fool who fought an enemy ten to one when he could fight him a hundred to one.' " And he laughs again. " You may be sure that at Trafalgar Nelson smiled cheerfully when he saw the French and Spanish admirals exchanging signals that they didn't understand." This, with reference to the doubtful value of allies in naval warfare, for his references and anecdotes are never idle—they always have their bearing in actualities, which are the only things that interest him.

What sentiment or emotion dwells behind this astonishing energy of mind, this gay and fluent talk, I do not know, and can only guess. Certainly not the emotion of humanitarianism. "War should be terrible," he says, and I have heard him defend that terrible act of Togo on the eve of the declaration of war between China and Japan, in sinking at sight a ship flying British colours, but which he knew carried 2000 Chinese. Perhaps it is the emotion of patriotism. "I am convinced that we are the lost tribes," he says laughingly, "for see how Providence has taken care of us." And he will point to a map and show in a few broad phrases the crushing geographical supremacy of Britain. And then, warming to his theme, "Do you know that there are five keys to the world? The Straits of Dover, the Straits of Gibraltar, the Suez Canal, the Straits of Malacca, the Cape of Good Hope. *And every one of those keys we hold.* Aren't we the lost tribes?"

"Isn't it wonderful?" he will say as he tells of some coincidence, some personal episode, some new invention, like wireless or submarines, that works to our advantage. "Isn't the hand of Providence in that?" We are the chosen people, and his God is the God of the Israelites. He sees the cloud by day and the pillar of flame by night. The language of the Bible, as I have said, is constantly on his lips, but it is the language of the Old Testament rather than the New, and preferably the comminatory language. He loves sermons better than anything else, except dancing. When he was a captain a visitor called at his town house one Sunday morning. "The Captain has gone to Berkeley Chapel," said the servant. "Will he be in this afternoon?" said the visitor. "No, he said he was going to hear Canon Liddon at St. Paul's." "Well, this evening?" "In the evening he is going to Spurgeon's Tabernacle."

And he is a man of omens, too, like most who go down to the sea in ships. When he became First Sea

Lord he refused to take up his duties until the 21st of October—the anniversary of Nelson's death. All his superstitions centre round that name. He entered the Navy as the nominee of Nelson's last captain. He served his apprenticeship on the *Victory*. And on the *Victory* as Commander at Portsmouth he finally hauled down his flag. "Isn't it wonderful?"

But at the bottom, I think, the governing emotion of the man is that of professional pride. It is that singleness of aim that gives him such driving power. His purposes are never deflected by side issues, never weakened by social, personal, or humane considerations. He has one goal, and goes straight for it all the time. Are you the best?—the best, that is, for your purpose?—not the best in a general sense, but in a particular sense? That is all he asks, whether of a ship, a gun, or a man. If you are a stoker, then you must be the best stoker that ever walked. It is no use pointing out that you are good to your aunt. The question is, Have you a genius for stoking? If you haven't, your aunt won't help you. He will look round with that genial, ruthless—it is both—glance of his, and he will find the man he wants though he be two hundred steps down the ladder. For, with defiant paradox, he will tell you that "Favouritism is the secret of success"—favouritism, that is, for the efficient, not for the personally or socially preferred. "If I haul a man up over the shoulders of his seniors, that man is going to take care to show I haven't made a mistake." He is the enemy of Buggins with his social and political backing. "Buggins' turn," he says, "is the curse of the Navy. Buggins is first cousin of the Duke of Dankshire, and can't be passed over. He is an ass, but he must have his turn." If Buggins has suffered an eclipse the fact is chiefly due to Lord Fisher's relentless *régime*. Efficiency, and again efficiency and always efficiency—that is his test. It is hard on the good weak man; it is hard on the stoker's impoverished aunt. But success is ruthless. It has no bowels of compassion. It takes its instructions from the head and ignores the pleadings of the heart. And so I come back to the one emotion—if indeed it is so warm a thing as emotion—of this remarkable man, his professional pride. He loves his calling and has no other love. It is not a means but an end. It is his whole life and outside that life there is no such person as Lord Fisher.

. . . . . .

Let us leave him pacing up and down the grass path in front of the figure-head of the old *Calcutta*, his forefinger raised to point his buoyant talk, his eye undimmed, his natural force unabated. He is taking his ease, and fighting his last great battle. And his foe is the veteran of the rival service. For in his struggle to establish conscription Lord Roberts's most formidable antagonist is the author of the *Dreadnought*, who sees in that movement a menace to the British Navy.

PRINCE KROPOTKIN

"AH, there were giants in those days," said my friend, "but now—" and he made a contemptuous gesture with his hands as if there were no words to convey the poverty of our time. "Now there are giants also," I answered, completing his sentence. "For example?" he said with a note of confident challenge. "Speak low," I said, "for my example is close by you." He turned in the direction I indicated, and amid the chattering company assembled in the studio his eye rested on the figure of a man advanced in years. He stood with the stiff precision and squared shoulders of the soldier, but the head, with the great brow, the wide-set eyes beaming with intelligence and benevolence, and the patriarchal beard, proclaimed the philosopher. He was talking with the nervous rapidity of a mind too swift for the slow medium of words, and as he talked he stirred unceasingly the cup of tea that he held in his hand but seemed never to taste. "Prince Kropotkin?" said my friend. "Yes." "But do you really think so?"

Yes, really. Seen in all their aspects, the personality and career of Prince Peter Kropotkin appear to belong to the realm of heroic fable. In a primitive world he would have become a legend, an Ajax defying the lightning of despotism, or a Prometheus chained to the Caucasus for bringing the lamp of liberty to earth. Poets would have made out of his exploits the songs of a people, and the imagination of children would have been fired by the tale of his perils and his escapes. There is a spaciousness and simplicity about the drama of this man that have no parallel in our day. As he

P. Kropotkin

stands there stirring his tea, the perfect picture of an amiable professor engaged in a little relaxation, one seems to catch a vision of all the vastness and tragedy of Russia—a vision, too, of the greatness of the soul of man. I see him a child in the old Moscow home of his father, an offspring of the house of Rurik, more ancient and more noble than the Romanoffs. It is the darkest hour of the night before the awakening of Russia. The hand of the terrible Nicholas I. is over the land; the people groan under the tyranny of serfdom. The wondering child touches life at its two extremes. At one, as a royal page-boy of eight, he follows in the train of the mighty Nicholas himself and falls asleep in the lap of the future empress. At the other, the horrors of serfdom scorch his sensitive soul. One day his father falls into a rage with the slaves of the household. His anger concentrates on poor Makár, the piano-tuner and sub-butler. He takes his seat at the table and writes a note: "Take Makár with this note to the police station, and let a hundred lashes with the birch rod be given to him." Terror falls on the child. He is suffocated with tears, and later in the day in a dark passage he awaits the return of Makár, who comes with pale, distorted face. The child tries to kiss his hand, but Makár tears it away and says, "Let me alone; you, too, when you are grown up, will you not be just the same?" "No, no, never," cries the child.

The scene changes. The night of Nicholas has passed away, but the pale dawn which had come with the abolition of serfdom has been swallowed up in reaction, and Russia is under the heel of a police tyranny. Thousands of innocent people are hanged; tens of thousands disappear in the prisons or go to a living tomb in Siberia. A pall of fear hangs over all the land. But beneath the surface Russia is awakening. Hang and exile as they may, the Trepoffs and Shuvaloffs, the police tyrants to whom Alexander II. has surrendered the government of the country, cannot suppress the mysterious movement that is flooding Russia with the literature of liberty and revolt. Through this underworld of unrest there moves the phantom figure of a wonderful workman clad in sheepskin—Borodin his name. If only we could lay Borodin by the heels, say the police, we should crush the head of the viper of revolt—Borodin and his colleagues, Tschaykowsky and Stepniak. But Borodin is elusive as a shadow. The faithful weavers and artisans among whom he moves will not betray him. They are arrested by the score, by the hundred; they are imprisoned, they are hanged. But they will not yield the secret.

It is a spring evening in 1874. All scientific St. Petersburg is assembled at the Geographical Society to hear the famous savant, Prince Kropotkin, reveal the results of his explorations in Finland, which overthrow all the old theories as to the diluvial period in Russia. The fame of the scholar is established. He has that vast range of mind that takes all knowledge for its empire. Mathematician and geologist, artist and author—he wrote novels at twelve years of age—musician and philosopher, familiar with twenty languages and talking easily in seven, he has at thirty become one of the intellectual glories of Russia. Compelled as one of the corps of pages—with whom he had served in the suite of Alexander II.—to enter the army, he had chosen Siberia as his field of action, and there through five years he had made himself known by his schemes of reform, his travels on the Amur, and his laborious researches, which had enabled him to upset all the old conceptions of the geography of Asia and the theories of Humboldt. To-night his triumph is complete. It is admitted frankly in a speech by Barbot-de-Marney, the first of Russian geologists, and Kropotkin is nominated forthwith as President of the Physical Geography section. He leaves in a cab, and as he passes down the great Perspective of Névsky another cab passes him. A weaver leans from it and hails him—" Mr. Borodin." The two cabs are stopped. From behind the weaver a detective leaps from the second cab—" Mr. Borodin, Prince Kropotkin, I arrest you." Policemen spring up at the detective's signal. Resistance is useless, and Kropotkin is taken back in custody. Judas follows behind in the second cab.

Two years have passed—two years of life in a solitary cell in that grim fortress of Peter and Paul, whose annals are the annals of the martyrdom of Russia's noblest and best, patriots and poets buried alive, condemned to slow death, driven to insanity in the loneliness of the dark dungeons. Two years and still Kropotkin awaits the trial that never comes—two years in which the only human intercourse he has had has been by a code of tappings which he has established, at the end of many months of deathlike silence, with prisoners in the adjoining cells. He has preserved his health by walking five miles a day in his cell—a thousand times from corner to corner—and by gymnastics with his stool. He has preserved his reason because, through the efforts of his much-loved brother Alexander, he has been allowed writing materials, and has completed his monumental work on the glacial hypothesis. But he has forgotten the sound of his own voice, for he is not permitted to sing, and has soon lost even the desire to preserve that contact with his old self. And now, at the end of two years, he has fallen ill, and is sent to the hospital of the military prison. Here in the afternoon he is permitted to walk in the courtyard with armed warders for companions, and here one day takes place that wonderful escape, the manner of which he himself had planned and had communicated to his friends outside—the gate open to let in the wood carriers, Kropotkin walking to and fro, hat in hand, as a signal that he is ready, the stranger talking to the warder at the gate, the sound of a violin from a neighbouring house playing Schubert's "Serenade" that gathers speed as the crisis comes, until it seems to shriek "Run! run!"—the dash for the gate, the leap into the carriage that sweeps up at the critical moment, the gallop through the streets, the daring dinner in a fashionable restaurant while the police are searching every hiding-place in St. Petersburg, the borrowed passport, the flight across Finland to Sweden, the Union Jack, and—England. There is no tale like it outside Dumas. It furnishes the most thrilling passage in the greatest autobiography of our time.

Throughout his career two dominant passions have possessed this remarkable man—the passion for intellectual conquest and the passion for human liberty. Ultimately, perhaps, they spring from one root, that love of mankind which warms you like sunshine in his presence. In this respect he reminds one of William Morris, who had the same radiant, all-embracing manner, and who, like Kropotkin, was very much more of an Anarchist than a Socialist. I mention the two facts because they seem to have some relevance to each other. The Socialist sees man in the abstract and society as an organism controlled by law, and the contemplation appeals to his intellect but leaves his humanity cold. The Anarchist, who is the Individualist carried to the logical extreme, sees man in the concrete, and his heart warms to one whom he can touch and hear and see. He is concerned, in a word, about a man; the Socialist is concerned about a system.

It is out of his scientific but warm-blooded thinking that his political thought emerges. In that memorable book, *Mutual Aid*, he combated the prevalent conception of the Darwinian theory as a doctrine that Nature is red in tooth and claw, and that all evolution is the outcome of the struggle for existence, of competition, of the "Hobbesian war of each against all." Against this doctrine he sets up the theory that evolution is the product of mutual aid, of co-operation, of social effort. "The fittest," he says, "are thus the most sociable animals, and sociability appears as the chief factor of evolution, both directly by securing the well-being of the species while diminishing the waste of energy, and indirectly by favouring the growth of intelligence."

And from this social motive that moves all things forward he deduces the gospel of individual liberty that, allowed free play, makes for that collective impulse. "We have more tears than our own suffering claims; more capacity for joy than our own existence can justify. The solitary being is wretched, restless, because he cannot share his thoughts and feelings with others. When we feel some great pleasure, we wish to let others know that we exist; we feel, we love, we live, we struggle, we fight. . . . It is the overflowing life which seeks to spread. . . . Power to act is duty to act. The moral obligation, thus stripped of all mysticism, is reduced to the conception: *the condition of the maintenance of life is its expansion.* The plant cannot prevent itself from flowering. Sometimes to flower means to die. Never mind, the sap mounts all the same. It is the same with the human being when he is full of force and energy. He expands his life. He gives without calculation, otherwise he could not live. If he must die, like the flower when it blooms, never mind, the sap rises if sap there be."

And so he arrives at his morality, which issues no commands, which will "refuse to model individuals according to an abstract idea, as it will refuse to mutilate them by religion, law, or government. It will leave to the individual full and perfect liberty." This morality leads to his conception of a society in which there is no restraint, in which is neither capitalism nor government, and in which each will have complete liberty of initiative and action for satisfying, by free groups and federations, the varied needs of life. It will be seen how much he is in the centre of the current of modern thought, how many of the tendencies of to-day have some of their sources in his teaching—the philosophy of Bergson, the practice of Syndicalism, the mediævalism of the young school of reactionaries, yes, even the *Passing of the Third Floor Back.*

No one obeys his morality more loyally than Kropotkin. He lives his own simple life with absolute independence, kindly and smiling, but indifferent to all gain or circumstance or distinction. Just as he surrendered his great estates in Russia to live the life of a fugitive, earning his bread by his scientific writings, so he has shed his princely title and has been the central influence in that great network of agitation, the International Working Men's Association. He has never returned to Russia since the day of his flight thirty-seven years ago; but Russia has not forgotten him. It drove him out from Switzerland, where he published his journal, *La Révolte*; it laid designs for kidnapping him which only failed through fear of exposure in connection with one who had made himself famous in English literature; when he published his book, *In Russian and French Prisons,* in 1887 the firm of publishers suddenly ceased to exist and the whole edition mysteriously disappeared.

Once it triumphed over him. In the Lyons riots of 1882—riots widely believed to have been incited by Russian *agents provocateurs*—bombs were thrown, and Kropotkin, who was in London at the time, and who neither then nor at any time has supported the doctrine of physical force, was accused of complicity in the crime. He returned to France, and with others he was sentenced to five years' imprisonment, ten years' police supervision, and other punishments. The

Russian Government in its glee bestowed decorations on all concerned in the prosecution. It was a disastrous mistake. It helped the agitation throughout Europe for his release. The French Government was obdurate, but conceded him the privilege of a small plot of ground within the prison, and here he began those experiments in intensive culture which have revolutionised agriculture and which are the basis of that striking book, *Fields, Factories, and Workshops.* But the outcry was continued, and M. de Freycinet was driven one day to confess that Kropotkin could not be released "on account of a question of diplomacy." The truth was out. "Is Kropotkin to be kept in prison to please the Russian Government?" was the question on every tongue. Faced with this challenge, the Government could no longer resist, and Kropotkin was released at the end of three years' imprisonment. Russia's comment was characteristic. The French Ambassador at St. Petersburg was, following the incident, treated with such marked discourtesy that he resigned and returned to Paris.

. . . . . .

"Well, what do you think of Kropotkin?" I said afterwards to my friend. I had introduced him to the Prince, whom we had left still stirring his tea.

"Well, I'm not sure whether he's a giant; but I think that he's a saint," was the reply.

LORD HUGH CECIL

THERE was thunder in the air of the House of Commons. Over the crowded benches and galleries reigned an ominous silence. Late-comers stole guiltily into the Chamber and, finding no vacant seats, sat down on the steps of the gangway. Across the floor the two hosts sat facing each other with an air of stony and implacable defiance. Mr. Asquith, wedged in the crowded Treasury bench between Mr. Lloyd George and Sir Edward Grey, showed by his flushed features and those movements characteristic of him in moments of stress—his body swaying gently backward and forward, his hands passing now over his knees, now across his face—that a moment of crisis had come. Presently he rose—rose to announce what everyone knew already, that the King had consented to create peers to over-ride the House of Lords, and to state his procedure in regard to the Parliament Bill.

With his rising the storm burst. The Opposition leapt on him with the snarl of hungry wolves. From out the pack, one figure emerged with a sort of white fury. He sat on the front bench below the gangway, a spectacle of passion incarnate; the face with its broad, high brow, deep-set eyes, and small chin, ashen and contorted; the slight body, with the bowed shoulders of the bookish man, swaying to and fro to the fierce rhythm of his cries, his fingers restlessly twining and untwining, his whole aspect a thing for wonder. Other voices faltered and failed; his never. Throughout that long duel his shrill voice chanted with deadly iteration the one word "'Vide, 'vide." Whenever the Prime Minister made a new start the chant was resumed. Mr.

Asquith stood at the table, facing the storm, his eye ranging over the tiers of screaming foes with a look of mingled scorn and wonder. It rested on the ringleader and stayed there with something of the fascination that one looks into the cage of a new and unknown species. Behind him his followers sat in outraged silence. For an hour the battle raged. Then with a shrug of the heavy shoulders Mr. Asquith turned to the Speaker and saying he would submit no longer to this degrading struggle sat down. Lord Hugh Cecil had won another of his fruitless triumphs.

Looking down upon that amazing scene, one felt that the familiar story of Lord Hugh and Mr. Gladstone was true. Gladstone was on a visit to Hatfield, and was left after tea to rest alone. Presently one of the servants heard a noise from his room, and entering found little Hugh assailing the old man with his infant fists and crying, "You're a very bad man." "How can I be a bad man when I am your father's friend?" Gladstone asked with characteristic ingenuity; but the boy was not to be betrayed into a fatal argument. "My father is going to cut off your head with a great big sword," was his implacable reply.

This intensity of conviction and ungoverned passion are Lord Hugh's peculiar contribution to the public life of his time. There are other men who are insolent in the House; but they are insolent without conviction. When Mr. F. E. Smith or Lord Winterton "raises the waters" no deeps are stirred, for deep only answers to deep. But the passion of Lord Hugh Cecil comes armed with the sword of the Spirit, hot with a message from Sinai. The message is mistaken, but it is sincere, and he would die to deliver it. He is like an ascetic of the fourteenth century emerging from his cell into a world that he sees thundering to destruction—a world given over to the false gods of material satisfaction, rioting along the ways of pleasure, talking its shibboleths of reform, clattering down a steep place to where God is not. He shrieks his warnings over our doomed heads, he wrings his hands, his face is contorted with a dreadful agony. To his monastic vision that figure before him, talking of the rights of the people, of old age pensions, of undenominational education, is very literally the *advocatus diaboli*. For he is leading the people out of the green pastures of the Spirit into the desert where the soul dies.

It is a perverted and a fantastic nightmare—the nightmare of a mind that sees the twentieth century from the fourteenth, of a mind that does not dwell in the broad day, but in the twilight of a feverish reverie. But we shall misunderstand Lord Hugh Cecil if we doubt his sincerity, if we confound his passion with the merely selfish interests of his class. He defends those interests with a sleepless vigilance, but he defends them not from selfish motives, but because they represent to him a social system that leads, as he believes, to the Kingdom of Heaven. He himself is of the stuff of the martyrs—a Crusader or a Quixote, charging the pagan world with spear and buckler. And beneath his mail is the hair shirt. His cause is lost and he knows it. The feudal baron has left the castle, and the beef baron has entered in. The monasteries have been despoiled—Lord Hugh knows the spoilers—and the beggars pass to the casual ward. Old Sarum is a green mound of memories, and the pulse of life throbs through the cities. The authority of the priest has passed, and man is alone with his own soul. We, the children of our time, accept all this as a matter of course. We thunder with the great world "down the ringing grooves of change," rejoice in the new scenery that opens up before our eyes, take the tunnels of darkness with delight, and look for the wonders that will burst on us when we emerge.

Lord Hugh, far away in the fourteenth century,

sees it all with horror and despair—sees in it the negation of God. What is this talk of Socialism and social reform but a will-o'-the-wisp leading poor humanity away from the Kingdom, diverting all our energies to material well-being and leaving the soul starved and perishing? What has the State to do with distributive justice? The State is but the policeman that guards to every man his own. It is the Church that must change society, the Church that must so charge the hearts of men with charity, that through charity they shall do justice. It is the dream of the idealist, who takes no account of facts—of the ecclesiastic and not of the politician. But the voice is not wholly vain. It is well in this eager time, when we are fashioning a new social machine, to be reminded that we shall not save society by abundance of food and raiment, that the temple is not made with hands, that we do not live by bread alone.

It is an old conflict—old as humanity. Change the heart of man, says the preacher, and society will be saved. Change the garment of society, says the reformer, and the individual will be saved. Change both, says the plain man, and each will save the other. When Dean Inge asked whether it was the pig who made the sty or the sty the pig, he insulted humanity and confounded the issue. Society has made the slum, and has doomed the slum child from its birth. It is for society to unmake the slum, and let the winds of heaven reach the flowers that are poisoned in its sunless courts.

Lord Hugh would leave the slum until he had changed the heart of the slum owner. He forgets that even under the walls of princely Hatfield he will find slums as noisome as anything in the great cities, hovels that are a shame, in the midst of the great solitude of pasture and woodland that the land monopoly has secured to his family. Yet charity is not wanting there. It is not wanting but it has failed, and only the State wielding the sword of justice can redress the social wrong.

It is the Church and the view of the Church that dominates all his thought. Parliament is but an antechamber of the Church—a sort of poor relation, a hewer of wood and drawer of water for Convocation. And by the Church he means the Anglican Communion. All other communions are but weeds by the wayside. Yet on his mother's side he comes of a line of Nonconformist ministers, and has ancestors who sleep, no doubt peacefully, in the Unitarian graveyard at Norwich. He has done his best to purge his blood of the heresy, and it is recorded that as a boy he went to his father with the grave news that he "feared nurse was a Socinian." He is prepared to pay the price of his exclusiveness, and in the midst of an election at Greenwich risked his seat by refusing to open a Nonconformist bazaar until he had the sanction of the local vicar to the countenance of schism.

The wrath that burns in him at so white a heat is the source of his power. There are few in these days who draw the curtain of the Unseen on the floor of Parliament. Hence the disappearance of oratory, for without the stop of the eternal, the organ of speech neither soars to the heights nor sounds the deeps. But Lord Hugh has brought back the name of the Almighty to the counsels of the Commons, and with it a certain exalted rhetoric that at its best—unhappily rarely heard—has no parallel in our time. One forgets the perversity of the argument, the ungainly gestures, the erratic voice at once harsh and musical—forgets them in the glimpse he gives of "the abodes where the eternal are." The peroration of his speech on the second reading of the Education Bill of 1902 will take its place among the finest flowers of Parliamentary oratory. Its close—directed, as all knew, to Mr. Morley, who sat opposite—has an elevation and a sudden thrill that would not be unworthy of Bright. He was pleading for the union of all the moral forces of the nation against the growth of materialism, and said:

"I hope also that it will obtain support from that other class who may be described as adopting the position of Christianity in everything except its theology, who possess the morality of Christianity, its sense of right and wrong, its delicate sensitiveness of conscience, though they are unable themselves to accept its theological basis. These men, it may be said, erect in the mansions of their hearts a splendid throne-room, in which they place objects revered and beautiful. There are laid the sceptre of righteousness and the swords of justice and mercy. There is the purple robe that speaks of the unity of love and power, and there is the throne that teaches the supreme moral governance of the world. And that room is decorated by all that is most beautiful in art and literature. It is gemmed by all the jewels of imagination and knowledge. Yet, that noble chamber, with all its beauty, its glorious regalia, its solitary throne, is still an empty room."

There have been some who, misled by his passionate Churchmanship, have prophesied that Lord Hugh Cecil would traverse the political path of Gladstone. It is true that he is the ecclesiastical successor of Gladstone in the House, and that he reverences his memory for the religious faith that saturated and coloured his mind. As he says of him: "The conscious dependence on unseen help; the inner vision which never was hidden from him that, great as were political affairs, there were much greater things going forward; the Mosaic sight of the Invisible, which is the strength of the religious character, gave him a steadiness of purpose and a dignity of bearing which no stress could subvert."

But the parallel is false. Gladstone was a great Churchman, but he was also a great citizen. In that spacious mind the sphere of the Church and the sphere of the State were truly separated and appreciated. He brought religion into politics, but he did not exalt the Church above the State. He would have kissed the toe of Hildebrand, but he would not have gone to Canossa. Lord Hugh is an ecclesiastic and not a citizen. He never doffs his cassock, for he is always on the way to the abbey. No path beckons him unless the spire is at the end. Education is nothing to him except as an instrument for making little Churchmen, and his famous phrase about "the school with two doors, one of which opened from the street, while the other admitted to the Church," represents his whole attitude to secular affairs. In a word, he is a fanatic. Hence that strange union of spirituality with unbridled passion, the sharp practice of a shady attorney, and the studied rudeness of a disappointed cabman. He moved the House to its centre by the sincere and touching eloquence of his speech against the Deceased Wife's Sister Bill in 1902, and then secured its rejection by the discreditable trick of loitering in the lobby with Lord Percy and other conspirators—an event which was commemorated in the jingling lines called *Festina Lente*, the first verse of which ran:

"Linger longer, Percy, linger longer, Hugh;
The House is dead against you and it's all that you can do;
So linger still and stop the Bill
To-day from getting through;
Ah, linger longer in the lobby, linger longer, Hugh."

The incident also attached the name of the "Hughligans" to the little group of insurgents and high-spirited young Tories who, under Lord Hugh and Mr. Winston Churchill, had combined to "study high politics on a diet of weekly dinners." "We shall dine first and consider our position afterwards," said Mr. Churchill. "It shall be High Imperialism nourished on a devilled sardine." Gone are those halcyon days—gone are the dinners. Earl Percy is dead, and across the floor of the House Lord Hugh flings his gibes at "the vicarious insolence" of the old comrade of devilled sardine days.

Lord Hugh Cecil

Of the five sons of Lord Salisbury, he alone is the inheritor of his father's sombre genius. He inherits, too, his father's mordant tongue. He has little humour, but a biting sarcasm, as when speaking of Lord Rosebery's failure as a leader he said, "He reminds me of an inexpert choir-boy who is always a little too late for the responses. He says what everyone else is saying, and, generally speaking, says it too late." He has all the sophistry of a schoolman, and would have been divinely at home in those controversies immortalised by Pascal. He can explain anything away—from a row in the House to a false signature to a letter. He has almost succeeded in explaining away the history of his own family—at all events that part of the history which it is inconvenient to remember when the "plunder of the Church" is under discussion. He has, in short, a mind of inexhaustible fertility in the invention of reasons for believing what he wants to believe. He can weave incantations on a theme until the brain reels, right and wrong have miraculously changed places, and the great globe itself seems a myth. It is the art of the Jesuit.

But, with all this, he is loyal, like the Jesuit, to his fundamental beliefs, and will suffer anything for them. There is no price on him. He is not in the market. And it is this fact which makes him indeed priceless. When Mr. Chamberlain raised the tattered flag of Protection Lord Hugh did not equivocate or count the consequences. He took his life in his hand, and fought the superstition with every weapon in his power, even carrying the light of economic sanity into the darkness of Birmingham. The lightning of Highbury descended on him, and he was driven out of the pale, banished from Parliament, made an outcast from the party which his father had led in the past and his cousin led then. No matter. You cannot break or coerce the stuff of which he is made. Though his head had rolled off in Whitehall, the last words would have been "I believe."

John Stuart Mill says somewhere that "one person with a belief is a social power equal to ninety-nine persons who have only interests." There is the secret of Lord Hugh Cecil's influence. On to a stage thronged with interests—personal interests, social interests, trade interests, party interests—he comes bringing a belief. It is a belief strangely out of touch with reality, aloof and remote from life, entirely anti-social—a belief that, carried out, would bring revolution and anarchy. But it is a belief for which he lives, and of which he would barter no shred for any reward the world could offer. And at its heart is a lofty vision of human life and a pure spiritual passion. His future is doubtful. Apart from Mr. Balfour, he is the chief intellectual asset of his party. But two things bar the way. He is the last of the Tories in a time when his party is following feverishly in the wake of what he believes to be the false gods of reform. And the Protectionist heresy cuts him off from full communion. Even if that heresy is purged and Conservatism returns to its true line of quietism and *laissez-faire* he will still find a bar to the leadership. For essentially he is not a politician, but a priest, and no party in these days can march under ecclesiastical insignia. His true place is below the gangway, breathing out his fiery spirit, sometimes in passionate eloquence, sometimes in fierce disorder; but always aloof—a voice crying in the wilderness of the world from the cell of the mediæval monk.

MR. ASQUITH

WHEN the history of these tempestuous days comes to be written, there is one figure that will emerge with a certain simplicity and aloofness that will dominate the story. It is the figure on the bridge. Pitt lives, rightly or wrongly, in Scott's phrase, as "the pilot who weathered the storm." It was the storm of a European convulsion. Mr. Asquith will be remembered as the captain who weathered the storm at home. No Prime Minister since Pitt has been confronted with so heavy a task as that which has fallen to Mr. Asquith's lot. Indeed Pitt's was the easier task of the two, for he was able always to appeal to the passion of patriotism and the fear of the foreigner. He had behind him the influence of the King. Democracy as we know it had not come to birth, and such opposition as found a voice was trampled under the heel of a ruthless repression. It was not Pitt but Fox who was the real hero of that tremendous time—Fox who spent his life in hopeless opposition, and struck that great note of liberty that has been the soul of English Liberalism for a century.

To Mr. Asquith has fallen the more difficult task of remodelling the structure of society at home. He did not seek the task. Temperamentally, I think, he would have avoided it, for he is not a man who loves action for action's sake. He prefers ease to conflict, and has none of that joy of battle which is characteristic of his brilliant lieutenant. His eye does not light up with any fine frenzy, and no tide of hot compassion engulfs him. He has little imaginative vision, a cold distrust of idealism and sentiment, a dislike of anticipating the future. You cannot get him to look into the middle of next week. He takes the situation as it presents itself, and deals with it honestly and plainly. It is the habit of the barrister who gets up his case overnight. Perhaps it would be more true to say that it is the habit of the judge, for the temper of his mind is wholly judicial. Nor has he that impulse of a compelling moral fervour which gave such driving power to Gladstone. He never believes—as Gladstone believed or as Cromwell believed —that he is a vehicle of Sinaitic revelation. He is saved from the self-deception which that frame of mind so easily involves, and he is too scornful of pretence to walk on moral stilts. Mr. Roosevelt's talk about Armageddon and "battling for the Lord" would be as unthinkable from him as Mr. Roosevelt's vulgarities about being "as bully as a bull moose." No man strips his speech so bare of appeals to emotionalism, ignorance, or passion. He will have no falsities. He will talk neither to the gallery nor to the side boxes, but to the general intelligence. If you cannot be reached by a plain tale and a clear argument, then you must go elsewhere. He has no lollipops for you. He brings you no jokes, and leaves fireworks to children. He is the russet-coated captain who must be taken for his merits, and not for a gay livery. If you will have him on these terms, good. If not, then there are other candidates for your patronage and support.

Nor has he the ambition which is the spur of lesser men. It is true that his aims have always been high. I have been told by one who knew him well when he was a boy at the City of London School, and whom he has since honoured, that young Asquith came to him one day and asked him to test his knowledge of the House of Commons, its members, and the seats for which they sat. His friend asked him the motive for such apparently idle knowledge. "I am going to the Bar and into Parliament," was the reply, "and I intend to be either Lord Chancellor or Prime Minister."

But ambition in the sense of reaching beyond himself he has never had. He was conscious of great powers, marked out a path for himself, and went forward to the goal without hurry or self-assertiveness. No statesman ever came to greater distinction with less pushfulness and self-advertisement, or with a more deliberate avoidance of the arts of the demagogue. He leaves the limelight to those who love it. He has a wholesome scorn of limelight, and a dislike for all the insincerities and affectations that make for popularity. His public bearing is somewhat stiff and unsympathetic. It is the attitude of one who is always on guard over himself, who fears that geniality is only another word for weakness, and who refuses to wear his heart on his sleeve for daws to peck at. He does not invite enthusiasm nor easily respond to it, and if he makes a railway journey he avoids wayside demonstrations and draws the window-blind of the carriage.

It is the custom of his enemies to speak of him simply as an intellectual machine. "He talks like a barrister from a brief," said Mr. Chamberlain bitterly in those memorable days of the Protectionist revival when Mr. Asquith pursued him from place to place and blew his case to the winds. It is true that his mind moves with a certain mechanical exactness and perfection. It is always adequate, never excessive. It wastes nothing and lacks nothing. Throughout, this intellectual mastery has been apparent. His master at the City of London School, struck by the boy's command of lucid speech; Jowett at Oxford, impressed by the undergraduate's capacious understanding; Sir Henry James, attracted by a statement of a case which some unknown junior had drawn up in three days, and which James declared might have taken three weeks — all bore witness to an incomparable intellect. In the House of Commons it is almost as though it works apart from his personality. See him at a time of crisis, wedged in the front bench between his lieutenants, his movements restless, his face a little flushed, his hands passing now over his knees, now across his chin. One might imagine him flustered and beaten. He rises. It is as though a machine gun has come into action. Every word finds its mark. His sentences seem to pour visible destruction into the ranks of the enemy. There is no rhetoric, no appeal to party passion, none of the sophistry with which Mr. Balfour loves to cloud his purposes, not a breath of emotion—nothing but the resistless logic of a powerful mind, that marshals its resources with incomparable ease and certainty. There have been more fascinating figures in the House. There has never been one more completely its intellectual master, nor one who gave the mind, as distinct from the feelings, a sense of more entire satisfaction.

But to regard him simply as an intellectual machine is wholly to misapprehend him. Behind the machine is a man of rare probity of character. Perfect honesty in politics is an uncommon achievement. When it is attempted it does not often lead to the front benches. A calculated honesty may do so, but I speak of real not of simulated honesty. And if it does miraculously arrive there it does not often survive the disintegrating influences of office. It did so in the case of Sir Henry Campbell-Bannerman, and it has done so in the case of Mr. Asquith. Mr. Asquith has not, it is true, the fundamental conviction of his predecessor: his roots are less deep in the democratic soil. Campbell-Bannerman was

> "True as a dial to the sun
> Although it be not shin'd upon,"

but Mr. Asquith has not that instinctive certitude in great crises. He trusts his intellect where Campbell-Bannerman trusted his faith. His inferiority is spiritual, and when he fails, as in the case of the South African War, he fails, like all the men of the Jowett tradition, because, trained in a purely academic view of politics, he bases himself upon the calculations of the material factors and the motives of expediency, and is deaf to the promptings of the primal instincts of men. But if his mind works within a more limited circumference than that of Fox or Gladstone, it is within that range marked by a rare integrity of purpose and performance. No man is more scrupulously loyal to his word, more exact in the fulfilment of his engagements. It is not enough to fulfil the letter: he must fulfil the spirit. It is not the judgment of others that he fears; but the judgment of his own mind. He can stand abuse and slander and misrepresentation with cold and silent disdain, for he has that type of mind which is more at ease when it is attacked than when it is flattered. In the days when he used to be pursued with the cry of "Featherstone"—a crime for which he was no more responsible than I am—he used to stand silent with folded arms and head flung back in scornful challenge until the storm died away. He would not stoop to explain or reply. And so in that great scene in the House after the Parliament Bill had triumphed, when for an hour the Opposition howled at him like shrieking dervishes, he uttered no word of resentment or anger, made no appeal for fair play. He bore the outrage with a certain noble detachment of bearing, struggled with patient endeavour to gain a hearing, and when Lord Hugh had triumphed and he had to sit down defeated, he did so with only one sentence of grave and dignified protest. His persecution by the militant suffragists has been borne with the same disciplined restraint. He does not reply or argue. He will keep his bond. He will neither subtract from it nor add to it though they pull the knocker off his door and the epaulettes off his shoulders.

But when he suspects that he has misled the public then he is profoundly moved. The Albert Hall incident came nearer to breaking him than any episode of these stirring years. His speech contained a passage which was construed into a declaration that if the Liberals won the election the King would create the Peers necessary to pass the Parliament Bill. The truth about that passage will perhaps never be known. But we know that Mr. Asquith had no guarantees from the King on the point. He won the election, but that misunderstanding stood between him and the nation. Other men would have slurred it over with a light hand, and trusted to the development of events and the forgetfulness of the public mind. He was urged to leave the facts to reveal themselves with the progress of the drama. But no, whatever befell he must clear his account with the public. Those who saw him in those days know how unnerved he was—how he paced his room, agitated and distressed. He went down to the House on the opening day of the new Parliament, and in terms as bald as he could make them announced that there were no guarantees, and that guarantees in such circumstances would have been unthinkable. Never was there such a cold douche for a triumphant party. It seemed as if the victory had vanished into thin air—as if Samson had pulled the temple down over his doomed followers. The members went out into the lobby and discussed the date of the next election. And for weeks the pall of that desolating speech hung over the sky of the new Parliament.

This meticulous sense of honour governs all his public conduct and all his dealings with Parliament. No public man has eaten fewer of his own words than he has done. This is due not only to the probity of his mind, but to the precision of his speech. He does not spill over with words. They are weighed and counted, and every one has its specific value. His vocabulary has little colour and no poetry. It is copious and sufficient; but formal and professional. He "does not hesitate to assert," and he will "venture to deny." He has even been known to speak "with no uncertain sound," and the guarded locution "if and when" is so frequently on his lips that I have heard of the gayer spirits of the House making bets on its appearance in any given speech. He uses words, in fact, not as a luxury, but with business-like directness, and for the simple purpose of making himself understood, and no man ever succeeded better. His brevity is as remarkable as his lucidity. As Lord Morley says of Tacitus, he seems to aim at putting a book into a chapter, a chapter into a page, a page into a sentence. The result is that no one can afford to quote him loosely against himself. If he does, he is impaled on the question, "When did I say that?" And there is no answer.

Few men seek less to score merely dialectical points, for, unlike Johnson, he does not argue for argumentative victory, but for practical results. But if he is attacked no one can deliver a more smashing blow. He does not suffer fools gladly, and his retorts to idle questions are apt to be abrupt and rough. "Arising out of that answer, may I ask the Prime Minister, etc.?" "The hon. gentleman's question does not arise out of my answer." Or: "Am I to draw the conclusion—?" "The hon. gentleman may draw what conclusion he likes," and as the heavy jaws snap together one seems to see the head of the unhappy questioner disappear within.

It would be unfair, nevertheless, to conclude that he is hard and unsympathetic. The manner is hard, it is true, but it is a manner that is worn as a shield. Sometimes we get behind the shield, and discover a man of sensitiveness and humanity. There was such a moment towards the end of the great coal strike. For weeks he had been labouring to bring about a settlement. Then one afternoon he came into the House from one of the innumerable conferences. At once he rose to make a statement. As he proceeded the air seemed to darken. His story was of failure, and the sky became overshadowed with the menace of an incalculable catastrophe. He made a last appeal to the patriotism of masters and men, and then speaking of his own efforts that had failed his head fell, his voice sank into a broken whisper, he stopped. With a struggle he finished his sentence and sank into his seat. I have only seen one man unmanned in the House of Commons. It is significant that it should have been the man who is supposed to be the hardest metal of all. But, indeed, the iron mask is only a public disguise. " He is *so* good-tempered," is the verdict of the one who probably knows him best, and I have been told by the uncle who took charge of him and his brother after their father's death in Yorkshire that the comradeship between the two boys was never broken " even by the lifting of an eyebrow."

As a parliamentary leader he will take rank with the highest. He has not the omnipotence of Pitt, nor the eagle flight of Gladstone, nor the Oriental magic of Disraeli, nor the fascination of Mr. Balfour. But he has a rare combination of qualities that make him invaluable as a leader in these days. Not the least of these are what one may call negative qualities. A brilliant woman once said to me: " Asquith has three great virtues. He has no egotism, no jealousy, and no vanity." His freedom from jealousy is one of the rarest and most precious virtues of public life. When Gladstone offered him the Solicitor-Generalship he declined the office. He would not take the post that belonged, in his opinion, to another, nor—though his relations with Campbell-Bannerman had been very strained as the result of their profound differences on the Boer war—did he support Sir Edward Grey in his attempt to send " C.-B." to the House of Lords in 1905. And all the efforts of the enemy to drive a wedge in between him and Mr. Lloyd George have failed. There is nothing in the history of this time more pleasing than his loyalty to his brilliant colleague. Without his unselfish support and the authority of his unrivalled logic, Mr. Lloyd George would have achieved nothing. It is Mr. Asquith's supreme claim to the nation's gratitude that he has never placed his own personality in the light of the national interests. He has brought no axe of his own to the parliamentary grindstone, nor has he imitated the example of Disraeli in surrounding himself with third-rate men as a chorus to his own heroic rôle. He yields a place in the sun to all who can do the work that needs to be done, and envies no man the plaudits of the crowd. Perhaps, indeed, he drives his team with too light a rein, leaves them too much latitude for personal exploitation, is, in a word, too easy-going.

But his freedom from all paltry motives has made him a perfect instrument for the great reconstruction that he has carried through. It has kept his mind receptive to the vision and initiative of others. He is himself the least experimental and adventurous of men; but he has brought to the schemes of his colleagues a disinterested criticism, and a powerful judgment governed by a high sense of public duty, and only his stability of mind and constancy of purpose could have made those schemes possible. There have been many greater political seers: there has been no greater political engineer.

MR. ANDREW CARNEGIE

THERE is probably no more impertinent task than that upon which I have so cheerfully entered in these studies. It is a task that is at once easy and impossible. We love to weigh each other in the balance and to deliver solemn judgments that dismiss this man to the sheep upon the right hand, that man to the goats upon the left. Of only one thing can we be sure: that is, that our judgments will have no likeness to the judgments which will be passed upon us in the Valley of Jehoshaphat.

Take that bright, beady-eyed little man at the end of the table for example. Grey and pallid, with broad brow and a mouth that closes with the decision of a rat-trap, vivacious as a boy, full of jokes and morals, maxims, assertive, combative, clear-headed, masterful —what will be the ultimate judgment passed upon him? For this is Andrew Carnegie, the wonderful Rich Uncle who has emerged from the mephitic glooms of Pittsburg and scattered largesse over all the earth. Seen through that dazzling rain of dollars he appears radiant and aureoled; seen through the smoke of Pittsburg he is less radiant, and the aureole is dim. Your judgment of him will be governed by whether you take the rainy or the smoky view, whether you think of him in terms of libraries and universities, Peace Palaces and Hero Funds, or in the light of the thousands of men working twelve hours a day and seven days a week in the furnaces of Pittsburg. In either case your judgment will probably be wrong.

It will certainly be wrong if you do not remember that there are two Andrew Carnegies—at least—and that without the one we could not have the other.

Andrew Carnegie

Mr. Andrew Carnegie

There is the business man, ruthless, hard as his own pig-iron, who is the maker of millions, and there is the philanthropist, filled with the abstract love of humanity, who is the spender of millions. Neither has any dealings with the other. Each has an atmosphere and a hemisphere of his own. "Business is business," said Mr. Andrew Carnegie, the great Ironmaster, when he smashed the trade union at Homestead and prepared the way for the gigantic serfdom of the Steel Trust. "Humanity is on the march," says Mr. Carnegie, the philanthropist, as he scatters libraries o'er a smiling land, and in his study paints in gold letters his motto: "All is well, for all grows better."

There is no conscious conflict between the two. There is no conflict because they never meet. Each comes into action at the word of command and vanishes when his task is done. "Business," and up springs the Ironmaster keen as a razor. "Humanity," and up springs the Philanthropist bursting with benevolence. The phenomenon is familiar. It was exhibited in its extremest form in the late Mr. Passmore Edwards, whose passion for economy, even penuriousness, in business was at least as remarkable as his splendid generosity to the public.

The two motives are distinct. Mr. Carnegie does not differ from the ordinary millionaire in the object with which he pursued wealth. He pursued it because he liked the pursuit, because he had the passion of the industrious apprentice to "get on." It was only when he had attained it that he parted company with the millionaire type. It was only then that the Friend of Humanity discovered himself. No doubt the idealist was always dormant in him; but it was not the idealist who had anything to do with making the money: that was the work of a simple, frugal Scot with a swift eye for an opportunity and the instinct for turning it to account.

It is this duality which should be kept in mind in dealing with Mr. Carnegie. On the making side he is no better and no worse than the average millionaire. The fact that he destroyed trade unionism by the help of thousands of soldiers gives him a bad eminence in the mind of the industrial world. It is an achievement that will never be forgotten or forgiven though the sky rain libraries and temples of peace. It is true that Mr. Carnegie was touring in the British Isles in the midst of that thrilling drama and that he disclaims all responsibility for the shooting. But it was he who wrote the letter declaring war on the union, and it is he who for good or evil must bear the burden of all that followed. The Steel Trust has its heel on the neck of labour, and it was Mr. Andrew Carnegie who placed it there.

But though as a maker of wealth he has the defects of his class, as a steward of wealth he has set a rare example. And he has done it without any affectation of sacrifice. In his address at the opening of the Institute in Pittsburg in 1907 he said, speaking of his gifts:

"It is true I gave some pieces of paper, but they do not represent anything in my mind, because I do not part with anything that I could understand. It is true that these bits of paper represented bonds, but I had never seen these bonds. I cannot feel that I own a mountain. I don't think any man can really feel he owns a stretch of land. Let him walk over mountains or heather and say to himself, 'These mountains are mine,' and he will not be able to make himself understand the meaning of the words. So it is impossible to make one's self understand that he owns a great fortune. So far as I know there are as many bonds in the safe deposit vault as there were before."

This is the language of a plain and sincere mind. And it is because he has never become obsessed with wealth, but has always remained its master, that Andrew Carnegie has secured so unchallenged a place among the millionaires. The Pierpont Morgans and the Rockefellers are simply gigantic shadows of men unintelligible apart from their millions. But this bright-eyed little man at the table would be noticeable anywhere. He does really own his millions and is not owned by them. "Millionaires who laugh are rare," he says, but he laughs always. He laughs because he has had the wisdom not to mistake riches for life. "Huge fortunes," he says, "so far as their owners are concerned, are as useless as a Star or a Garter are to their possessors and not so ornamental."

His habit of mind and point of view belong to an earlier generation. He is not afraid of those commonplaces which are the great truths of life and his talk and writing are garnished with well-worn maxims—"Virtue must bring reward, vice punishment, work wages, sloth misery." Against tobacco he carries on an unceasing warfare, and it was only after long hesitation that he so far yielded to the necessities of hospitality as to provide a smoking-room for his friends at Skibo Castle. His politics are of the same pattern as his morals. He is an Individualist of the most uncompromising kind. Like the self-made man generally, he sees in his own triumph convincing proof that a career like his is open to everyone who deserves it. Virtue is its own reward. Look at me. "No young man ever lived who has not had a chance" is a favourite saying of his. This frame of mind naturally makes him intolerant of Socialism. But, on the other hand, he sees that the State must break down the tyranny of the plutocracy and through taxation effect a juster distribution of wealth by graduated income-tax and death duties. All wealth, he holds, is due to the operation of society, and is therefore justly subject to its laws according to its ability to pay. Moreover he approximates to the modern view of the functions of the State in his advocacy of Industrial Courts to control the Trusts by fixing the maximum prices in the interests of the consumer. This hardly seems distinguishable from Socialism, though Mr. Carnegie would probably not admit it.

There is about him the not unpleasant vanity of the successful man. He loves—like John Burns, whom he resembles in so many particulars—to regard himself as a bookish man, and talks much of Shakespeare and Robert Burns. And he loves, too, to win his game at golf or at billiards; it makes things more comfortable if you lose. He would rather be remembered as an author than as an ironmaster, and he declares that "if he had his life to live over again he would be a librarian." His enjoyment of life is unceasing. "I never found my business anything more than mere play," he says.—"Golf is the only serious business of life." "It's worth ten thousand dollars to make a drive like that."—"Making one hundred thousand dollars is nothing to the sport of landing a monster pickerel."—"I would give all the millions I own and all I could get credit for if I could only be a boy again." It is the eager, vivacious talk of a young man.

His youthfulness is shown also in his open-minded enthusiasm for new subjects, especially subjects which are looked at askance by the conventional. Thus he has thrown himself into the cause of "Speling Reform," and not only advocated it for others but adopted it himself. He delights in the triumphs of science, and when his new observatory at Mount Wilson brought 60,000 new worlds into the range of vision he was as pleased as if he had manufactured them at Pittsburg. One of his pleasures is to feel that the Carnegie yacht, the first ever built with bronze substituted for steel so as not to deflect the magnetic needle, is going over all seas year after year, "putting the world right. That one service," he says, "will give ample dividends upon the five millions"—the five millions sterling, that is, that he has given to the Carnegie Institute at Washington.

Mr. Andrew Carnegie

Like the philanthropist generally, Mr. Carnegie would not survive the very searching question in Mr. Chesterton's ballad—"But will you lend me half a crown?" He will not lend you half a crown. "If you ask him for an autygraf," says Mr. Dooley, "he'll send ye a free libr'y." That is not quite true; but he would probably rather give you a free library than half a crown. He is even said to avoid the perils of indiscriminate giving by going about with empty pockets.

The famous saying attributed to him that "the man who dies rich dies disgraced," is really a paraphrase of a passage in his *Gospel of Wealth,* in which he says that "the man who hoards his wealth instead of administering it as a fund for the service of his fellows should die 'unwept, unhonoured, and unsung.'" If Mr. Carnegie did indeed use the briefer and more emphatic saying, he is in danger of dying disgraced. For so far it is estimated that he has made no serious breach in his millions. He has given away something like forty millions sterling; but as fast as he dispenses the balance accumulates. Once, it is said, he did seem to be shifting his golden mountain; but then came an appreciation in his Steel Trust securities and again he was foiled. It is a pitiful thing to be struggling all one's days to get a little poorer and to struggle unavailingly. I wonder what those thousands of Steel Trust workers who earn sevenpence an hour—which is less than a living wage in America—think of it. Their struggle is in quite another direction.

Yes, on the whole, that seems to suggest the best way out for Mr. Carnegie. He has failed to get rid of his fortune by building his fifteen hundred libraries and his six thousand church organs and his palaces of peace and his institutes, and by founding his Scotch University schemes and his Hero Funds in all countries. Why should he not try another method? Why should he not spend the rest of his days and his resources in warring against the twelve-hour day and the seven-day week of the Steel Trust? That Trust is the most colossal monument that the Mammon of modern industry has conceived. Its capital of 1,400,000,000 dollars is half water. Upon that water vast dividends are paid out of the excessive hours and under-payment of thousands of unhappy serfs. That cannot be a pleasant thought for Mr. Carnegie as he wakes to the sound of the bagpipes at Skibo Castle. For it was he who broke the union that gave the serfs at least a fighting chance.

The smoke of Pittsburg rises again between me and the bright-eyed figure at the end of the table. The aureole grows dim.

MR. WALTER LONG

MR. WALTER LONG is the most brilliant touch of colour in the House of Commons. The general appearance of that Assembly is grave, almost funereal. It is a study in greys and blacks—grey heads and black coats, black heads and grey coats. The average member of Parliament, like the average Englishman, has a horror of display, and conceals his vanity as carefully as he does his affections. It is only rebels like Mr. Keir Hardie who dare to profane the solemnity of the Chamber by appearing in a suit of white flannels. But Mr. Walter Long is decked in colours always. He cannot help it, for nature has painted him with the tints of the rosy-fingered dawn. As he reclines on the Front Opposition Bench, his head flung back, his eyes closed in happy dreams, he seems like an idyll of the countryside. He carries the mind out of this dusty atmosphere to the ploughed lands and pastures of the billowy Wiltshire country, to jolly meets of the hounds on crisp, bright mornings, when his coat is as far-shining as his countenance, to harvest homes and country markets, and all the wholesome activities of the England that endures. In the midst of so much that is transitory, here is a figure that speaks of the permanence and continuity of things, that takes the mind trippingly through the centuries, and links us with a past that fades into the twilight of legend.

It was just such a Walter Long as this, I fancy, that came up to represent Wiltshire in the time of the Wars of the Roses. It was another Walter Long that helped to hold down Mr. Speaker in his chair during the reading of Sir John Eliot's "Tonnage and Poundage" Declaration. Hard by, in the Abbey, sleeps that Robert

Long who was Secretary of State to Charles II. There was a Long at the Field of the Cloth of Gold, a Long who fought in the fields of Picardy, a Long who was Master of the Buckhounds to Henry VIII. Tough, downright fellows all of them, I fancy; not brilliant, but honest, bluff, plain-spoken men, sound in wind and limb, loyal to their word, innocent of that subtlety and ambition that laid the foundations of the great houses of the Russells and the Cecils.

It is these homely qualities that make Mr. Walter Long so pleasant a figure to dwell upon. In politics, as in other spheres, character is of more consequence than intellect. And it is, unhappily, more rare. It is certainly more rare on front benches. It is the agile, subtle, often the intriguing mind that arrives there, the mind that uses public causes as instruments of personal advancement, that directs its course not by fixed stars but by the weather vane, and drops a principle as lightly as the mariner drops ballast from the hold. Now Mr. Long never dropped anything that he believed in, nor adopted anything that he did not believe in. He is an entirely honest man, whose "thoughts lie clear as pebbles in a brook." He does not try to deceive either himself or the public, and his motives are as transparent as his utterance. He must not be confounded for a moment with mere reactionaries like Sir Frederick Banbury. The scope of his mind is limited, it is true. It is a bucolic, unimaginative mind. But within its scope it is singularly sincere and public-spirited. It is motived not by personal considerations of his own class, but by real devotion to his country, to his conception of justice and duty, to his sense of humanity.

Perhaps the incident of the Steeple Ashton water supply seems to qualify this view. He had asked the village for something approaching £1000 for an acre or so of land whose market value was only about a tenth of that price. The incident occurred, appropriately enough, to point the moral of the land campaign in connection with the famous Budget. It was exposed as an illustration of the operation of the land monopoly. Mr. Long was touched in his most sensitive spot, and challenged me to go and argue the matter out with him before the villagers. But the attack was not on him : it was on the system. The case showed the injustice which the land monopoly inflicts on the community even when it is administered by men who desire to be just. It showed that Mr. Long was not more enlightened than the system that produced him.

But I should not despair of him even here. His mind is slow to receive ideas, for centuries of tradition encrust it, but its inherent honesty makes it ultimately accessible, and when once convinced it faces the facts with something of that undemonstrative candour which was characteristic of the late Duke of Devonshire. You may see a Tory prejudice dying, as it were, heroically upon the scaffold. It sweats blood, but it goes through the ordeal unflinchingly. It was so in the case of his legislation for the unemployed, the experience of which led him afterwards, step by step, to the conclusion that its basis must be the public funds and not voluntary contributions. It was an agonising conclusion, but his loyalty to facts triumphed.

It follows that he has the courage to be unpopular. He came into prominence by an act which made him the best hated man in the land. Hydrophobia had made its appearance and was spreading. He issued the most drastic muzzling order on record, and aroused a storm of incredible fury, not least among his own political followers. It was as though hydrophobia had attacked the whole dog-owning community. Mr. Long faced the storm with a stiff obstinacy that neither argued nor placated. He had a task to perform, and he would see it through though the heavens fell and not a Tory dog barked in the land. His victory was complete, and hydrophobia has been extinct for twenty years. And his courage does not take the form of exaggerated frenzies, for he is the least hysterical of men. In the midst of the frantic dementia of the "wild men" he kept a cool head, and would have nothing to do with the "Die-Hards." While there was profitable fighting to be done, no one more active than he. It was he who founded and engineered the Budget Protest League, and in that struggle as well as in the struggle against the Parliament Act he really believed that he was fighting to defend the foundations of society. But when he was beaten he took his defeat like one of the Old Guard. The ship of State was going down, and he was going down with it, but he would not go down screaming. His heart was sad, but it was not in his boots.

He has, indeed, none of the neurotic tendencies of the "new style." He is just a plain squire, who sees his country going to the dogs under the baleful influence of the Radicals, but is determined to hold his head up, and to "stop the rot" according to the rules of the game. If he cannot stop it fairly, then he will take his beating with a stiff upper lip; but at least he will not kick down the wicket or abuse the umpire. He learned his cricket at Harrow, for which he played against Eton, and he has never departed from that healthy spirit of the game embodied in a later maxim of the Harrow Song Book: "Play up, play up, and play the game."

The most fatal mistake the Tory party have made in recent years was when they passed over Mr. Long for Mr. Bonar Law. What the party needed was not a "new style," but a return to the old style. It wanted a leader whom it could trust and whom it could understand, one whose "Yes" meant "Yes," and whose "Certainly" did not mean "Certainly not." It had been wearied by the intellectual gymnastics of Mr.

Balfour and the intrigues of the Protectionists, and it wanted less cleverness and cunning, and more plain dealing. In the face of a Government whose activity was without parallel it sought to convince the world that its own aims were even more drastic than those of the enemy. "Codlin's the friend," it declared, "not Short." Short's reforms were a mere shadow compared with the reforms that Codlin contemplated—if only he could have office and a tariff.

In this eagerness to out-Herod Herod, to be more Radical than the Radicals, the Tory Party not only made the path easy for the Liberal Government by admitting the whole case for great changes and habituating the public mind to their necessity: it destroyed the spirit of Toryism. The Tory does not want more activity: he wants less: he wants none at all. He wants leaders who will mark time and a policy that will sleep in a pigeon-hole. He wants, in fact, Toryism which is the natural alternative to Radicalism. But the Chamberlain influence had captured the caucus, and the Chamberlain influence has no contact or sympathy with Toryism. It has been many things, but it has never been Tory. And the result was that at a time when a confident appeal to the *vis inertia* of society, to sheer unadulterated Toryism, would have met with an eager response, the party became frantically adventurous. Mr. Austen Chamberlain was not strong enough to make himself leader, but he was strong enough to keep Mr. Walter Long out and put Mr. Bonar Law in. It was a happy stroke for Liberalism, but it was one more nail in the coffin of Toryism.

Mr. Long would have given the party precisely the note it needed. He would have restored its traditions and rehabilitated its character. It is the falsity of the Unionist Party that has destroyed it: it has become an unintelligible sham to the plain man. He is bewildered by its dark *séances*, by the incoherences of its policy, by the levity with which it makes solemn undertakings and repudiates them, by its plunges into violence, and by what one of its supporters in the Press called " its pot-house methods." Mr. Long would have saved it from the gutter into which Mr. Bonar Law has led it. He would have saved it not because he is a brilliant leader, but because he is sensible of the traditions of public life and because he knows that there is a certain level below which no man and no party can stoop and retain the respect of the country.

It is too late for Mr. Long to rescue his party now. It has sunk into the morass too far: it awaits a man of genius to bring it out and make it clean and stand it on its feet again. And Mr. Long is not a man of genius: he is almost the antithesis of a man of genius. He speaks with great fluency; but he has never said anything in his life that anybody remembered. His speech is a stream of the obvious and the commonplace. It flows as fluently as water, and it makes about as much impression on the hearer as water does on a duck's back. Nor has his mind the momentum and mobility necessary for an heroic task. But it is his spirit that must be recovered if Toryism is ever to become a reputable force in English public life again. And it needs no enthusiasm for Toryism to recognise that, as exemplified in him, it is a wholesome element in affairs.

There is, says Emerson, an ultimate Tory in all of us. If ever that ultimate Tory discovers himself in me, I should like him to resemble, in the qualities of honesty and conscientiousness, that rosy-featured squire who slumbers gracefully on the Front Opposition Bench.

THE JAM SAHIB OF NAWANAGAR

THE last ball has been bowled, the bats have been oiled and put away, and around Lord's the grand stands are deserted and forlorn. We have said farewell to cricket. We have said farewell, too, to cricket's king. The game will come again with the spring and the new grass and the burgeoning trees. But the king will come no more. For the Jam Sahib is forty, and, alas, the Jam Sahib is fat. And the temple bells are calling him back to his princely duties amid the sunshine, and the palm trees, and the spicy garlic smells of Nawanagar. No more shall we see him tripping down the pavilion steps, his face wreathed in chubby smiles; no more shall we sit in the jolly sunshine through the livelong day and watch his incomparable art till the evening shadows fall athwart the greensward and send us home content. The well-graced actor leaves the stage and becomes only a memory in a world of happy memories. And so " hats off " to the Jam Sahib—the prince of a little State, but the king of a great game.

There have been kings before him to whom we have joyfully bowed the knee. There was he of the great black beard who first captured our idolatry in the far-off days when the Three Graces arose in the West. What a Vulcan the man looked! What a genius he had for the game! " I put the ball where I like," said Carpenter after bowling to him, " and then he—well, he puts it where *he* likes." And F. R. Spofforth—who can forget those thrilling days in the 'seventies when he came like a scourge from afar and swept British cricket before him? What a revelation he was of pace and passion. How stealthy his approach, how astonishing his leap into the air, how terrific the bolt he sped! And Lohmann of the many gifts, so easy, so various, so fresh and original. And Johnny Briggs, that incomparable comedian. What duels of cunning and resource have we seen between him and Abel in the old days at the Oval. And A. G. Steel—do you remember that 148 against Australia at Lord's in the early 'eighties? Grace had failed, and Lucas had failed and the day was dark for England. Then, supported by dour Richard Barlow, Steel slowly retrieved the game, broke the bowling, captured it, smote it. Thrice in succession he drove—was it not the great George Giffen himself?—into the crowd, and with each stroke the temperature rose higher, and the ring was a vision of waving hats and handkerchiefs, and the sound was like the breaking of a great sea on a ringing shore. I think we must have been more intense in those days. Perhaps it is that we were younger.

Yes, there were giants before the Jam Sahib. And yet I think it is undeniable that as a batsman the Indian will live as the supreme exponent of the Englishman's game. The claim does not rest simply on his achievements, although, judged by them, the claim could be sustained. His season's average of 87 with a total of over 3000 runs, is easily the high-water mark of English cricket. Thrice he has totalled over 3000 runs, and no one else has equalled that record. And is not his the astonishing achievement of scoring two double centuries in a single match on a single day —not against a feeble attack, but against Yorkshire, always the most resolute and resourceful of bowling teams?

But we do not judge a cricketer so much by the runs he gets as by the way he gets them. "In literature as in finance," says Washington Irving, "much paper and much poverty may co-exist." And in cricket, too, many runs and much dullness may be associated. If cricket is menaced with creeping paralysis, it is because it is losing the spirit of joyous adventure and becoming a mere instrument for compiling tables of averages. There are dull, mechanic fellows who turn out runs with as little emotion as a machine turns out pins. To watch them playing is as deadly an infliction as it was to see Peall making his interminable breaks with the spot-stroke. There is no colour, no enthusiasm, no character in their play. Cricket is not an adventure to them; it is a business. It was so with Shrewsbury. His technical perfection was astonishing; but the soul of the game was wanting in him. There was no sunshine in his play, no swift surprise or splendid unselfishness. And without these things, without gaiety, daring, and the spirit of sacrifice cricket is a dead thing. Now, the Jam Sahib has the root of the matter in him. His play is as sunny as his face. He is not a miser hoarding up runs, but a millionaire spending them, with a splendid yet judicious prodigality. It is as though his pockets are bursting with runs that he wants to shower with his blessings upon the expectant multitude. It is not difficult to believe that in his little kingdom of Nawanagar, where he has the power of life and death in his hands, he is extremely popular, for it is obvious that his pleasure is in giving pleasure.

In the quality of his play he is unlike anything that has been seen on the cricket field, certainly in our time. There is extraordinarily little display in his methods. He combines an Oriental calm with an Oriental swiftness—the stillness of the panther with the suddenness of its spring. He has none of the fine flourishes of our own stylists, but a quite startling economy of action. The normal batsman, obeying a natural impulse, gets into motion as the bowler starts his run. He keeps pace as it were with his foe, and his movements are a crescendo culminating in a crisis. At the end of the stroke the bat has described a circle, the feet are displaced, the original attitude has been lost in a whirl of motion. It may be an ordered whirl, conventional and academic as in the case of Hayward, who has all the correctness, monotony, and efficiency of a book of rules, and like a book of rules sends one to sleep. Or it may be a whirl of fine frenzy like that of John Tyldesley, who is a glorious empiric, and who plays as though he had never heard of a rule, but meets every situation with a swift and dazzling inspiration. But in either case the whirl of bat and batsman is unfailing. The style of the Jam Sahib is entirely different. He stands moveless as the bowler approaches the wicket. He remains moveless as the ball is delivered. It seems to be on him before he takes action. Then, without any preliminary flourish, the bat flashes to the ball, and the stroke is over. The body seems never to have changed its position, the feet apparently unmoved, the bat is as before. Nothing has happened except that one sudden flash—swift, perfectly timed, indisputable

> " Like the lightning, which doth cease to be
> Ere one can say it lightens."

If the supreme art is to achieve the maximum result with the minimum expenditure of effort, the Jam Sahib, as a batsman, is in a class by himself. We have no one to challenge with our coarser methods that curious refinement of style, which seems to have reduced action to its barest terms. It is the art of the great etcher who with a line reveals infinity. It is the art of the great dramatist who with a significant word shakes the soul. Schiller, said Coleridge, burns a city to create his effect of terror: Shakespeare drops a handkerchief and freezes our blood. The typical batsman performs a series of intricate evolutions in playing the ball; the Jam Sahib flicks his wrist and the ball bounds to the ropes. It is not jugglery, or magic: it is simply the perfect economy of means to an end. His batting may be compared with the oratory of Mr. Asquith, who exercises the same thrift in the use of words as the Jam Sahib exercises in the use of action, and achieves the same completeness of effect. The Jam never uses an action too much; Mr. Asquith never uses a word too many. Each is a model in that fine art of omission of unessentials, that concentration on the one thing that needs to be said or done.

It follows that in all sports in which success depends upon truth of eye and swiftness of action the Jam Sahib has won distinction. At lawn tennis he has in his time beaten Renshaw, and as a shot he takes rank among the most instant and deadly of his time.

Probably no cricketer has ever won so peculiar a place in the affections of the people. They loved him from the first for the novelty of the thing. It was as though a pet kitten had begun to talk Tariff Reform. Here was what the late Lord Salisbury would have called " a black man " playing cricket for all the world as if he were a white man. Then they realised that he did not play it as a white man, but as an artist of another and a superior strain. And so they came to reflect, and to catch through this solitary figure in our midst some vision of that vast realm which we govern without knowing anything about it. It is the Jam Sahib's supreme service that, through his genius for the English game, he has familiarised the English people with the idea of the Indian as a man of like affections with ourselves, and with capacities beyond ours in directions supposed to be peculiarly our own. In a word, he is the first Indian who has touched the imagination of our people. He has released trains of thought in the common mind that cannot fail to influence beneficially the popular feeling in regard to the greatest task that belongs to us as a nation.

And if India had sought to make herself heard and understood by the people who control her from afar, she could not have found a more triumphant missionary than the Jam Sahib, with his smile and his bat. Great Indians come to us frequently, men of high scholarship, rare powers of speech, noble character—the Gokhales, the Bannerjees, the Tagores. They come and they go, unseen and unheard by the multitude. The Jam Sahib has brought the East into the heart of our happy holiday crowds, and has taught them to think of it as something human and kindly, and keenly responsive to the joys that appeal to us. In the narrower circle of those who know him his influence has not been less fruitful. He is as engaging with his tongue as with his bat, a lively raconteur, and a man of thoroughly democratic sympathies and serious purposes. It was he who first set himself to break down the practice of professionals and amateurs lunching separately, providing thus a curious commentary on our vague conceptions about caste. The castes of India have at least some basis in great traditions and fundamental ideas. The caste system of our own cricket field as of our own society has only a basis in riches. You cannot be a Runjeet-Singh—to give the Jam Sahib the true rendering of his much-abused name—unless you had the blood of the Lion race in your veins, but you may join the old nobility of England if you have made a brilliant speculation in rubber, or have exploited the oils of Baku or the gold of the Transvaal. Perhaps, after all, the Jam Sahib has more right to correct the caste traditions of our land than we have to deplore the caste system of his own.

He goes back to his own people—to the little State that he recovered so romantically, and governs as a good Liberal should govern—and the holiday crowds will see him no more. But his name will live in the hearts of hundreds of thousands of British people, to whom he has given happy days and happy memories.

Johnston Forbes-Robertson.

SIR JOHNSTON FORBES-ROBERTSON

WHEN the well-graced actor leaves the stage and the last plaudits die away and we turn to go, it is not the player alone to whom we bid farewell. We take farewell also of something of ourselves. The curtain has fallen like a guillotine upon the pictured past, the vision has faded, the cloud-capped towers and gorgeous palaces have shrunk to the dimensions of a dream. There will come other falconers' voices, but not for us. The light will still shine upon the morning hills, but our sun is sloping to the west. The actor does not leave the stage alone. We, too, are going into retirement. The illusion that was once a rapture has become a memory.

It will be a noble memory in the case of Forbes-Robertson. It will be a memory of how great and elevating a thing the stage may be in the hands of one who appoaches it with reverence and high purpose. There is much loose talking and thinking about the stage. There are good people who avoid it as though it were invested with some original and ineradicable sin. The old Puritan who like the anchorite regarded the senses as the enemy of the soul had a logical objection to the drama. He distrusted all æsthetic emotion and suppressed every sensuous appeal. He built himself a cell without windows to the world—with only a skylight through which he could contemplate eternity. He suppressed the stage, but he also suppressed art and literature and music and all carnal things. He had a complete philosophy—in its way a noble one. But the people who place the stage under a ban to-day have not that philosophy. They admit that the senses may be the vehicle of precious things—that Millet's "Sower" is worth many sermons, that the Ninth Symphony may sunder the soul, that a fine novel may inspire to fine purpose. Only when they come to the stage do they say: "Away with the unclean thing." They are less wise than Luther who "would not let the devil have all the good tunes." They say, "Let the devil have the stage; it belongs to him."

There could be no better corrective to this mistaken view than a course of Forbes-Robertson. It would reveal the stage at its highest, and it is by its highest that it should be judged. There have been more sensational actors than Forbes-Robertson—actors whose imaginative intensity has carried them beyond the gamut of his art. We may suppose that Edmund Kean was one of them. "To see Kean," said Coleridge, "was like reading Shakespeare by flashes of lightning." Irving, too, touched a note outside the range of Forbes-Robertson, a note of impending horror, of unimaginable things. One felt that the whole cosmos was involved in his fate, that the very elements were mixed up with the drama. It was largely a theatrical illusion, an illusion, that is, produced not by real emotion, but by profoundly considered effects, aided by perfect external attributes, the tragic, doomed face, the sepulchral voice, the strange, shuffling gait, as—in Sir Edward Russell's phrase—of "one walking hurriedly over ploughed fields." There was an air of mystery and detachment about him, a suggestion of unfathomable memories. Here was one surely who had lived with ghosts, or been with Dante into hell. You felt that he might take you aside, as Eugene Aram took the boy, and tell you the secret of some hidden pool. Whether on or off the stage, he was always an actor, a noble actor. His art had so absorbed his faculties that it had become the only reality. He is linked in the mind with the other supreme actor of his time—Disraeli. They were very brothers in their art, equally wonderful in their mastery of the technique of mystery, in suggesting an alien and unexplored realm of experience and emotion—a realm that never was on sea or land. They differed only in this, that the one was subdued to what he worked in, the illusion had become his existence; the other was a conscious player to the end.

Now Forbes-Robertson has none of this superb legerdemain. There is not a trick in his repertory. There is study, of course, study which through his teacher, Samuel Phelps, links him up with the classic tradition of English acting and makes him easily the foremost representative of that tradition, remote alike from the limelight school, which reduces the drama to the level of Doré, the "just-walk-on-and-be-natural" school, which makes it the refuge of incompetence, and the fresh and beautiful simplicity which the Granville Barkers have discovered for us in their Shakespearean revivals. But his studied effects are not designed to mystify: they are the instrument less of an emotional than of a spiritual purpose. His influence on the mind is stimulating, quickening, cleansing. The excitement is intense, but it is healthy and vital and in a very real sense ennobling. You may be "borne darkly, fearfully afar," but you return refreshed and enriched—not with the headache with which you emerge from Sarah Bernhardt's chamber of mysteries with its purple hangings, its heavy perfume, its opiates, and its witchcraft.

For, just as Irving was wholly an actor, there is a sense in which it might be said that Forbes-Robertson is not an actor at all. The idea may be conveyed, perhaps, in this way: it would be difficult to conceive Irving in any relation other than that of the stage. You cannot think of him in the terms of any vocation except the actor's. Forbes-Robertson is only incidentally an actor, just as Watts was only incidentally a painter. You may think of him with propriety in a score of possible connections, as an artist, as a preacher, as a poet, even as a politician. Irving's world in short was on one side of the footlights; Forbes-Robertson's is on the other. He is a moralist before he is an actor, a spiritual influence more than an artistic satisfaction.

And yet the stage has rarely seen a more complete artistic endowment, whether of temperament or equipment. One may be forgiven in the case of an actor for dwelling on his physical traits, for they are a considerable source of the impression he creates. In the case of Forbes-Robertson they are profoundly important. His presence brings with it a certain air of distinction and refinement. It suggests a world of chivalrous passion and romantic ideals. The horizon of the mind is widened, the emotions are tuned to a lofty theme, and one feels what Hazlitt calls a hurry of the spirit. The magic casements are open, the muddy vesture has fallen away, we are launched on the great deeps—

> " It may be that the gulfs will wash us down,
> It may be we shall touch the Happy Isles."

But whatever the end, the adventure will carry us into that larger atmosphere where the conflicts are not the conflicts of the flesh, but the nobler conflicts of the spirit. The eager motion, the swift, delicately modulated speech, the rapid gesture, at once forceful and restrained, all convey a sense of urgency and compulsion, as of a mind winged with thought and carried beyond the confines of words and the encumbering flesh. The face is at once serene and sensitive, the brow high and significant—not one of those " large, meaningless foreheads " of which Turgenieff speaks—the eyes grave, with that slight inequality of focus which suggests the dreamer, the nose bold and shapely, the lips delicate and close pressed, the chin firm, but hardly adequate to the scale of the face. It is a face immortalised in Rossetti's great picture, "Dante's Dream," in which Forbes-Robertson, then an art student at the Royal Academy, represents Dante. For it was only an accident that made him an actor. He had played Macbeth as a child with his brothers and sister, one of whom, it is said, acted the part of the army of Macbeth, another the army of Macduff, with instructions to create an impression of numbers by rushing wildly from wing to wing, a device that worked admirably until they collided, and the poverty of the battlefield was revealed. But at Charterhouse, where he was a contemporary of Cyril Maude, his interest was not in acting but in art, which he adopted as his career. But one day, forty years ago, W. G. Wills was complaining to Forbes-Robertson's father, the art critic, of the inadequacy of one of the younger players in his *Mary Stuart*. "Why not try Johnston?" asked the elder Robertson. The suggestion was acted on and Forbes-Robertson became an actor, never, however, wholly deserting his first calling in which he achieved considerable success, as his well-known picture of the Church Scene in *Much Ado*, painted for Irving, witnesses.

To this arresting presence Forbes-Robertson joins a golden voice of rare range and flexibility and with a quality of sympathy that does not pass into maudlin sentiment on the one hand or into hysterical excess on the other. It has a lower register than Gladstone's, but it has the same sonority and something of the same thrilling power. It seems to make the whole house resonant with music, and, though the utterance is unusually rapid, the cadence is so wonderfully preserved, the articulation is so clear and penetrating and the emphasis so just, that nothing is lost either to the ear or the mind. It is—as in the case of Coquelin—as though the words leap out in visible characters before the inward eye. There is no speaking voice comparable with it to-day, either on the stage or in public life, for in addition to the beauty of tone and magnitude of volume it has been cultivated to a rare degree of refinement that expresses the swiftest transitions of feeling with unfailing propriety.

It is the perfect instrument of a temperament both sensitive and reflective. This combination of feeling and thought in just balance is the quality that gives him his unique place on the stage. It is the quality that makes his Hamlet the most convincing presentation of that part, certainly in our time, possibly in the history of the English stage. The obscure psychology of the Dane places the character outside the range of the merely emotional actor who can render its phases, but cannot give it the unity that springs from a fundamental conception which makes all the parts intelligible. Kean himself failed conspicuously in this supreme test. Flashes of lightning are not enough to illuminate so subtle and complex a spiritual landscape. Forbes-Robertson triumphs because he has both Hamlet's quick sensibilities and Hamlet's philosophy. Lamb, it is true, denied philosophy to Hamlet. He saw in him only a power of excitement, as painfully vivid and as transient as the lightning's. " His sorrow is as wayward as his mirth; he lives in a world of imagination; his projects have little of the solid and consecutive architecture of the earth; his castles are of the clouds and he sees shapes forming into pomp and beauty, and rejoices, or melting away and grieves, where the general eye sees nothing but the measureless rolling of vapours." Forbes-Robertson's Hamlet is deeper and truer than this. He is responsive to the outward show of things, and to the pageantry and pomp of life; but under all he feels the burden and the mystery of this unintelligible world and in reflection a palsy falls upon the will. It is in this eternal aspect of the human conflict that the appeal of Hamlet touches the supreme note of drama; and it is because Forbes-Robertson is a thinker as well as an artist, a philosopher as well as an actor, that he has realised that conflict so subtly and nobly. He who has seen Forbes-Robertson in the part can think of Hamlet in no other terms. There is a temptation to endow the actor with the genius of the play of which he is, after all, only the momentary vehicle, but it is also true that the great actor is a revealer as well as a borrower, and the chief debt we owe to Forbes-Robertson is that he has deepened our understanding of Shakespeare. He has carried the torch of his genius into that vast world of the imagination and has illuminated it anew. It is the highest tribute to his reverence and the fineness of his artistic conscience that when we emerge from his Hamlet or Othello we think less about the actor than about the mighty mystery which we call Shakespeare.

But it does not much matter what he plays in: he shapes it to his own fine mould. It becomes something gilded with "skyey-tinctured grain." No matter how mean the material that has come from the playwright it catches from that contact a suggestion of a spacious world and a chivalrous time and a note of personal sincerity curiously rare on our stage. I do not mean sincerity of acting. That is rare, too, but less rare. Mr. Bourchier has it in *Henry VIII.*, for example. But the impression which Forbes-Robertson has always conveyed to me from those far-off days when I first heard him play Claudio in Irving's *Much Ado* is that of an actor who sees the world beyond the stage, and would fain make the stage an instrument by which to ennoble and dignify life.

Perhaps it is this quality of high seriousness, joined to a modesty which cannot stoop to the cheaper forms of advertisement, that deprived him of the full recognition of his genius in London until he came to take his farewell, and the fullness of his powers burst like a revelation on critics and public. We do not like humour in our politicians or seriousness in our actors, and Forbes-Robertson's intensity of conviction on the suffrage question is only typical of the general gravity of his mind. It is no accident that the great success of his career, *The Passing of the Third Floor Back*, should have been achieved in a play which is almost frankly a sermon. It was because it was a sermon that he was so profoundly attracted by it; it was because he was essentially a spiritual preacher that he was able to invest it with so moving a quality. I remember, just when it was being produced, meeting him and Mr. Jerome one Sunday afternoon at the house of the late W. T. Stead, and there we talked of the problem of the Better Self. I found both the author and the actor full of this means of regenerating humanity. Mr. Jerome told us an episode of his own with a horse dealer which was as wonderful as, I am sure, it was true. I hope he will tell it some day in print *pour encourager les autres*. And then Forbes-Robertson followed with a memory of his own, so poignant and moving, told with such tenderness and restraint, that I could not help feeling as I listened that in him the world had lost a preacher of quite unusual power.

This quality of seriousness, which had perhaps put him a little out of touch with the London taste, has certainly helped to make him the most popular actor in America. "I am going out to your country," said a friend to him one day as a way of intimating that he was going to America. And, indeed, in the professional sense America is his country. With all its shrillness and what seems to some of us its crudeness, the American people still has a passion for ideals. It is not afraid of the moral maxim. It loves to hear from its public men those great commonplaces—the truths of existence, as Stevenson reminded us—which are no longer good form in our more *blasé* world. The American people even suffered no shock when Mr. Roosevelt opened his campaign by conducting a vast political meeting in the singing of "Onward, Christian soldiers." In that country, with its hunger for moral purposes and visions, Forbes-Robertson—who has been a constant visitor to America since he first played there with Mary Anderson a quarter of a century ago—has carried on what is only comparable to a religious revival. *The Passing of the Third Floor Back* has ceased to be a play. It has become a school of thought, a moral cult, a new evangel.

It is fitting that Forbes-Robertson should pay America the compliment of taking his final farewell of the stage in the country which has been most responsive to his elevated appeal. That farewell is a shadow across the future. It should, as Mr. Bernard Shaw said in writing to the farewell dinner to him in London, be celebrated, not by a feast, but by a fast. When the curtain falls finally upon him it will not only close the career of a great actor; it will take from the stage a high-souled man. We shall not look upon his like again.

SIR EDWARD CARSON

Just as in the Golden Age we knew that there were good and bad fairies, so when we come out of dreamland we know that there are good and bad heroes. There is even a bad hero in *Paradise Lost.* Brougham was so captured by his courage that he said he was sorry he did not win. That sympathy with reckless adventure, divorced from moral considerations, is a very human trait. There is no shorter cut to the idolatry of men than by the path of courage, let the motives be good or bad.

Now whether Sir Edward Carson is a good or a bad hero I leave for the moment. But that there is the quality of heroism about him is undeniable. Without him the cause of Ulster would be contemptible; with him it is almost formidable. His figure emerges from the battle with a certain sinister distinction and loneliness. He is fighting for a bad cause that is in full flight, but he is fighting as men fight who count nothing of the cost. The dawn is up in Ireland, but he will not yield to it. He prefers to go down with the darkness.

If you would understand the Irish question you must understand Sir Edward Carson. Few Englishmen do understand him. Generally speaking, he is dismissed under one of two categories. In this he is simply an Old Bailey lawyer with a brief; in that he is a patriot ready to die in the last ditch for his country. He is neither. His sincerity is the sincerity of the fanatic, but his passion is not the passion of patriotism, for he has no country. He has only a caste. He does not fight for Ireland; he does not even fight for Ulster; he fights for a Manchu dynasty. But to doubt his earnestness is to make a fundamental miscalculation. It is true that his record led even Mr. J. M. Robertson to doubt whether Unionism was not adopted by him as a policy of expediency.

The charge emerged out of the famous "turncoat" incident. "There is nothing," said Sir Edward with his customary coarseness, *apropos* of Mr. Churchill's visit to Belfast—"there is nothing that the men of the North of Ireland hate more than a turncoat, whoever it be, T. W. Russell or Winston Churchill." "What about Sir Edward Carson himself?" asked Mr. Hamar Greenwood in the *Times* next day. "He was once a Liberal and a member of the National Liberal Club." It was a palpable hit, but when Sir Edward retorted, "On the day that the first Home Rule Bill was introduced I telegraphed to the National Liberal Club to take my name off the roll of members," it seemed that the victory was his. Mr. Greenwood, however, had the curiosity to go to the records of the National Liberal Club, with disastrous results for Sir Edward. For the records showed that he was elected a member two months after the Home Rule Bill was introduced, and that he did not resign until fifteen months later, on Oct. 21, 1887.

In the meantime he had become the Judge Jeffreys of the great reaction in Ireland. "Twenty years of resolute government," was Salisbury's grim prescription after the defeat of the Home Rule Bill; not freedom, but a gaol. He sent his nephew to direct the campaign, and the sword of vengeance was put in the hand of the young Dublin barrister. Ireland has always been a generous land to those lawyers who have been willing to serve the Castle. "Ireland may be a poor country, but it's a rich country to sell," said an Irish judge who owed his own success to "selling" his country. Lecky's pages illuminate the saying. "Twenty-three practising barristers," he says, "voted for the Union in the House of Commons in 1800. In 1803 six of them were on the Bench, while eight others had received high honours under the Crown. Thirty-two barristers voted for the Union (166 against) at the Bar debate in 1799. In 1803 not more than five of them were unrewarded." What a squalid tale it is!

But though Mr. Carson profited, like many a hungry lawyer, by his loyalty to the Castle, though he swept through the country as the Crown Prosecutor and imprisoned a score or more of Irish members for daring to address their constituents, though he was promptly rewarded for his services by being appointed Solicitor-General of Ireland—in spite of all this it is not, I think, true that he adopted the cause of Ulster as a matter of expediency. It is the breath of his nostrils, the fire in his blood. It makes him shed tears—real tears—on the platform. It makes him talk treason, set up a provincial government to defy the Crown, and utter wild threats about marching from Belfast to Cork. It makes him put himself deliberately out of the running for the highest office in the State to which he might have aspired. It is not expediency which works this miracle. Good or bad, it is something deeper than that.

In most men there is an ultimate passion that is capable of transfiguring them. Awaken it and you have a hero, "ready to do battle for an egg or die for an idea," in the fine phrase of Stevenson. It may be the child of an ancient prejudice, or of a new theory, or of a cherished faith. Lord George Hamilton sat in the House of Commons for a quarter of a century a model of blameless mediocrity. Like the Northern Farmer, he just "said what he ought to ha' said and coom'd awaäy." It seemed that he would go to his grave without giving the world a moment's interest or concern. Then the Fiscal issue arose. It touched the springs of reality in him. He rose in stature as if by magic. He made speeches which still rank among the most convincing and profoundly felt statements of the case for Free Trade. He relinquished office—he, who had seemed but a limpet of office. He went out of public life. The issue had found him a mere party echo; it left him a hero. It is fine to think that in the vague hinterlands of most of us there is this latent passion for something for which we are ready to die if the call comes—this latent heroism, to balance, perhaps subdue, the darker possibility that also sleeps or wakes within us.

Now I can imagine no head around which an aureole would look more ridiculous than Sir Edward Carson's. He is the very perfect knight not of the Round Table, but of the Bar mess, learned in the crooked ways of men, cynical, abounding in animal spirits, loving equally a joke or a row, with something of the gay swagger as well as the brogue of the squireen of the West—a man of the type who takes his meat red and his whisky without water. An ideal would wither in his presence. Even Joseph Surface would not have tried a "sentiment" on him, and a poet before him would be dumb—hypnotised like a rabbit before a python.

There is something in the mere presence of the man that is shattering and masterful. The retreating forehead, with the black, well-oiled hair brushed close to the crown, the long, hatchet face, the heavy-lidded eyes, at once dreamy and merciless, the droop of the mouth, the challenging thrust of the under-lip, the heavy jaw—all proclaim the man *capable de tout et pire*. He might pass for a Sioux chief who had left his scalps at home, or for an actor who plays the bold, bad baron, or for a member of another and still more strenuous profession.

A barrister, said Carlyle, is a loaded blunderbuss; if you hire it, you blow out the other man's brains; if he hires it, he blows out yours. Sir Edward Carson is the most formidable blunderbuss to be found in the

Temple. He is one of those men who always have easy cases. With a weak man on the bench he simply walks over the course. It is so much easier for a judge to agree with him than to differ from him—so much pleasanter; and after all, does not the maxim tell us to let sleeping dogs lie? "Live pleasant," says Burke, and the old judge nodding on the bench and smiling down at Sir Edward, finds himself in entire agreement with Burke. In these circumstances the great advocate is graciousness itself. He is sweet and kindly even to the poor plaintiff, who sees all his hopes vanishing before some magic solvent. Vainly his counsel wrestles with this intangible influence. He advances his most powerful line of attack. Sir Edward gently drums his fingers on the table and murmurs, "My lord, I must object." And the court holds its breath, as if there is thunder in the air. But the judge averts the storm and nods a nod of profound conviction. It is all a delightful comedy, and everyone goes away happy except the poor plaintiff, who takes a walk on the Embankment and thinks with some bitterness of Lord Halsbury. Perhaps he looks at the water. But if the judge is of harder metal then the note is changed. He must blow the plaintiff to pieces himself; he must overawe the jury himself. Then who so ruthless as he, who so artful in playing upon the political string, who so subtle in suggesting hidden motives? The heavy, vibrant voice fills the court, the blows fall with a ruthless crash, all the resources of his dominating personality are brought into play to stampede the silent men in the box.

He has the gaiety of high animal spirits and the rough wit of the street. "Ar-re ye a teetotaler?" he asks of the bottle-nosed man in the witness-box. "No, I'm not," says the bottle-nosed man with resentment. "Ar-re ye a modtherate dhrinker?" No answer. "Should I be roight if I called ye a heavy dhrinker?" "That's my business," says the bottle-nosed man stiffly.

"An-ny other business?" It is the knock-out blow of the sparrer who plays lightly with a poor antagonist and sends him spinning with a scornful flick of the finger. But when he is engaged with more formidable foes his methods are coarser. No one in politics has a rougher tongue than he or uses it more freely. "I am not paid £5000 a year for spitting out dirt," he says, referring to Mr. Birrell, who has spat out less dirt in a lifetime than is contained in that one sentence. "I have taken the opportunity of congratulating Sir John Benn that Ananias is still flourishing," is his retort to a mere statement of facts and opinions. "There is nothing but a farce going on at Westminster," he says elsewhere. "It is called 'The Gamblers, or come and get ninepence for fourpence.' Come and see Lloyd George, the magician. He must be inspired, you know, because he preaches in tabernacles." It is crude stuff. You will search his speeches in vain for a noble thought or a flash of genial humour. It is all hard and grinding. But in that it is the true note of Ulster. Not that Sir Edward Carson is an Ulster man. Orangeism never produces a great leader in Ulster. If a man of distinction is born in Ulster, he is, like Mr. Bryce or Canon Lilley, usually a Home Ruler. The Orange democracy have never produced a voice or a personality, and but for the Dublin barrister they would to-day be dumb. But the Carson spirit is the spirit of Ulster in its harshness and lack of humour. There was never such a group of smileless politicians in the House as the men of Ulster. You will get more fun from "Tim" Healy in five minutes than you will get from all of them in five years. They never make a joke, though, like Falstaff, they are the source of humour in other men. "I respect the hon. gentleman," says Mr. Birrell. "We don't want your respect," says the incorrigible Mr. Craig. "The hon. gentleman can't prevent me respecting him," says Mr. Birrell genially. And the House rocks with delight. What can one do with men who have no laughter in their souls?

But with all his defects Sir Edward has one supreme quality for a leader. He is a first-class fighting man. He would be magnificent at Donnybrook Fair, and the blackthorn, decorated with the Orange colours, presented to him at Portadown, in the midst of his famous review of the rebel warriors of Ulster, is the perfect symbol of the man. He is always for the blackthorn argument. When the Parliament Bill rent the Tory Party he was the most enthusiastic of "Die-hards," and gave his leader of to-day, Lord Londonderry, no quarter. "We are told that though we run away to-day," he said, "we will fight hereafter—I prefer to fight to-day, to-morrow, and hereafter." That is the man. His blackthorn is never idle.

Withal, he is—such is the perversity of popularity—one of the most popular of men with friends and enemies alike. "Who is the most popular man in the House?" I once asked a member of the present Cabinet. "Younger," he said, without hesitation. "And next?" "Well, it's between Ure and Carson, but I don't know which has it." The truth is that the House takes kindly to the man who has no reserves, no affectations, and loves the smoke of battle.

What is the motive that converts this masterful man of the world into a passionate crusader? Why does he shed tears on the platform? It is not, as I have said, expediency; nor is it patriotism, nor is it even the Union for its own sake. The motive is the Ascendency of his caste, established and maintained by the Union. For a century or more the Orangemen have had Ireland under their heel:

> "The crown of the causeway in market or street,
> And the rascally Papishes under our feet."

With the Castle at their back they have held Ireland

like a conquered province—they have held it as the British hold India. They have planted their nominees in every fat job; they have controlled the administration; the police have been an instrument in their hands; justice has been the tool of their purposes; the law has been of their fashioning and the judges of their making. And now the Ascendency is done. The outworks have gone; the walls are crumbling. Landlordism has been put to flight. The Irish people are emerging from the dust. They have their land; they have their local councils; they stand erect and ask for full freedom in their own household. The whole fabric of Ascendency is collapsing before our eyes. A new Ireland is dawning across the Channel. And against the dawn there stands a figure baleful and heroic, challenging the new day—a figure emblematic of an ancient tale of wrong and of a night that is past.

PROFESSOR GEDDES

You remember the man at the Breakfast Table whom Holmes called the Scarabee. He sat absorbed and silent over his meals. Nothing that was said reached the remote fastnesses of his being until one day someone mentioned beetles. Then, to the amazement of everybody, he awoke to the world around him. The key had been found that unlocked his prison, and he came out into the daylight—only to return to his solitude and abstraction when the subject that was his one contact with life ceased to hold the table.

In that quaint figure, Holmes satirised the specialist—the man who in pursuit of one microscopic phase of being becomes divorced from the splendid pageant of life. In some degree most of us are victims of this myopy of the mind. It is one of the diseases of civilisation. It is the price we pay for that wonderful subdivision of labour, that intricacy of relationship, which removes each of us farther and farther from the centre of the wheeling universe of things. As the artificial structure we create becomes more vast, more complex, a more cunning contrivance of machinery, the individual man diminishes in stature and authority. The primitive shepherd, shearing his sheep, spinning his wool, weaving his cloth, making his rude coat, was nearer the heart of things than the multitude of clever mechanics, salesmen, labourers, and clerks who each carry out some detail of the modern industry. We are like Frankenstein in his laboratory. Out of our necessities and our ingenuities we have constructed a monster who makes us his slaves; a monster so enormous, so amorphous, that we can neither measure nor control him. All that we know is that we are caught in his intangible toils.

The remedy for this tragedy of civilisation, which exalts the machine and belittles the man, is in education. Since we cannot have the joy of creation which the old craftsman had, we must learn to let the mind expand outside the scope of our daily work. And, alas, when we come to education we find the Scarabee! The same principle of specialism which reduces the artisan and the clerk to a tiny function in a structure he does not see or understand reduces scholarship to water-tight compartments—mechanics divorced from art, economics from ethics, medicine from education. Yet all are only phases of one theme that is universal—the art and practice of life. It is the full light of the sun we want, not the broken fragments of the spectroscope. We should use pigeon-holes—not live in them.

And it is to bring the world out of its dusty pigeon-holes that Patrick Geddes comes like a Crusader with his Masque of Learning, his astonishing enthusiasm, his eloquence, and what someone has called his "elfish fantasy." To meet Patrick Geddes for the first time is an intellectual red-letter day. It has all the fascination of an adventure. It is like stepping over a stile into a new country—like passing, let us say, out of the tunnel at the top of Glengariff Pass and seeing all the wonders of Kerry spread out before you. Perhaps you discover him at some Town-planning Exhibition. You have gone in without emotion, and have wandered round the rooms hung with great maps and diagrams and charts. You find them very important and very dull. You are glad that you have come; but on the whole you will be more glad to go. Then good fortune brings you Professor Geddes and the whole place is illuminated. The maps cease to be maps and become romantic visions. His talk envelops you like an atmosphere; your mind becomes all windows—windows into the past and windows into the future. The old city leaps to life again; the map echoes with the tramp of armed men; it becomes a pageant of history, a sudden interpretation of the present. But it becomes more: it becomes a promise of the future, a vision of the City Beautiful, with squalor banished, with learning and life no longer divorced, but going hand in hand to the complete triumph over the misery and confusion of things.

Or it may be around the fireside or in the lecture room that you fall under the spell as he reveals the significance of the Greek mythology, translates it into a complete philosophy of life, and applies it to the living present and the problem of the making of the great city. For he is, before all things, the prophet of citizenship. He is the enemy of the great capital that absorbs all the power and authority and splendour of the State to itself, leaving the rest to become vast overgrown factories, hewers of wood and drawers of water to the insolent capital. We want proud, defiant cities all through the land. What is the evil of France to-day? It is in the centralised power of Paris imposing its unobstructed will, the creation of a few politicians and journalists, upon a great nation. Or of Spain? And he seizes a sheet of paper and draws—for he always thinks pictorially—a diagram of Spain with Madrid sitting like a spider in the centre of its web, and making the great provincial cities dance to any imperialistic tune it may choose. Germany is better. There the capital has not yet degraded the provincial cities. They stand erect, with a proud, independent life each rich in its own culture and traditions, and scornful of the parvenu vulgarity of Berlin. But even there the centralising of national power is beginning to work its maleficent purpose.

And the chief value of Home Rule in his eyes is that it will qualify this tyranny of the capital. It will make Dublin a new centre of civic patriotism and independence: it will make Belfast discover that it is a great

Irish city and not an encampment on foreign soil. In the same way Scottish Home Rule will serve for the revival of the city—not of Edinburgh alone, for he would not have Edinburgh absorb all the functions of government, justice, and administration. They should be distributed to add lustre and dignity to many cities.

But above all, the new city with its independent life and vigorous patriotism must have its own culture—not a University that is aloof and remote, the property of a small caste; but a University that penetrates the life of the community in all its activities, ennobles it, inspires it, has no meaning except to become the soul of the city. For learning is a living and not a dead thing. It is not a multitude of separate secrets, done up in bottles and labelled "Poison" to scare off the uninstructed. It is the common stock of the general life; it is the vital atmosphere of every society that is to grow and not perish.

But what do we find? The people do not want to be educated: they want to be amused. Bereft of our old spiritual appeal (it is he, the Professor, who is talking now), our philosophic or learned authority, we fall back for the mass on compulsion and on fear, on greed of small rewards for a bright minority, or on personal ambition for the highly gifted few. At best we form small groups and coteries—in one age grinding at grammar, in another at psychology, and always convinced of the rightness of our intellectual methods and the inherent wrongness of popular demands.

And meanwhile it is not the people, but our education that is wrong—our education that gives them stones for bread, dry bones for wholesome meat, dead stalk and thorns for fruit and flowers. "I was a student of bones myself once," he says, laughingly, recalling the days when he was assistant to Huxley, and the debt he owed that great man. "But with all his commanding grasp of the skeleton through Nature,

Huxley never came to Life. Indeed, as he once said to me, 'I should have been an engineer.' He made us, his pupils, comparative anatomists—ay, and good ones—but not naturalists, as Darwin mourned." The dead bones of knowledge would not satisfy Patrick Geddes. He must escape from the letter that killeth to the spirit that giveth life. And so, side by side, with his achievements in many branches of science—biology, mathematics, botany—he became a pioneer in the great task of applying learning to life—making it the instrument of the culture, not of coteries, but of peoples. As a young man, he wandered through Europe like a mediæval scholar, passing from one university to another and enjoying contact with the greatest minds of his day. Haeckel and Virchow declared him to be one of the most brilliant young naturalists in Europe, and his subsequent works on the *Evolution of Sex* and various biological subjects established his reputation finally as a scholar.

But a mere scholar he was not content to be. And so, concurrently with his professional duties, he plunges into great social experiments with the splendid heroism of a man who is careless of all save the pursuit of his ideal. He gathers together the students of Edinburgh to a common life and founds University Hall, which becomes the model of all the universities that are springing up in the country on the modern secular plan as opposed to the cloistral plan of Oxford and Cambridge. The Outlook Tower becomes a beacon that is seen from all lands. It symbolises the unity of the arts and sciences and their application to the immediate life around. He organises the university summer meeting at Edinburgh, and from that seed springs the great university meetings movement everywhere. It was he who twenty years ago began to talk about town-planning, of which all the world is talking to-day. And he not only talked about it, but did it, carrying out that transformation of the Closes which has done so much to redeem old Edinburgh. It was he who, with Mr. Victor Branford, founded the Sociological Society; he who was at the birth of the eugenic movement, though now out of sympathy with some of its developments; he who saved Crosby Hall from the despoiler and brought it down to Chelsea where he has founded another University Hall.

His mind is a seedplot of ideas. They spring up with a bewildering fertility which would be disquieting if one did not remember that they are all connected at the root. It was said of Coleridge that his talk seemed nothing but detached gems and irrelevances unless one was able to follow the vast arc of his theme. Then it was discovered that the sequence was perfect. And so with Professor Geddes. His talk flits through history and science and life and art, but the thought is always connected and illuminating. "He thinks in such various quantities," said one of his old fellow-students of him, "and has such a unique mental idiom, that it is difficult for the heavy-footed to follow him." And yet, however baffling and elusive he seems, the fascination is unfailing.

For, indeed, his actual achievements, great though they have been, do not form his real contribution to his time. That contribution is spiritual. It is as an inspiration that his influence has been most profound —it is as an inspiration that he is working through scores of channels to-day. "You may trace Geddes in many places where he has never been," said a distinguished educationist to me. "I sometimes say to a student, 'Ah, you have been under Geddes, I see.' 'No,' is the reply, 'I have been with So-and-so at Oxford.' 'Ah, the same thing,' I say; 'I was with So-and-so at University Hall under Geddes, twenty-five years ago.' There are dozens of reputations to-day which owe their inspiration to Geddes, just as there are many movements and ideas, unassociated with his name, that truly belong to him. Take the subject of regional geography, which has been transformed by him, or the classification of statistics, or the wonderful development in the teaching of craft in our technical schools—all Geddes. Whenever I am barren of ideas I go to that surprising book of his, *City Development*, which he wrote at the time he was asked to lay out the public gardens for Dunfermline under the Carnegie Trust. It is the very text-book of citizenship and education, and I never turn to it without fresh inspiration."

It is natural that a man of such original and wayward genius should have had little material reward for services which the future will appraise as among the most considerable done in this generation. It is natural because we are distrustful of genius, and also because Professor Geddes has never made concessions to a dull world. He has obeyed his own imperious impulses, has followed his own splendid vision, without counting the cost or the consequences. Posterity will thank him for it, for the dreamer of to-day will be the prophet of to-morrow.

MR. F. E. SMITH

THERE is no stage on which a reputation can be made or lost with such startling swiftness as the House of Commons. You may rise unknown and sit down famous. You may rise with the prestige of a distinguished career in other fields behind you and resume your seat without a future. And the tragi-comedy of it is this, that the victory may exalt a trivial man for a trivial achievement, and the defeat may thrust a fine soul into outer darkness for a *faux pas*.

Two incidents will illustrate what I mean. They occurred in the session that followed the memorable earthquake at the polls in 1906. A man of fine character and high public service, pure, disinterested, able, rises to deliver a maiden speech. The House listens with respect and expectation, for here is one who is marked out for high office. Unfamiliar with the traditions of the House, he makes some slight departure from the decorum of the occasion. He offends against "good form." From the other side rises Mr. Joseph Chamberlain. It is the hour of his humiliation. He has fallen, never to rise again; but he can still slay with that terrible tongue. He turns with all the authority of his past, and with all the passion of failure, and rends the nearest symbol of the triumphant and derisive enemy. He pours upon him a stream of bitter contempt, and a career that should have added a rare combination of character and capacity to the resources of Parliament was gravely checked—checked by a momentary slip in deportment, and the resentment of a powerful foe.

Take the other case. From the thinly-peopled benches of the Opposition there rises a figure also new to Parliament—unlike the other, new to public life. He could hardly rise in more depressing circumstances. Around him are the forlorn remnants of the great wreck. They sit broken and dispirited by an incalculable disaster. They have fallen so low that they have lost even the instinct of retaliation. They are in that chastened frame of mind that possessed Mr. Tom Lofty when he had been exposed and was told that he ought to have his head stuck in a pillory. "Stick it where you like," he said; "it cuts a poor figure where it sticks at present." "Kick us as you like," the Opposition seem to say; "we are poor cowed creatures, and shall never kick back again." And from this dreary host of the routed there emerges, as there emerged from another stricken field, one who still declares war against high heaven. A young man, elaborately dressed, slim and clean shaven, with long hatchet face, scornful lip, defiant eye, and hair oiled and smooth. He stands with his head thrust forward and his hands in his pockets, and in suave, self-assured voice delivers a speech of brilliant insolence and invective. It is elaborately studied. It scintillates with "impromptus" that have done splendid service at the Oxford Union, as Mr. Belloc and Mr. Simon, sitting on the other side of the House, doubtless recall. But it acts upon the depressed ranks like magic. "All is not lost—the unconquerable will and study of revenge." They are a party yet. They sit up, they laugh, they cheer. A leader is calling them back from flight. A new star is emerging from the gloom. And Mr. F. E. Smith sits down with his political fortune made.

If you examine the speech to-day you will find the wit thin and the insolence vapid. It depended for its success on the circumstances in which it was delivered—the gloom of the party and the sudden revelation that it was still possible to be gallant and combative. But it would be a mistake to attribute Mr. Smith's success to chance. "My pork pies don't turn out good by accident," said Aunt Priscilla, and Mr. Smith might appropriate the saying. He did the right thing for the occasion because he knew what the right thing was and had the pluck to do it. He would have emerged in any case and in any career, for he has that rare combination of audacity and calculation which is assured of success. Some men fail because they have too much respect for the world and too modest an estimate of themselves. Mr. Smith has no respect for the world, and no one ever accused him of exaggerated modesty. His philosophy is the philosophy of Disraeli, upon whose career his own is modelled. "To govern men," said the great Israelite, "you must either be superior to them or despise them." You must on the lower plane see the world not as a vast collective intelligence before which you shrink; but as a mob of purposeless children, a flock of sheep ready to follow the bell-wether into any path. You must not be terrorised by the past, but must, in Ben Jonson's phrase, be "one of those pragmatick young men" to whom action is the only valid gospel of life. In short, you must be an adventurer. Then you will find that the oyster of the world will open to your sword.

It is in this spirit that Mr. Smith has conquered. Ever since he was a boy at school at Birkenhead he has attacked the world with a high-spirited intrepidity and insolence that have marked him out from his fellows. Adventure was in his blood. His father had broken with his family as a youth, had enlisted in the army, served in India, retired as a sergeant-major, joined the Bar, established a practice at Liverpool, and died—all by the time he was forty-two. The fatherless boy was left to carve his own career, and from the first he aimed high. "If I applied myself closely to my books," he has said, "it certainly was not from any disinterested love of them." The books were stepping-stones to higher things in a social sense. He was going to get on. He was going to be among the best, and since fortune had denied him a golden key he would force the door with the crowbar of hard work. And so, scholarships and Oxford, a fellowship at Merton, success at the Bar, Parliament, a triumphant maiden speech, and his name on every lip.

A less astute man would have attempted to repeat the *tour de force*. A brilliant member on the Liberal side had made that mistake. He had delighted the House with a maiden speech of glittering epigrams. He gave it another in the same vein, and the House was amused; a third, and the House ceased to discuss him. Not so Mr. Smith. He knew that no solid career can be built on a foundation of brilliant *jeux d'esprit*. He was not out to be a Parliamentary humorist. He was out for the highest game that was going. Wit and insolence had given him a hearing and established his reputation. Now he had to justify it by showing that he was a serious politician. And so, one afternoon a little later, when members crowded into the House at the news that "Smith is up," hoping for another entertainment, they found the young man discussing a dull subject with portentous gravity and with an air of sweet reasonableness that was quite disarming.

That is characteristic of the man. There is no touch of real passion or spontaneous wrath about him. He is audacious, but his audacity does not spring from deep emotions. It comes from calculated purpose. He eyes a political situation as he eyes a jury. What is the best method of attack? Will it be better to be truculent or persuasive, to abuse the plaintiff or to shed tears over the misfortunes of the defendant, to reveal the black iniquity of Jones or to lay stress on Brown's suffering wife and family? You may hear the same accents, almost the same phrases, from him both in the courts and in Parliament. "Some of you are fathers yourselves," he says with tears in his voice, while his client in the dock looks at the jury with an air of surprised innocence. "Those of you who are parents," he says in the House in pleading accents—and the stranger in the gallery says, "Is this the terrible Mr. Smith?—is this he?"

His view of politics, in short, is purely barristerial. His wrath and his tears are both conceived in the spirit of Serjeant Buzfuz. He would lay down his life for Mrs. Bardell—such is the admiration he has for that noble-minded woman. As for that recreant Pickwick, he is a blot on the escutcheon of mankind, a shameless, unconscionable, black-hearted villain. In his heart, it may be, he knows that Mrs. Bardell is an impostor, and that Mr. Pickwick is an amiable old gentleman whom she is trying to blackmail. But his duty is to win a verdict for his client, right or wrong, and win it he will if indignation or tears can prevail.

It is this fact which explains why a personally amiable man, as Mr. Smith is, can assail his opponents in the language of Billingsgate—if Billingsgate will forgive the comparison. It explains why, for example, speaking of Mr. Ure, whom he knows to be one of the most high-principled and respected members of the House of Commons, he describes him as "A clever spokesman who, if the facts are not convenient for his case, does not hesitate to invent them." It explains why he goes down to the Taunton election and referring to Mr. Acland's criticisms of Lord Roberts, proceeds as follows:

"What happens? A priggish underling, a man not of the slightest account anywhere, who, while Lord Roberts is saving the Empire, I will undertake to say will be losing the only thing he has got—his seat—has the insolence to come forward and lift his tiny little tongue and squirt out his feeble little venom at a man old enough to be his grandfather and great enough to make people forget that Mr. Acland was ever born."

Now he doesn't really feel like this. I daresay he is

privately rather ashamed of it. But he conceives that Mrs. Bardell's interests require that he should abuse Pickwick, and he is not the man to desert his client from fear of being vulgar. "Mr. Smith is invariably vulgar," said Mr. Churchill on one occasion, and it is true that if he ceased to be vulgar he would cease to be witty. For all his jests depend upon a certain coarseness for their humour. "The Socialists had better not cheer the name of Mr. Churchill," he says at Huddersfield, "for he will most likely in the end steal their clothes when they go bathing—if they do bathe, which I doubt." This is typical of the crude quality of his persiflage. It is not irony, because it reflects too nearly what is in his mind. It is not good-humoured, for it is meant to hurt. It has the same relation to humour that a boy's ragging has: its fun is in the pain it gives.

And yet, appropriately enough, it was Mr. Smith who invented "Slimehouse speech" as a description of a speech which has probably been more grossly slandered than any speech ever delivered. For in the Limehouse speech there is not one word of abuse, not one word which is even strong, except the word "blackmail" used justly and frankly in connection with the Gorringe case. Yet upon the legend of its scurrility a certain type of journalism has largely existed for years. It is that type of journalism of which we have had such an amazing revelation in the Marconi inquiry—a journalism that lives upon the scandals that it invents about its political opponents, now charging one Liberal Minister with having "squared" a divorce case, now another with having broken his parole, now several of them with having used their official knowledge in order to make money on the Stock Exchange. Why is it that these libels always come from the Conservative party? Why is it that it is left to the Kinloch-Cookes of Toryism to call a member of the Government a "mud-slinger"? Why should it be a

Tory privy councillor who tells the Socialists they don't wash themselves? Why should it be the Tories who howl down a Prime Minister and hurl books and papers at the Ministry? What is the meaning of this association of the Conservative Party with the manners of the pot-house? It is worth consideration, for the fact is significant of much. It would reveal among other things what is wrong with the Conservative cause.

But the barristerial outlook goes deeper than his humour, and it is then that the calculation, which is so successful in tactics, fails. It explains the unreality and shiftiness of his policy. He asked one day why Mr. Lloyd George did not invite the Opposition to join him in the settlement of the land question. That would have raised the issue above party, he said grandly, and his audience cheered. It had forgotten the Insurance Act. That was brought in frankly as a non-party measure. "Let us do it together," said Mr. Lloyd George, and this is what Mr. Smith replied, in a speech at Birmingham:

"I welcome in its main features Mr. Lloyd George's Bill without any reservation whatever. . . . No temptation born of party spirit, no desire for an Opposition advantage, will induce me to oppose the main features of the Bill for a single moment. It binds the employer, the State, and the employee with a common bond, and it recognises the solidarity of the nation."

That was when it seemed that the Bill had stampeded the country, and that it was safer to support it than to oppose it. We know what followed, and a year later we find Mr. Smith at Hanley declaring that "No measure more unfair and more oppressive in its incidence to the agricultural community was ever conceived."

He declares for social reform, and says the "luxurious classes" must pay for it, and when old age pensions are introduced he assails them with flippant jokes—

"One section of the community lives to enjoy old age pensions; the other has to die to pay them." Or, "The pious Liberals—they give you seven-and-six a week for living with your wife, and ten shillings for living with somebody else's."

Take him on the question of the unearned increment. In his election address when he entered the House of Commons he declared that he was in favour of an examination of the whole law of rating with a view to the more equitable distribution of its burdens, and he added, "I am an advocate of the taxation, upon equitable conditions, of vacant land sites in cases where the land has been increased by communal expenditure." And when the famous Budget gave expression to these views it was he who was most vociferous in his attacks on it, who encouraged the Lords to throw it out, and who, when the Lords resisted the Parliament Act, joined the Die-Hards and the Halsbury Club, and hinted that in two years the streets would run with blood. The two years have passed and no blood has flown. But Mr. Smith is not depressed. England has failed him, but Ulster remains, and he rejoices in "prave 'orts" like these: "Violence and bloodshed in Ulster would be an incomparably smaller misfortune than cowardly acquiescence. . . . We will shrink from no step, however extreme, to repel the plot in which Mr. Redmond has involved a cowardly Government."

But it is always Buzfuz talking—Buzfuz doing the best for his client. That is the final impression that Mr. Smith leaves. He carries no conviction to the mind because his utterances are so mutually destructive. He always seems like a man trying to walk in two opposite directions. Now he is hallooing at the head of reactionary Toryism; now he is denouncing "a policy of negation and inactivity," proclaiming the wrongs of society, and declaring that ostentatious luxury is the cause of the prevalent discontent. Perhaps the truth is that he enlisted on the wrong side. There is a legend that when he and Sir John Simon were at Oxford they tossed to decide which party either should join, since no party could contain both of them. It is a good story. It may be true so far as Mr. Smith is concerned. It may be that he tossed—and lost.

MR. ST. LOE STRACHEY

If you turn out of the Strand into Wellington Street you can hardly fail to notice a certain house which is painted white. There are many houses which are painted white, but the white of this house is more white than the whiteness of any other house. It is like a house dressed in a surplice—a house that stands in conscious rebuke of a naughty world, wearing the white paint of a blameless life. The impression will be deepened when you read the legend inscribed in modest characters across the front, "The Spectator," and realise that over the threshold Mr. St. Loe Strachey must pass daily to the pained contemplation of the wickedness and folly of men.

That contemplation is lightened by one thought—the thought of his own rightness. This thought enables him to bear with fortitude the burden that destiny has cast upon him. The world is very evil. Radicals and Socialists and other strange breeds without the law encompass him on every side. The hosts of Midian prowl around. Providence in its inscrutable purposes has permitted these strange weeds to grow in the garden. He is puzzled by their presence. He cannot doubt the wisdom of Providence; but he shares the respectful perplexity of the little girl who, troubled by the news of the depredations of wire-worms in the garden, asked me the other day, "Why does God make wire-worms?" I found it difficult to give a plain answer to that plain question. Even the *Encyclopædia Britannica* evaded the point. And I doubt whether the same authority will explain to Mr. Strachey the purpose of Providence in making Radicals, Socialists, and the like. Perhaps Portia's "God made him: let him pass for a man," may help him; but it is not an explanation, it is only an excuse.

In this perplexity, however, Mr. Strachey is sustained by the sense of his own unswerving rectitude. "Every right-thinking man" is the note of the *Spectator*—and when one speaks of the *Spectator* one speaks of Mr. Strachey, for his spirit breathes in every line of that organ. He appeals to "the right-thinking man" with a firm assurance that the right-thinking man is with him. Indeed, he must be with him: how else can he be "right thinking"? And "the right-thinking man" will have his reward in a blessing of pontifical solemnity. If he has written a letter to the *Spectator* charged with right thinking his heart will leap with joy on finding appended to it one of those editorial footnotes which are an unfailing delight—footnotes which perspire with right thinking, footnotes which, with portentous gravity, call the universe to witness the beauty of the truths which the right-thinking correspondent shares with the right-thinking editor. But if the correspondent, being perhaps a poor, uncertain wanderer in this quite unintelligible world, writes a letter hinting doubts about things as they are, then terrible is the flaming sword that is turned upon his heresies. "No sensible person, we are sure, will agree . . ." Or, "We are confident that we express the view of every right-thinking person . . ." And as the poor, uncertain wanderer turns away, one sees with the mind's eye the right-thinking reader of the *Spectator* raising his eyes in thankfulness that he is not as other men are, and that he has had the wisdom to take Mr. Strachey as his guide, philosopher, and friend.

This congenital rightness of view, of course, imposes a heavy burden of responsibility on Mr. Strachey. He is conscious that it has its dangers, that it may lead to self-pride and censoriousness, sins that he would fain guard against. It is difficult, because he knows no other example so pertinent as his own. He is compelled, in the interests of right conduct, to refer to himself, to tell what he said in certain circumstances ten years ago, to show how he acted when faced with temptations that others have failed to resist, to dwell upon the enlightened and patriotic example of the High Sheriff of Surrey (himself, modestly but ineffectually veiled) in some moment of national crisis.

Thus, in discussing the Marconi case, he writes a moving story of how he was tempted to buy oil shares. He saw the opportunity of making money. The probable abandonment of coal for oil by the British Navy, and the prospect of a tremendous extra demand for oil, promised a great rise in oil shares. But his disposition to buy was checked by another and a loftier consideration —" namely, that as a newspaper man the editor would have to consider and discuss, and to some extent to direct public opinion in regard to, such a problem as to whether the Navy ought or ought not in future to take to mineral oil." And he tells how with that thought he waved the temptation aside. Some men would have felt a glow of pride at this act of renunciation. They would have boasted about it. But Mr. Strachey checks the motion with resolute humility. He refuses to be proud. He has done a thing which must be told as an inspiration to right thinking and as a rebuke to Radical Ministers, but he will not be praised for it.

" No sensible person," he continues with beautiful modesty, " will think that this was a noble or a self-sacrificing act. It was nothing of the kind. It was simply a piece of prudence and common sense, coupled, if you will, with a high instead of a low view of the functions of an editor. But surely if it is the standard for a journalist—and here we are sure we speak for all responsible journalists—it is clearly not asking too much to expect Cabinet Ministers to adopt a similar way of looking at investments. And here, though perhaps it may open us to the accusation of unctuous rectitude, we wish to say a word in season about oil."

"Unctuous rectitude." . . . "A word in season about oil." . . . How reminiscent it all seems. Mr. Strachey himself is conscious of the reminiscence, for with perfectly shattering *naïveté* he proceeds to anticipate that he will be accused of "self-righteousness and abject Pecksniffian cant." But even that terror shall be faced. "We will indeed supply our critics," he says, "with a quotation from Mr. Pecksniff which will seem to them very apposite, but which they will probably miss if we do not recommend it to their notice. 'Do not repine, my friends; do not weep for me, it is chronic.'"

Such candour disarms criticism. When a man proclaims in print that he reminds himself of no one so much as Mr. Pecksniff, what is there to be said?

It follows perhaps naturally that the thing that most stirs Mr. Strachey to indignation is hypocrisy. He cannot "abide" it, any more than the bear in *She Stoops to Conquer*, which would only dance to "the genteelest of tunes," could abide any music that was "low." It is not the politics of his opponents that shock him so much as their hypocrisy. And it is the misfortune of his opponents always to be canting hypocrites. The whole Liberal Party is an "Organised Hypocrisy." That phrase runs through his paper like a refrain. You cannot escape it. If you dodge it in one connection you are sure to encounter it in another. It is this moral censorship that makes Mr. Strachey so unique a controversialist. He always has the victory over you, for, like Johnson, if he fails to shoot you with his pistol, he knocks you down with the butt end. If, that is, he fails to prove that your intellectual views are wrong, he falls back on his second line of attack, and shows that your character and conduct are not what they ought to be, and that you belong to an "Organised Hypocrisy."

"When I have said 'Malaga,'" said Planchet, "I am no longer a man." When Mr. Strachey has pronounced you to be an "organised hypocrite" your views no longer count. You are politically dead. It is a simple way of getting rid of opposition.

With all this censoriousness, Mr. Strachey combines a carefully-studied air of moderation and sweet reasonableness. He can brand a whole party as "canting hypocrites" and still preserve a touching faith in his own freedom from extravagance of view or violence of statement. His self-respect is invulnerable, his escutcheon without a stain. He can prove at inordinate length that everything he has done has been quite refined and gentlemanly. When the *National Review* and the rest were exploiting Mr. W. R. Lawson's romantic fancies about Marconi, Mr. Strachey gave the exposures a dignified welcome in his columns. When Mr. Lawson in the witness-box withdrew practically every serious statement he had made, Mr. Strachey explained how careful he had been to take no responsibility for Mr. Lawson's statements. He had only printed them. One gathered that his behaviour, in fact, had been, as usual, that of a perfect gentleman. And again when Mr. Maxse, sheltering himself behind the plea of editorial confidence, refused to divulge the source of rumours to which he had given currency involving the honour of public men, Mr. Strachey eloquently defended him. He justified a plea which, if admitted, would enable an editor to blast the reputation of any man he chose on authority which could not be disclosed and indeed which need not exist at all. It was not because he did not know the falsity of the position. He knew as well as Mr. Maxse knew, as well as every editor knows, that you have no right to destroy a man on evidence which you cannot produce. But what was such a consideration worth, put in the balance against an opportunity to strike a blow at the Government?

For the "morral waxworks" of Mr. Strachey only furnish a disguise for a very ordinary and a rather acrid politician. His moral fervours usually coincide with his political purposes, and play the part of lackey to them. What those political purposes are needs little explanation. He is the arch-enemy of social reform legislation. Old age pensions, insurance, small holdings, minimum wage, housing—what has the State to do with these things? The business of the State is to leave all this to voluntary action and to concentrate on "A New Way of Life." Now the New Way of Life set forth in Mr. Strachey's book of that title is—Conscription, or, as he prefers to call it, National Service. In a word, all he asks of the State is that it shall teach every boy to use a gun and obey a drill-sergeant. He shares, one feels, the common view of his type that the answer to democracy is militarism. It is conscription which keeps the Russian despotism in being; it is conscription which maintains the antiquated constitution of Germany; it is conscription to which we must look in order to suppress the insolence of the British workmen. Mr. Strachey, in short, is of the school of Sir Frederick Banbury, with the exception that, having some economic knowledge, he happens to be a Free Trader.

But while his curiously unsympathetic and unimaginative mind makes him merely a geological curiosity of politics, he has a considerable influence in a certain section of society. He has got the measure of that comfortable person who wishes to remain comfortable and undisturbed and still to preserve a conscience—the sort of person who, as Tolstoy said, will do everything for the poor except get off their backs. These people are terror-stricken at the idea of land taxes, housing, old age pensions, and similar revolutionary measures. But they do want to feel that "something is being done for the poor." It need not be anything that will be of any use; but it must be something that will be an anodyne to the troubled conscience. It must not be a minimum wage for the sweated worker, but it may be a consumers' league; it must not be a serious housing scheme financed by the State, but it may be a nice model exhibition, where landowners can get hints that they don't want; it must not be old age pensions from the State, but it may be doles from the benevolent; it must not be justice, but it may be charity.

Of all this class Mr. Strachey is the prophet. He supplies their double need—a sense of protection against the perils of change and an easy conscience about their duty to society.

I think there is deep significance in the decoration of a house-front.

MR. CHURCHILL

TRAVELLING to Portsmouth to the Naval Review one day I met in the train a nice, rosy-faced old gentleman who, I gathered, had a house in the Isle of Wight and shooting in the North. His political views were of a sort not uncommon in such circumstances. His attitude towards labour, which at the time was giving much annoyance to the comfortable classes, may be comprehensively summed up in the phrase, "Shoot 'em down." As to the Government his language was strong, but not stronger than, as a pillar of the Constitution, he felt to be necessary.

"I hope," said he, speaking of the review—and in that tone that one uses in regard to the lower animals—"I hope that they will put Lloyd George on a nice leaky submarine, and if they can give Asquith a place on it, too, so much the better."

"And Churchill," I suggested, "wouldn't it be as well to include him?"

"Yes," he said, with some reluctance, as though moved by sudden pity.

"But," said the lady who accompanied the nice, rosy-faced old gentleman, "it is thought that he will be the next Unionist Prime Minister."

The old gentleman looked thoughtful. "Well," he said, shaking his head, "I am not sure about Prime Minister." Short of that he seemed cheerfully acquiescent.

The incident is doubtless unjust to Mr. Churchill, but it illustrates a very significant change in public opinion in regard to him—a change due in part to his remarkable and continued reticence in the party con flict and in part to his baffling character. He is the unknown factor in politics. You may cast the horoscope of anyone else; his you cannot cast. You cannot cast it because his orbit is not governed by any known laws, but by attractions that deflect his path hither and thither. It may be the attraction of war or of peace, of social reform or of a social order—whatever it is he will plunge into it with all the schoolboy intensity of his nature. His loves may be many, but they will always have the passion of a first love. Whatever shrine he worships at, he will be the most fervid in his prayers.

He is the typical child of his time. It is a time of feverish activity, of upheaval and challenge, of a world in revolt. The dams have broken down and the waters are flooding the land. The old continents are submerged, and new and strange worlds are shaping themselves before our eyes. In one of his letters, written during those astonishing days when Chatham was sweeping the French out of India with one hand and out of Canada with the other, Horace Walpole said that on waking in the morning he was in the habit of asking what new world had been conquered to-day? We might in these times ask daily what ancient fabric has fallen, what venerable tradition has been jettisoned, what new gospel has leapt into the saddle. It is as if we are in a world that has awoke from a sleep and has set out on a furious march with sealed orders. Labour is marching, the women are marching. Religion, politics, journalism, literature—all are seething with a new and unintelligible life. Harmony has gone out of music and beauty out of art. The Ten Commandments are challenged and the exploitation of self is elevated into a religion. Even Toryism is seized with the fever of action. Mr. Balfour stands aloof as the last standard-bearer of *laissez-faire* —the last believer in the futility of human endeavour to shape the channels of humanity. He is all reflection and no action. The new Toryism is all action and no reflection. " Let us do something—never mind what it is, but do it." The prophet of all this unrest is Bergson, who tells us that our minds are " orientated towards action rather than pure knowledge." Don't reflect: Act. That is the gospel.

Into this vast turmoil Mr. Churchill plunges with the joy of a man who has found his natural element. A world in transition is a world made for him. Life is a succession of splendid sensations, of thrilling experiences. He rushes from booth to booth with the delight of a boy at a fair. And each booth is more wonderful than any other. He must shoot at every gallery, shy at every cocoa-nut, see every bearded woman and two-headed man. He is reckless of his life and of his money, indifferent to consequences. All that matters is this magic world of which he has become the momentary possessor, and which he must devour ere the curtain is rung down on the drama and the dream.

With this abnormal thirst for sensation, he combines an unusual melodramatic instinct. He is always unconsciously playing a part—an heroic part. And he is himself his most astonished spectator. He sees himself moving through the smoke of battle—triumphant, terrible, his brow clothed with thunder, his legions looking to him for victory, and not looking in vain. He thinks of Napoleon; he thinks of his great ancestor. Thus did they bear themselves; thus, in this rugged and most awful crisis, will he bear himself. It is not make-believe, it is not insincerity: it is that in that fervid and picturesque imagination there are always great deeds afoot with himself cast by destiny in the Agamemnon rôle. Hence that portentous gravity that sits on his youthful shoulders so oddly, those impressive postures and tremendous silences, the body flung wearily in the chair, the head resting gloomily in the hand, the abstracted look, the knitted brow. Hence that tendency to exaggerate a situation which is so characteristic of him—the tendency that sent artillery down to Sidney Street and, during the railway strike, despatched the military hither and thither as though Armageddon was upon us. "You've mistaken a coffee-stall row for the social revolution," said one of his colleagues to him as he pored with knitted and portentous brows over a huge map of the country on which he was marking his military dispositions. His mind once seized with an idea works with enormous velocity round it, intensifies it, enlarges it, makes it shadow the whole sky. In the theatre of that mind it is always the hour of fate and the crack of doom.

It is this impressionableness that makes him so vital and various. He astonishes by his accomplishments. How, we ask, has one so young, whose years have been years of breathless action, acquired this large mastery of ideas, this power of statement, this grasp of facts, this air of authority? It is not by application and industry alone that he has succeeded, though he has these in an unusual degree. He labours at a subject with the doggedness of Stonewall Jackson. He polishes a speech as the lapidary polishes a stone. He will have no loose ends, no unfortified assertions or slipshod phrases, none of those unconsidered asides with which Mr. Lloyd George invites attack. When after one of his speeches at Dundee a friend of mine called on him on an important matter at one o'clock in the morning, he found him sitting up in bed immersed in Blue books. His father when Chancellor of the Exchequer asked, according to Sir Algernon West, the meaning of the decimal points, and when told replied, "I've often wondered what those d——d dots meant." Perhaps it was his fun; but he was certainly ignorant. Mr. Churchill always knows what the dots mean.

But more potent than his industry is his astonishing apprehension. He flashes through life taking impressions, swift, searching, detached. He absorbs a moral or an intellectual atmosphere as another man absorbs the oxygen of the air, and he gives it out as if it were his own vital breath. He is what the Spiritualists call a "medium"—a vehicle through which some vision, some doctrine, some enthusiasm finds temporary utterance apart from himself. No one has stated the principles of Liberalism with such breadth as he has done; no one has preached peace with more fervour economy with more conviction, and social reform with a more thrilling break in the voice; or, on the other hand, presented an unexampled naval expenditure with such an adroit and disarming appearance of sad necessity. Each task, however subversive of former tasks, finds him perfectly equipped, for he always knows his subject, and convinces himself first. He is direct, rests his case on a plain argument, and avoids all the dialectical cobwebs by which the Cecils delight the intellect and bewilder the public. In saying this I do not wish to exaggerate the importance of consistency. A pedantic consistency is a sterile frame of mind. We all change if we are alive; we can all say with Whitman:

> "Do I contradict myself?
> Very well then, I contradict myself:
> (I am large. I contain multitudes.)"

It is not that Mr. Churchill is more multitudinous than others. It is that one seems to look in vain for that fundamental note that makes the discords of the supreme men plain. Ruskin was full of contradictions; but the ultimate Ruskin—the Ruskin with soul aflame for beauty and justice—emerges triumphant out of them all. It is the ultimate Churchill that escapes us. I think he escapes us for a good reason. He is not there.

In short, brilliantly as he preaches, he is the man of action simply, the soldier of fortune, who lives for adventure, loves the fight more than the cause, more even than his ambition or his life. He has one purpose

—to be in the firing line, in the battles either of war or peace. If he cannot be there in one capacity he will be there in another. When the Cuban war broke out he got leave from his regiment, went out as a newspaper correspondent, and fought as a soldier. When the Malakand rising took place, his regiment not being engaged, he again got leave, again took service as a correspondent, again fought as a soldier, and got mentioned in the despatches for "courage and resolution at a critical moment." Back from the Tirah expedition, in which he had got himself appointed orderly officer to Sir William Lockhart, he went straight to the War Office and begged to be sent out with the expedition to the Soudan. Thence he returned to fight Oldham, missed it, and plunged into the South African War. That over, he galloped up to Westminster to "have his shot at politics." Never has there been such hustle. At twenty-five he had fought in more continents than any soldier in history save Napoleon, and seen as many campaigns as any living general.

Nor is it purposeless hustle. It always has a strict business basis. When in the Soudan he was attached to the 21st Lancers—known, I believe, as the "Saucy Devils"—there was resentment against this precocious intruder. Instead of giving him a troop to lead they put him in charge of the mess store, and one has described how he met him one day in charge of a decrepit mule and two donkeys. "Look at that. There is a trust for a British officer. It is not even a job for a noncommissioned officer. They have said, 'We'll break young Churchill's heart if he comes to us.' Poor little men! They think I'm as small as they are. But it's my object to write a big book on this campaign, and as long as I get up I don't mind in what capacity they employ me. Even if they give me a sweeper's job I should not demur." It is a fine story—as fine in its way, given the inferiority of motive, as that of Lincoln when General McClellan, according to his rude habit, had kept the President waiting for him. Someone expressed anger at the indignity. "Never mind," said Lincoln, "I will hold McClellan's horse if he will only bring us success."

It is more difficult for a Churchill than for a Lincoln to pocket his pride; humiliation no more than danger can check him, and the boy of twenty-three produced in *The River War* not merely the best history of the campaign but one of the best military books in the language, a book, moreover, that in its attack on Lord Kitchener for the desecration of the Mahdi's body illustrated the courage, physical and moral, that is so conspicuous a virtue of Mr. Churchill. He is never afraid to risk his life. He showed that in his defence of the armoured train, but not less in the circumstances of his visit to Birmingham in the most feverish fiscal days. The howling crowd had assembled round the Town Hall to deal with him perhaps as they had dealt with Lloyd George. Lord Robert Cecil, who was to speak with him, went to the hall unobserved on foot, accompanied by a plain-clothes detective. Not so Mr. Churchill. Suddenly a carriage and pair drove into the midst of the hostile crowd. It contained only Mr. Churchill; open, palpable, flagrant; a challenge that might mean lynching. For a moment there was a pause: then the crowd, captured by the spirit of the thing, burst into cheers. It was another triumph for the Churchill audacity—that union of recklessness and calculation that snatches victory out of jaws of danger.

And he has not only courage but the will to discipline himself and to triumph over grave defects. His appearance and his utterance are against him. There is still no better pen picture of him than that which the Boers issued in the warrant for his arrest after his escape from Pretoria: "Englishman, twenty-five years old, about 5 ft. 8 in. high, indifferent build, walks with a bend forward, pale appearance, red-brownish hair, small moustache hardly perceptible, talks through the nose and cannot pronounce the letter 's' properly." It is not a flattering picture. That defect of speech alone would have destroyed most men. Mr. Churchill makes you forget it by the sheer energy of his mind and manner. He rides, as it were, roughshod over himself. And so with his temperament. His natural habit is ebullient and provocative. He used to be rude and defiant: he has changed all that. He has become as discreet as a family lawyer, as decorous as a churchwarden. The spirit is still there, but it is curbed and bridled and obedient to its imperious master. He cultivates silence. And his silence is not less eloquent than his speech and far more significant. It is not an accident, for, with all his impulsiveness, nothing is accidental about this remarkable man. Behind all his actions, however sudden or headlong, there is the calculation of a singularly daring and far-sighted mind—a mind that surveys the field with the eye of the strategist, weighs the forces, estimates the positions and, when the hour has come, strikes with deadly sureness at the vulnerable place. "Keep your eye on Churchill" should be the watchword of these days. Remember, he is a soldier first, last, and always. He will write his name big on our future. Let us take care he does not write it in blood.

LORD STRATHCONA

If your way of life carries you in these days to the great public dinners and functions of the London season, there is one figure that will be more memorable to you than any other. It stands out from the background of conventional figures like a solitary snow peak from the browns and greens of the valley. It seems divided from all the rest by an immeasurable gulf of years. We are of to-day and yesterday, but from what remote past does this venerable guest come into our midst? What tale does he bring of far times and far lands? The figure is bowed, but still agile; the head a splendour of white—hair white as the driven snow, heavy white brows overhanging the keen and searching eyes, white beard, complexion white. It is like an allegory of the Great White North. And the suggestion is not wholly fanciful. For this is Lord Strathcona, and it is from the frozen shores of Labrador that he brings the snows of winters of long ago.

Sydney Smith said of Macaulay that he was "like a book in breeches." One may say of Lord Strathcona that he is like Canada in swallow-tails. He is not so much a man as a legend—the legend of half a continent. You shake hands with him, and it is as if you shake hands with a section of the British Empire. You talk with him, and it is as if Canada is before you telling her astonishing story. And if the accent still betrays some hint of the Highlands, that only makes the impression more complete, for the eminent Canadian usually has his roots in Scottish soil. There have been two great currents westward from these islands across the Atlantic. One has flowed from Ireland to the United States; one from Scotland to Canada. Both have had their source in the same tragedy—the tragedy of the land. The Highlanders fled from their burning homesteads to find ultimately a refuge in the solitudes north of the great lakes, and to lay there the foundations of a mighty nation. The straths are desolate, and the deer wander over the ruins of the crofters' homes: but across the Atlantic the seed blown from those straths has made the plains to stand thick with corn and the desert to blossom as the rose.

And in the track of the exiles of the eighteenth century followed the adventurers of the nineteenth. One day, seventy-five years ago, about the time when the girl-queen, Victoria, was being crowned in the Abbey, there reached Labrador, to take up duties under the Hudson Bay Company, a lad from Forres, in Morayshire—his name Donald Alexander Smith. When you find an indisputable Highlander claiming kinship with the great family of Smith you may suspect that there is a tale "of old, unhappy, far-off things" behind the disguise. Many a Highlander who had been "out" in the lost cause of the Stuarts in the '15 and the '45 re-emerged under some homely patronymic that spelt safety; and the ancestor of young Donald was probably among the number.

The lad reached the solitudes of Labrador alone, unfriended, and poor, having travelled hundreds of miles on snow-shoes. It was the loneliest outpost of a lonely land. Canada, three-quarters of a century ago, was still an undiscovered country, far more remote than Australia is to-day. The sailing vessel that carried young Donald thither had occupied six weeks over the journey, and it was not until later in the year that the first passenger steamer from England, the *Great Western* arrived in New York harbour. West of the settlements on the St. Lawrence there stretched a solitude to the far Pacific shores. Over the vast territory, afterward known as the province of Rupertsland—the Manitoba, Alberta, and Saskatchewan of to-day—the Hudson Bay Company held dominion. Here and there, but at incredible intervals, a little fort of the Company was planted in the trackless wilderness—one, as it were, in Kent, another in Lancashire, a third in Scotland. Outside these tiny shelters, the primeval forest and the wandering Indian. One of the chief of these oases was Fort Garry, with a white population numbering a few score. To-day Fort Garry is the great city of Winnipeg, the centre of the chief agricultural industry in the world.

In this mighty transformation no single influence has played so great a part as Lord Strathcona. Canada would have developed without him, of course. But it would not have developed so rapidly or in the same direction. He brought to it at a critical time a constancy of purpose and a steady faith that were of incalculable service. His very limitations were largely the secret of his power. Romantic though his career has been, there is no touch of romance in his temperament. He is neither a man of genius nor an idealist. He is just an ordinary man in an extraordinary degree—simple, honest, clear-sighted, practical as a plumber, stable as the hills. He himself would be the last to claim any kinship with the superman. What he has done has been done with weapons within the reach of all—"honesty, frugality and perseverance," the lessons of that frugal home where eighty years ago he sat reading his Horace by rushlight. "A mother's early training," he will tell you, "has everything to do with a man's career. I know mine had with me. She taught me to work when I was young, and to save money—two very important things in a man's life."

There are other important things, which were not forgotten in that humble school. He learned the lesson of generosity. It is not difficult for a man whose riches are beyond calculation to be a public benefactor. In this country one might think it was, for our rich men have lost the fine tradition of public munificence. With all their faults the American millionaires have that trait, and Lord Strathcona shares it. But it is not his great benefactions—the gift and endowment of the Victoria Hospital at Montreal, the equipment of Strathcona's Horse for the Boer War, the millions he has spent on the M'Gill University and other institutions—that are the true witness to his generosity; but the habits of a lifetime. "When he was a poor man," said one who knows him well to me, "he had the same generous instincts. If he had only two rooms there was always one for a guest." And there is an incident on record from his childhood which shows that, though his mother taught him to save money, she taught him also something even better. When he was a boy of nine the Findhorn and the Spey broke their boundaries and flooded the country. Many of the peasants, with their families, came into Forres to seek relief, and amongst them the parents of one of Donald's playmates who had been drowned in the floods. After school Donald called upon them, and with a gravity far beyond his years condoled with them, and on leaving handed to them his riches, amounting to one shilling and some odd coppers. That is as convincing a witness to this pleasant phase of his character as the M'Gill University.

And in addition to work and thrift his career has been founded on two other homely virtues—duty and constancy. He is never tired of inculcating duty. "Don't go to Canada to have an easy time," he says. "You will not find any of its streets paved with gold. But work hard and do your duty and you must succeed." He himself would put his success on no higher plane than that, and if he is proud of anything it is of telling how he did his duty under difficulties. There is one typical story he tells of those grim, hard years he spent on the coast of Labrador, where he laid the foundation of his fame as one of the best fur dealers in the Company's service, and acquired that intimacy with the Indians which served him so well when he became the chief administrator of the Company in Rupertsland. Being threatened with snow-blindness, Donald Smith, with three Indians, made a journey of 500 miles by dog-sledge to Montreal, where an operation on his eyes was successfully performed. It was the depth of a winter of exceptional severity even for those latitudes, and his friends tried to dissuade him from returning to his post, for the journey almost certainly meant death. But young Smith had a guiding principle which admitted of no exceptions.

"I had my duty to perform," he says in telling the story. "Everything must give place to one's duty, you know. The Indians insisted that they could never reach the post alive, the snow was so deep. They were right, poor fellows—two died from the cold and the hardships we were forced to endure before we had gone half-way; the other succumbed when we were over one hundred miles from the post. . . . I went on—alone. I don't like to think of that time: it was too horrible. However, my rise in the Hudson Bay Company was very rapid after that. I am glad I took the trip." There is a *naïveté* in that frank confession which is very illuminating. Perhaps another sense of duty would have suggested a doubt as to the right of risking the lives of others in one's own affairs, but the incident shows the unflinching loyalty of the man to an unalterable though narrow code of duty.

But after all, it is his steadfastness that has been his chief contribution to Canada. And the supreme memorial of that steadfastness is the Canadian Pacific Railway. The late Sir Charles Tupper once publicly declared that but for Lord Strathcona that railway would not have been constructed. It is true that it would not have been constructed then, and perhaps, ultimately, it would have been well for Canada if it had not been constructed then. The surrender of vast tracts of the richest land in Canada as a bait to the financial interests to carry out the work was a concession which the future will deplore, and the political influence which this great corporation has brought to bear upon the life of Canada is a fact of great and sinister import. The truth is that the railway should have been made by the State, and that, I believe, was the view of Lord Strathcona himself. But, conceding the necessity of the undertaking, his claim to gratitude cannot be overstated. The idea of driving a railway through thousands of miles of pathless forests and mountain ranges to a desolate shore—where Vancouver with its noble streets and bustling life stands to-day there was then not even a log cabin—was one before which the most courageous adventurer might quail. It was a more daring idea than the Cape-to-Cairo railway which united two great centres of world activity. The Canadian Pacific was a plunge through nothing to nothing. It was a stupendous guess at the future.

But Donald Smith never faltered for a moment. He had reached middle life, and an affluence that would have turned most men's thoughts to repose. Thirty years of work and thrift had brought him out of the wilderness and made him the financial King of Canada. He was supreme in the great Company that had held half Canada in fee, but had now surrendered its sovereignty to the State, and through the Bank of Montreal he controlled with Lord Mount Stephen the only resources at all adequate to the enterprise. He staked everything upon the venture with a quiet fortitude that has few parallels. At every crisis, as was said of a greater man in a greater connection, "hope shone in him like a pillar of fire when it had gone out of all the others." There was one such occasion when it seemed that the difficulties were finally insurmountable.

Donald Smith, then in England engaged in communicating his own confidence to financiers, received a long letter from the Company couched in terms of despair. He cabled back one word. It was a Highland clan cry, "Craigel-lachie," its meaning "Stand Fast." And when finally the victory was won, and the two sets of constructors met in the Eagle Valley in the heart of the second of the great ranges which had made construction so difficult, the place was named "Craigel-lachie," and it was here that "Stand Fast" Smith drove in the last spike that bridged a continent.

This constancy extends to his personal associations. When John J. Hill, who is now one of the great railroad kings of America, made his *coup* of the St. Paul and Pacific Railroad, it was Donald Smith's financial backing and loyalty that saved him. He wanted a railway to Winnipeg to open up the Hudson Bay country, and he believed in Hill's schemes as well as his honesty. No temptation would induce him to desert him. The American magnates determined to capture the undertaking at all costs. Up bounded the shares higher and higher. Hill's fate hung on Donald Smith. A huge fortune was in his grasp if he chose to sell, but he had placed his confidence in Hill, and would see him through, and not a share could be wrung from him, no matter what monstrous price was offered. Indeed, no share ever is wrung from him. He is one of the men who "never sell," however black the sky. In the days when Canadian Pacific shares slumped to 50, and there was an almost universal *sauve qui peut*, "Stand Fast" Donald was immovable as ever.

From this security springs a courage not less admirable because it is entirely matter-of-fact and undemonstrative. The story of his intervention in the first Louis Riel rebellion—how he journeyed, mostly by dog-sledge, two thousand miles away from Montreal to Fort Garry, which Riel with his half-breeds had captured; how he was held prisoner for two months; how he refused to yield his papers, and finally, through the well-affected French, forced the holding of a meeting of the people; how in the open air, with the thermometer twenty degrees below zero, and in circumstances where one rash word would have set the country in a flame, he won the people from the rebel leader, so that when, later, Sir Garnet Wolseley appeared at the head of a military expedition, the first Riel rebellion was at an end—all this stands as a witness not only to his practical wisdom but also to his personal and unaffected courage.

It will be seen that his character is one of rare simplicity of thought and motive. If you do not like the Smiles ideal, which certainly has its limitations and has fallen into some disrepute in these days, your admiration for this Grand Old Man of Canada will be qualified. For he is the sublimation of the industrious apprentice, and he remains to-day, with his vast wealth, his palaces on both sides of the Atlantic, his pictures, and his great reputation, unchanged in intellect and outlook from the honest lad who sailed westward to make his fortune long before you and I were born. His moral philosophy is still that of the frugal home and the frugal mother. "Every mother should teach her children to be honest and work and save their money," he says. "When I was earning only fifty cents a day I saved half of it." And his respect for men is governed by these considerations—Carnegie working and saving as a telegraph operator, J. J. Hill, as a mud clerk in the levee at St. Paul, with fifty cents a day, saving on his clothes in order to buy books and "prepare himself," these are the heroes of his simple creed. And with these admonitions to be industrious and frugal he mingles warnings against the pursuit of wealth for itself. "Great wealth cannot bring happiness," he says. "Real happiness must come from a contented mind and hard work. Great wealth is a burden, for one has to think very hard how to make the best use of his money. I would not advise any man to strive after great wealth. I would rather be a very good man than a very rich man."

It is all in the style of Benjamin Franklin and the hagiology of Smiles. And, after all, a philosophy that produces a life like this, though it may be inadequate, cannot be wrong. When I see him with his burden of nearly a hundred years leaving his office in Victoria Street after his industrious day, and when I think of the vast span of his activities, of the kindliness of his bearing, of the splendour of his munificence, and of his indomitable loyalty to his early faith, I feel that though the fashion of his life is old it can never become outworn.

MR. AUSTEN CHAMBERLAIN

On a certain evening in May in the year 1883—to be precise, on May 29—there was a tumultuous rally to the Union Society at Cambridge. It was a rally to a familiar bugle-call. The House of Lords was in danger. Out in the great world a mighty demagogue who had sprung into an equivocal fame as Citizen Chamberlain, the Republican Mayor of Birmingham, was abroad thundering his anathemas against the House of Lords. "They toil not, neither do they spin," he cried. "Away with them! Why cumber they the earth?" And the echoes of that ringing challenge—which to some was the portent of revolution and to some the message of a new hope—penetrated the academic calm of Cambridge and sent a shudder through the souls of the undergraduates.

To-night the House of Lords was to be saved if Cambridge could save it. The motion before the Union was this: "That in the opinion of this House the existence of the House of Lords is injurious to the welfare of the country." The mover was a young man of pleasant, if somewhat heavy, features and of immaculate dress. He wore an eye-glass in his right eye, and in his button-hole there was an orchid. His hair was brushed neatly across his forehead, and his clean-shaven face and solemnity of bearing suggested thoughts infinitely removed from barricades and revolution. But his name had in it the ring of the Red Terror. For this was Mr. Joseph Austen Chamberlain, the eldest son of the great Radical who was casting his baleful shadow over the comfortable homes of the aristocracy. He spoke in rather a muffled, ponderous voice, not fluently, but with the air of one who had got up his case industriously and would go through with it or perish. And what a formidable case he made—what ruthless measures he proposed! Why should men who had done nothing for their country, except being born into it, have such power over the lives and fortunes of millions? Why should a free political workhouse be kept up for the relief of the destitute, who, disloyal to their principles and their party, were shown to what was sarcastically termed the Upper House? Look at what we had suffered from it. Look at what Ireland, poor Ireland, had suffered. Reform? No. Let us sweep it away: let us make an end of the unclean thing.

I do not recall this speech in order to brand Mr. Chamberlain as a turncoat. Most of us are turncoats. Most of us can be convicted of inconsistency—all of us ought to be convicted. A pedantic consistency is the most arid and profitless frame of mind. One might as well be proud of never having grown since one was five. It is quite clear that if, with all the developing experience of life, you never changed an opinion on anything, you can never have had an opinion to change. You can only have had prejudices derived from the opinions of others. But if the fact of inconsistency is of small moment in itself, the reasons of the inconsistency are vital to an estimate of character. It does not matter in the least that Wedderburn turned his coat so often; but it does matter that he turned it for the basest motives. We discriminate between the inconsistency of Burke and that of Charles James Fox, because that of Burke was the result of a narrowing vision, while that of Fox came from a splendid enlargement of vision. Gladstone and Disraeli were both inconsistent; but what a gulf between the motives of the two!

Now the motives of Mr. Austen Chamberlain's inconsistency are neither reprehensible nor splendid. They are, in a way, admirable; they are also, in a way, pathetic. For he is the victim of a fatal devotion. He is the *pius Æneas* of politics, who has followed Anchises down those facile slopes of Avernus to the nether glooms where the shores of Phlegethon are lined with the ghosts of dead causes. Or, less poetically—as F. C. G. expressed it in a famous cartoon: "When pa says 'Turn,' we all turn." Filial piety and the spirit of obedience are good things, but they are not enough to make a leader of men. Even fathers are sometimes wrong, and there is a duty to rebel as well as a duty to obey.

The other day I was walking near the ponds at Wyldes Farm on Hampstead Heath, when a small boy approached me and said, very appealingly, "Please, sir, may I fish for tiddlers in that pond?" I was flattered by this evidence that my appearance had some distinction and authority about it. I felt momentarily something of that glow of proprietorship that the Duke of Sutherland must feel when he goes to a high place and surveys his million acres of moor and valley, mountain and forest. Strict integrity would have replied: "My boy, you are as free to fish for tiddlers in that pond as the Lord Mayor of London or the Archbishop of Canterbury." But that momentary pride of possession checked the impulse to be honest. I gave him the permission with an air of noble recklessness, and with it a caution—not to tumble in. And as he ran off I felt that whatever sort of splash he made in the water, a boy who needed authority to fish for tiddlers in a pond would never make much splash in the world.

Mr. Austen Chamberlain has always been asking for permission to fish for tiddlers in the political pond. He has lived under the dominion of the imperious and masterful personality of his father. He has never had a real political existence of his own. He is not a voice, but the echo of a voice. Just as he echoed the fulminations of Highbury on that May evening thirty years ago, so he echoes the will of Highbury to-day. Now, an echo is a very pleasing, even a romantic thing; but no one ever girded on his sword to follow an echo, no one ever shed his blood in the last ditch to please an echo. And the trouble is that, when the voice falls silent, there is not even an echo.

Hence the decline in Mr. Austen Chamberlain's star. While the sun of his father was still in the heavens he shone with some reflected radiance. The sun being withdrawn, he passes into eclipse. He has made the mistake of being merely imitative. And in politics, as in art, imitation is a snare. It is at once easy and fatal. The world demands originals, not copies: it demands them because it needs them, because it cannot remain fresh and vital without the individuality and energy that imitation cannot give. "To equal a predecessor," says Chamfort, "one must have twice his merits." Mr. Austen Chamberlain is not twice as good as his father. He is only the pale shadow of his father. He has, it is true, some of his externals, but they are curiously softened. In the House you could not escape the hypnotism of Mr. Joseph Chamberlain's presence. It pervaded the Chamber. The glance of that ruthless eye was like a sword-thrust. It seemed to search out its enemies and leave them dead. The challenging nose, the sharp features, the swing of the long arms, the sibilant intensity of his utterance—everything about him attracted you, held you, perhaps filled you with fear.

Now, no one ever feared Mr. Austen Chamberlain. You couldn't fear him if you tried with both hands, as they say in the immortal *Alice*. For he is really as gentle as a dove. His temperament is as remote from that of his father as one temperament can be from another. Nature made him an amiable gentleman, naturally considerate of the feelings of others, entirely without venom, honourable and veracious in intention, anxious above all not to stoop below a certain level of "good form" and decorum. It is not without significance that his tastes in literature run in the direction of the gentle musings of which *Elia* is the supreme example. We have only to try to conceive his father sitting down by the fireside with Lamb to understand how widely separated their temperaments are from each other. And Nature gave him also a suitable intellectual equipment, a mind clear and honest, but slow—sometimes painfully slow, as when in one of his Budget speeches the House on both sides shouted an obvious correction of a clear inaccuracy again and again while he stood before it puzzled and wondering—and an utterance that keeps pace with his thoughts. It is slow, and the voice entirely lacks that sharp, incisive quality that made his father's voice stab like a stiletto.

And in spite of all these obvious indications that he was cast for another rôle Mr. Austen Chamberlain has sought to understudy his father's method—to be the masterful man who rides roughshod over all opposition, the sayer of hard things and biting sarcasms. He is like young Gourlay in that great and terrible book, *The House with the Green Shutters*. The timid boy saw how his rough-hewn father "downed" his foes with his terrific glower and his scornful "Imph," and he pictured himself "downing" his own foes in the same way. But he had not the glower. Nor has Mr. Austen Chamberlain the glower that "downed" his father's foes. No matter how hard the things he says, they fall softly. When Mr. Joseph Chamberlain said that Mr. Dillon was "a good judge of traitors" he stung his opponents as though he had hit them across the face with a whip. But when Mr. Austen Chamberlain says that the Government are traitors, that they are guilty of fraud and every crime in the calendar, no one seems a penny the worse. It is all as harmless as Bob Acres' oaths. It is not enough to say hard things if you want to hurt. You must have the will to hurt. And the will to hurt is obviously not in Mr. Chamberlain. He pumps up his indignation with evident labour as a duty that has to be done, but there is no joy to him in the blows he gives and no distress to those who receive them.

Not that he is negligible as a debater. He has untiring industry, and has probably worked harder than any politician of his time to improve his modest talents. He is one of those men who are always just about to "arrive," and whose latest speech is welcomed on all sides as an evidence that at last he has "found himself" and is coming to his kingdom. The welcome is largely the measure of the very sincere desire of men of every party to see him succeed. It is illusive, and the more he advances the more he is found to be stationary. The truth probably is that alone he would not have emerged from the rank and file. It is his "right honourable friend, the member for West Birmingham," to whom he owes the rapid advancement that made him Chancellor of the Exchequer at forty. Lord Morley once said that Mr. Chamberlain had a genius for friendship, and he has in a marked degree also the gift of family affection. Everyone recalls how moved he was when Gladstone complimented his son on his maiden speech, and said it was "a speech that must be dear and refreshing to a father's heart." And a not less pleasant memory is that in which, during Mr. Austen's bachelor days, his father spoke of his own house as the place where his son "gave him the pleasure of his company." Mr. Chamberlain never performed a more adroit manœuvre than when, in those sensational days of the raging, tearing propaganda, he at one stroke secured his own freedom to force the pace outside the Cabinet, made his son the Chancellor of the Exchequer, and got rid of the Free Fooders from the Ministry. It was a brilliant feat of strategy, and not the least of its attractions to Chamberlain *père* was the fact that it seemed to secure the reversion of the leadership of the Unionist Party to his son. His own career had been a series of disappointments, but in that vicarious triumph he would have his reward. He would reign in his son.

That dream has vanished. Mr. Balfour has been dethroned at last—beaten after fighting the most subtle and skilful battle for the soul of a party that any leader has fought; but Mr. Austen Chamberlain does not reign in his stead, and the Chamberlain cause is sinking rapidly into disrepute. We have in these days the unfailing sign of the sinking ship. They are not brave men who are leaving it, but they are good judges of a sinking ship. When the ship goes down, however, there will still be at least one loyal soul on board, one hand to keep the flag of the doomed vessel flying. Whoever else may desert the cause of food taxes, Mr. Austen Chamberlain will remain faithful to it, not, perhaps, because he believes in it, but because his father did. He will be a faithful echo to the end. And being an echo he will never be a leader.

LORD COURTNEY

It was said long ago that Leonard Courtney had only two weaknesses. One was to fancy that everyone had the same intellectual advantages as himself, the other was to dress in the evening as if he were employed to advertise the *Edinburgh Review*. Now, the latter is no weakness at all; it is a very conspicuous virtue. In the first place, there is courage in wearing a blue coat and a canary-coloured waistcoat in these days. To wear them naturally and unaffectedly is a triumph not of vanity, but of character; it is the sign not of a love of admiration, but of an independent mind. Lord Courtney does not affect bright colours because he wishes, like the young Disraeli, to attract attention, but because he likes them, and is unconscious of what the world says or what it wears. Falstaff said of Justice Shallow that he was "always in the rearward of the fashions." Lord Courtney, with his canary-coloured waistcoat and his low-crowned silk hat, comes down into these bustling times like a reminiscence of the days of our grandfathers. It is not because he loves new things, but because he loves old things, that he looks so gay. It was so men clothed themselves when he was young: it is so he clothes himself to-day.

To see him on some sunny afternoon walking along the Embankment to his home at Chelsea affects one like the smell of lavender in a drawer, that brings back with a sudden magic the memory of old days and forgotten faces. He is redolent of these fragrant suggestions. You may take him for a prosperous farmer who has come to town from the West Country: one seems to see him on the Corn Exchange taking handfuls of grain from a bag and letting it run with grave deliberation through his fingers. He may be an elder of some country church, for he preserves the old fashion of the bearded face and the shaven upper-lip which bespeaks the elder. Or one might take him for a Quaker of other days if his garb were not a thought too illuminated for the ancient traditions of that body. But whatever the conclusion, your eye, if it has any perspicacity, will pick him out from the throng of commonplaces and rest on him with a sense of repose and pleasure. For he has the distinction not merely of separateness, but of a certain primeval dignity and security that arrests the eye and the mind. The tide of humanity sweeps by with its restless ebb and flow. The newsboy shouts the latest sensation from the pavement; the motor-car hoots the authentic note of modernity from the street. But here, one feels, is something enduring in the midst of so much that is transitory, something that speaks of continuity in the midst of so much that is changing, something built on rock in a world of shifting sands.

Perhaps to those who count success only by visible achievement, Lord Courtney may almost be reckoned a failure. He seemed capable of so much and has accomplished so little. Second Wrangler of his year, and Smith's Prizeman nearly sixty years ago, fellow of his college, familiar through his early connection with his father's bank with finance and statistics, a member of the Bar, one of the most distinguished leader-writers of the *Times* in the great day of Delane, Professor of Political Economy at University College, a political philosopher, and in his rather massive, unpretentious way an orator, he seemed destined to supreme place in the service of the State. There was in him the promise of an incomparable Lord Chancellor, or of a great Speaker, or of a Premier who might have challenged Gladstone himself in the eye of the historian.

And instead, his record consists of a few inconspicuous Ministerial appointments, culminating in the Financial Secretaryship to the Treasury, a brief but memorable tenure of the Chairmanship of Committee, and finally a decent interment in the House of Lords.

And yet, viewed in a larger way, there is no career of our time more admirable or indeed more splendid. It is a career whose failures are nobler than the successes of most men, for they are the failures of a great spirit devoted with rare purity of motive to the service of public ends. Lord Morley once lamented that we had lost the strain of the great private member. He did not ask for a Burke or a Cobden; he would be content with a Bradlaugh, a powerful critic, with a large sweep and a bold utterance, whose disposition or circumstances place him definitely outside the pursuit of office. Lord Courtney belongs to that lost strain. He made no self-denying ordinance against office; but Nature made it for him. He has that type of mind which is uncomfortable on front benches. Front benches mean compromise, petty surrenders here, suppressions of the truth there, equivocations, legerdemain. And there is no such word as compromise in the stern vocabulary of Lord Courtney. His principles are ruthless taskmasters, who must be obeyed though the heavens fall and he be buried in the ruins. He is impossible as a party man, and has ploughed his lonely furrow across the field of politics without swerving a hair's-breadth to please anyone or to secure any personal end. He is the least jesuitical man in the public life of his time. He will have no circuitous routes to the millennium, no present falsities to achieve an ultimate good. If the thing isn't right in itself then no supposititious consequence will make it right. He will play no tricks with his conscience, offer no sacrifice at the altar of party unity. When Gladstone brought in his Redistribution Bill of 1884 Mr. Courtney resigned the Financial

Secretaryship to the Treasury and ended his Ministerial career because the Bill proceeded upon the plan of the single-seat constituency. He had been seized with the idea of proportional representation, and would rather sacrifice all his hopes of political advancement than be faithless to that pale abstraction.

And in the same way, though he broke with Gladstone on Home Rule, he never harnessed himself, as Mr. Chamberlain and Goschen did, to the Unionist chariot. He is the only Liberal Unionist who has emerged from the great disruption with his Liberalism unshaken. And when the war came his was the weightiest voice raised against that great crime, just as, when Sir Edward Grey had revealed to the country his practical adoption of the theory of two European camps, it was Lord Courtney's speech in the House of Lords which showed the sinister gravity of that step, and stated with the authority of a prophet the historic doctrine of the Concert of Europe.

In short, he is a party of one. It is not that he is perverse. He is quite content, it is true, to be in disagreement with the world. Indeed, he is probably happier when he is in disagreement with the world, for he has a wholesome distrust of popular judgments. He has something of the quality of Tolstoy, who fought for a cause with all his passion while it was unpopular, but began to doubt its validity when it became successful. It is indeed the quality of the thinker in all times—the quality that makes Plato the critic of the Athenian democracy, and Burke the critic of the French Revolution. The philosopher is free from the hypnotism of party cries and party shibboleths. He doubts all great popular emotions, and is more sensitive to the defects of a system than captured by its excellences. The movement of his mind is the movement of the tide, not of the tidal wave. His habit is to be in opposition to the general tendencies of the time, no matter whether they be Liberal or Conservative. Lord Courtney has in a conspicuous degree this philosophic contrariness. But while he is happy to stand alone, he does not do so perversely. There are some men who are so impartial that they are always a little partial to the other side. There are others who have a congenital tendency to disagreement. They are the converse of the man in *John Bull's Other Island*, of whom it was said, " Sure, he'll say what gives most pleasure to you and least trouble to himself." They are only happy when they have blighted your hopes or chilled your warm enthusiasms. Thoreau was an example of this not uncommon type. Emerson said of him that he found it easier to say " No " than " Yes." Lord Courtney can say " No " very well; but he says it without that temperamental negation which was characteristic of Thoreau. He says it because, governed entirely by principle, and wholly indifferent to expediency, there is nothing else to say. In the rare atmosphere in which he dwells the emotions of the street and of the passing hour do not touch him. His judgments come, as it were, from another sphere. Hence their occasional blighting effect upon the enthusiasms of the moment. When, after the General Election of 1880, the Liberals were wild with delight at the magnitude of the triumph, Mr. Courtney's characteristic comment was that he distrusted these big turnover majorities. It is a chill air, but healthy.

It might be said of him as Hazlitt said of Cobbett, that he is " a sort of fourth estate of the realm." But there is this difference between him and Cobbett, that while the latter was tossed about by every wind of doctrine, Lord Courtney stands four-square to all the winds that blow. It cannot be said that he has never changed an opinion: he has changed his opinion on Home Rule. But he has never changed a principle, or been false to one that he held. He is the keeper of the national conscience—a sort of barometer that tells us unfailingly whether we are set "foul" or "fair." You cannot bribe that barometer into returning a false verdict. Tap it or coax it as you may, it will say the truth that is in it and no other.

It is probable that Lord Courtney has never been quite so much at home anywhere as he has been in the House of Lords. The atmosphere of that chamber, which acts with such subtle alchemy upon the Radicalism of most men, only serves as a tonic to Lord Courtney's stern spirit. He rises like a prophet of Israel at some Belshazzar feast, and reads the writing on the wall to the doomed revellers. He was at his best in the great conflict of the Lords with the Commons, when he warned the peers of the perilous path they were treading. He suffered the usual fate of the prophet. The revellers scoffed at his prophecies. But the prophecies came true.

Except in his native Cornwall, which loves him, and whose love he returns, he has never been a popular figure. He is caviare to the general. Popularity is rarely the reward of the gold of character, but of its alloy. The Athenians, who made a popular hero of Alcibiades, banished Aristides because they got tired of hearing him called the Just. We have not been able to banish Lord Courtney; but we have done our best. We have ignored him. It is true that he makes no concessions to our weakness. Queen Victoria said that Gladstone spoke to her as if he were addressing a public meeting, and she took her revenge by a whole-hearted dislike, while she lavished her affection upon Disraeli, who inquired after the health of the royal babies, and in his own phrase laid on his flattery with a trowel. It is so with the public. It reserves its affection for the man who inquires after the baby. Lord Courtney never does that. He deals in abstractions, in ideas, in theories. He pays the public the compliment of thinking it is as serious and as learned as himself, and the public yawns and passes to some more popular performer for its entertainment. Delane is reported to have said that when Courtney has walked for three hours and written for two he was fit company for ordinary mankind. And it must be confessed that there is something formidable in those beetling brows, that heavy voice, and that colossal gravity. Yet he is not without humour, and a smile, which some men have felt to be the smile of the superior person, but which seems to me singularly gentle and winning, constantly plays over his massive features. And he can make a joke, too, in a rather elaborate Socratic way as befits him. Thus when, at one of his election meetings, he was asked if he were in favour of legalising marriage with a deceased wife's sister, he replied, all smiles, "May I ask whether the gentleman who puts the question is married?" "I am." "Has your wife a sister living?" "She has." "Is your wife present?" "No." "Well, my wife *is* present, and she, too, has a sister living."

He is the lay preacher of national righteousness. Mr. Lehmann once likened him to Isaiah, and the parallel is not inappropriate. He is the Isaiah of our day—Isaiah in a canary-coloured waistcoat. He moves through our feverish time with the cloud of prophecy about him—a figure significant and inspiring, firm as a rock, free from all rancour and littleness, speaking the truth, and working without thought of reward or praise for all noble ends. When we have lost a certain reverence for such a figure we shall have lost the soul of goodness. We shall have forgotten that

> 'Thrice blessed are the things that last,
> The things that are more excellent."

His eyes have grown dim almost to blindness, so that he has to rely on others to read to him; but the inner vision remains clear and undazzled. It is the vision of the seer who looks beyond the street and the moment, and scans far horizons and the unalterable stars.

SIR WILLIAM LEVER

It was a dramatic coincidence that made Sir William Hesketh Lever and Lord Northcliffe the antagonists in the greatest libel action of our time. It was as though Hector and Achilles had each scoured the battlefield to find the foeman who challenged his supremacy and had come into collision by a kind of natural law. For Sir William Lever and Lord Northcliffe are the most significant products of our time. They are the Cæsars who bestride our world like a Colossus. While we petty men have been creeping about to find ourselves dishonourable graves, these great adventurers have shot up in our midst like portents. Their heads strike the stars. They levy tribute on us like the despots of a subject people. You can hardly wash your hands or shave yourself in the morning without paying toll to the one; you can hardly learn who was at Lady Midas' ball last night without paying toll to the other. They hold us all in fee. They are the potentates of our modern world. The king of old ruled us by capturing our territory and making us his serfs; the king of to-day rules us by controlling our commodities or our finance and making us his customers or his tools. And Sir William Lever and Lord Northcliffe are the pioneers in the new kingship of trade. They saw an empire awaiting exploitation: they entered and took possession.

These men are worth considering, for they represent the new material forces that have come into our modern life. They are our conquerors—the princes of the new régime. They are singularly alike in the qualities that have won their triumphs—in their clear vision of material possibilities, their swiftness to take occasion by the hand, the high-vaulting ambition of their flight, the masterful will with which they drive fullsteam ahead to their goal. But while they are alike in methods they are widely separated in motive. In a former book I have described Lord Northcliffe as the type of success ungoverned by moral purpose. He has a passion to be powerful and the means to be powerful, but he does not know what he wants to be powerful about. His career is thronged with thrilling incidents, but it has no direction. It is like that wild night-drive on which Tony Lumpkin charioted his mother. It was full of sensations and adventures, but at the end Mrs. Hardcastle found she had only careered round and round the domestic pond. Now Sir William Lever is all moral purpose. He reminds one of Benjamin Franklin. I can see him putting himself through the same hard moral discipline, taking himself in hand with a certain grim joy, and subduing himself to his own maxims with relentless firmness. He is a moral athlete who has trained himself down to the last ounce, and wins the race by first winning the victory over himself.

The successful man lives under a perpetual challenge. There is always a *primâ facie* case against him. He may have an honourable acquittal from the common jury who go into the details of his case, but the grand jury never fail to return a true bill. His success is enough to warrant the indictment. He is *ipso facto* a suspicious character. And the instinct, on the whole, though mixed in its origin, is sound. It is not that you and I, who may happen to be on the grand jury of failures, have a soul above material success. We haven't. We would be successful, too, if we knew how. In our several ways we are trying to be successful. It may, indeed, almost be said that the man who is not trying to be successful is not trying to be anything. But this common ground does not make us any more sympathetic with the man who has succeeded. To begin with, we are a little envious that he has got what we, who are obviously so much more meritorious, would have liked. We suspect that his success is the reward of methods we are too scrupulous to adopt, of a vulgarity we are too refined to stoop to, of a cold and calculating temperament that contrasts unamiably with the fine impulsiveness of our own. And so we watch him narrowly. Does he present a palace to the nation? Ah, we say, he has bought the Government. Now we know why he has got that concession in Africa. Does he treat his workmen with noticeable consideration? Just so; that is his artful way of stealing their souls. In all this distrust, unjust and mean though it often is, there is a sound social motive at work. We fear the absorption of power of any kind in a single hand. It is a vague menace to the commonwealth. And we know, too, that success is often rather a sordid thing. It is the failures who are interesting. It is Rembrandt in his garret, not Peter Paul prancing through the courts of Europe, whom we love. Who cares for the fat and prosperous Handel as a man? It is Beethoven, sinking under his weight of sorrows to the final *Commedia finita est,* who strikes the chords of our hearts.

But the judgment on the successful man may be reversed by one consideration. How did he use his success? That is the test by which we give him his sentence or his discharge. His success he could not help; his use of it he could.

Sir William Lever could no more miss material success than you, sir, with the retreating chin and the uncertain eye, or you with the doubtful, balancing mind can miss failure. Character is destiny. We say that, but for such-and-such circumstances, So-and-so would not have done such-and-such things. No, but he would have done something else. The qualities which made him successful here would have made him successful there. We are born either the masters or the victims of circumstance. And you cannot have a moment's doubt as to which category Sir William Lever belongs. You know him at once as the sort of person you would like to have at your back in a row. A taut, stockily-built man, with what a famous judge of men called " a good boiler "; head erect, with just a suspicion of defiance; the light blue eyes looking out at the world with fearless directness; tenacious mouth; a chin that will stand no nonsense. The sort of man of whom they say in Lancashire, " It's a word and a blow wi' him—and t' blow fost." For he has a great gift of eloquent silence. I have seen him sit on a garrulous committee without uttering a word, and at the end that cold, impassive eye and tightly-closed mouth formed the only comment I remembered.

Behind this masterful exterior there lurks a very human man, who loves simple joys and is at home with children. What is more significant is that children are at home with him. There is no better evidence of genuine good-nature than this, for children have an instinctive feeling for character that no elaborate arts can deceive. It is one of the most common and depressing experiences of mature life to find that you have lost the password to the child's garden, that the golden age has vanished, and that you are out in the cold among those sad Olympians who may be respected, but cannot be played with. Renan said that the final judgments on us will be those passed by women, countersigned by the Almighty. It would be truer to say that they will be the judgments of children, for women too are sophisticated, and it is easier to win their verdict by false arts than to enter the kingdom of the children by stealth. Now the children of Port Sunlight are not deceived by the formidable disguise that Sir William Lever wears to the world. They tear it away, they " make hay " of it, they turn it to derision. Their jolliest days are when Sir William invites them to descend on him at home, and they are his jolliest days too. Then you may see him swarmed over by children, riding a donkey with youngsters fore and aft, standing for leap-frog, playing the great and noble game of "making pretend," and beaming through it all with a perspiring happiness.

There is about him a severe, unrelenting simplicity of mind and conduct. "I was a grocer myself once," he said in the action to which I have alluded, and he preserves with a sort of proud challenge all the traditions of his origin. You could imagine him going back to the grocer's shop unmoved and unregretful, still master of himself and of circumstance. And out of that grocer's shop you know that that iron will would emerge again triumphant. You would have to buy his butter if you didn't buy his soap. If he had not built up the vast business of Lever Brothers, with its manufacturing centres in every continent, almost in every country in the world, from Japan to the United States, from Australia to Belgium and Germany, with its great enterprises for winning palm oil in the African forests, Nigeria, Sierra Leone, and the Congo, with its tens of thousands of work-people and its millions of capital—if he had not done this he would have been the Napoleon of tea or of oil or of sugar. For he is of the Napoleon breed, born to marshal big battalions and win empires, if not in war, then in peace.

The business man must have two common qualities in an uncommon degree. He must see truly and act decisively. He may be compared with the painter, who must have equal truth of vision and of hand. It is that double faculty in its highest expression that makes the veracity of Holbein so indisputable. The business man who has only the first quality is a dreamer; he who has only the second is a blunderer. Sir William Lever has both in a rare degree. His eye is always unscaled, and roves far horizons, and his mind is stored with an energy that makes action a joy and a necessity. A love of action—I mean not mere activity, but original action, initiative, adventure—is not a common trait. It is a very rare trait in fine minds—not because they are timid, but because they are apprehensive, imaginative, fear the consequences of the irrevocable word. A more distinguished son of Lancashire than Sir William Lever, speaking to me once about his retirement from a great office, spoke of that office as purgatory. The necessity of making grave decisions on vast issues preyed on his spirit until the burden was intolerable. Sir William Lever loves action as you or I, let us say, love to think about it. His earliest memory was a passion for tidying up the books on his father's bookshelf, big books to the left hand, the rest tailing down in beautiful symmetry to the right; his next was an attempt at intensive culture, covering the tops of rabbit-hutches with soil and endeavouring to grow corn in these ingenious plots. His father's shop would not give a field for so much energy. He opened a shop at Wigan; began to experiment with soap; prospered and bought a factory at Warrington; prospered and built Port Sunlight; prospered and girdled the globe with his enterprises until

> "The moving waters at their priestlike task
> Of pure ablution round earth's human shores"

seem to breathe his name and surge up his soap on every beach. And all the time, side by side with these great adventures of trade, he has pursued his own private enthusiasms with a thoroughness that seems to leave no room for other affairs. He has built at Port Sunlight a garden city which is one of the first and still one of the best object-lessons in the science and art of industrial housing; he has elaborated a great copartnership system which makes all his workpeople after certain service sharers in the prosperity of the firm; he buys a mountain and presents it as pleasaunce to his native town; he buys the town of Lymm and commences a great garden city enterprise; he buys an agricultural estate in Cheshire and begins roadmaking and experimental farming; he prepares an elaborate design for the reconstruction of the town of Bolton; he purchases Stafford House and gives it to the nation; incidentally—and at this I am grieved—he extends the outer ramparts of his house at Hampstead so that they dominate and despoil the most sylvan beauty-spot of the wonderful Heath.

In all this activity there is no trace of hurry or discomposure. He moves with the deliberation of a man who has plenty of time for everything and is always ahead of the clock. He wastes no words, and has the Lancashire man's faculty of saying "No" without circumlocution. And though he says that the art of business is to discover the capacity of other men and apply it to its right purpose, he is the architect of all his schemes—especially of any scheme that includes roadmaking and designing, which are his two special delights. Withal, he can find time for public affairs—though he found Parliament too great a demand on his time—to make speeches, to lead the Liberal party in Liverpool, and to write on Socialism. His reply to Mr. H. G. Wells on the subject of "Business and Socialism" was a remarkably acute dissection of the theory of the public ownership of the means of production, revealing a real mastery of economic problems and a faculty of lucid thinking and writing. He cultivates too the art of epigram. "Don't quarrel with a man," he said in one of his speeches, "because he is not suited for the work in hand. It is your business to find out what the man is suited for. It would be as logical to quarrel with the flowers in your garden because they are not watch-dogs." And again, "Don't believe for a moment that success is built on failure. Success is built only on well-laid, well-matured plans. I would alter the motto, ' If at first you don't succeed, try again,' to ' If at first you don't succeed, try another method.' " Like most rich men, he is very emphatic about the futility of riches, and he preaches self-conquest as the path to happiness, like the old-fashioned Puritan that he is.

A dangerous man to try a fall with. (Lord Northcliffe paid in all nearly £100,000 for the luxury, and that sum has gone to enrich Liverpool University.) Stiff, and a little challenging, with something of the watchful reserve of the self-made man, he goes his way, a plain, simple citizen, proud with the pride of conscious justice—a real russet-coated captain of industry. In him success presents its best front. We can almost forgive him.

MR. AND MRS. SIDNEY WEBB

If you were asked to call on the ablest woman in London you would, if you were a discerning person, hail a cab and proceed to Grosvenor Road, Westminster. But there your difficulty would begin. You would halt between No. 36 and No. 41, and remain like Buridan's ass when it stood transfixed between two bundles of hay. Probably you would give up the problem and call on neither. For at No. 36 lives Mrs. J. R. Green, and at No. 41 lives Mrs. Sidney Webb, and who shall make a choice between two such candidates? But if you were asked to call on the ablest couple in London, then you would have no doubt—then you would go confidently to No. 41.

There have been and are many cases of distinguished husbands and wives, but none in which the personalities of the two have been more completely merged than in the case of Sidney and Beatrice Webb. They are so entirely one that they seem to have dropped their separate identities—in spite of the startling dissimilarity in their personal appeal, the one so indisputably of the democracy, the other with the high-bridged nose, the thin lips and the wide-arched eyebrows of an authentic aristocracy. They have almost lost the use of the first person singular. They do not speak of "I," but of "we"—"We think," says Mr. Webb from his end of the table, and "We venture to take the view," says Mrs. Webb from her end. It is strophe and antistrophe; one intellect but two voices. It is as though they never disagreed, as though in that rare and passionless atmosphere of pure reason where they dwell, dissension is unknown and the stars sing together in eternal unison. It is true that in matters of the flesh Mr. Webb is the less celestial body of the two. He eats a chop and sips a little whisky and water with quite human enjoyment, while opposite him his wife dines off a plate of asparagus and a glass of mineral water. It is the only rift in that perfect lute.

Among the acolytes of the Fabian order there is a constant controversy as to which of the two is before or after the other. It is an idle theme, for you can never tell where one ends and the other begins—how much you are yielding to the eloquence of Mrs. Webb, and how much to the suggestion of Mr. Webb. It is she who weaves the spells, but he who forges the bolts. Between them they have an uncanny power of persuasion. Their knowledge overwhelms you, their sweet reasonableness disarms you. You are led captive in the chains of their silken logic, and they have the victories that fall to those whose knowledge is the instrument of relentless purpose, whose patience is inexhaustible and whose urbanity is never ruffled. Mr. Webb does not talk for victory in a dialectical sense. He understands as well as any man the difference between argument and persuasion. "So-and-so," said Mr. Lloyd George to me on one occasion, "argues too much in conference, and when a man argues he puts you on the defensive. He falsifies the issue. The struggle takes the form of a contest in which if you fail in the argument you suffer a sense of personal defeat. Mr. Balfour does not argue. He puts things before you. He keeps your mind open, and when your mind is open anything may enter." It is the same attitude which you feel in the case of Mr. Webb. He does not thrust his views down your throat. He offers them with an air of modest suggestion and inquiry. He keeps your mind disengaged and receptive. The element of personal conflict vanishes and you pass into an atmosphere of serene detachment where there are no false or reflected lights. He does not want a personal victory;

he wants your help in securing an impersonal end. No one yields more readily to a real point or surrenders non-essentials with a more liberal hand. But the pearl of price he does not yield. And so with Mrs. Webb. There is no cross-examiner at the bar more suave or subtle than Mrs. Webb. When I was called to give evidence before the Poor Law Commission I entered the room in the midst of her examination of Mr. Walter Long. The subject was the finance of the Unemployed Committees. Step by step she led him unconscious to his doom with gentle, innocent-looking questions. Suddenly he saw that he was being made to admit that voluntary effort was a failure and that the rates must be used. But it was too late to retreat. With a quiet "Thank you, that is all," she snapped the "bracelets" on his wrists, folded her hands, and sat back in her chair, the picture of demure, unexultant triumph.

It is this stealthy pursuit of their purposes, without haste and without rest, that makes them so powerful and so often distrusted. There is nothing that men dislike so much as being "managed." And Mr. and Mrs. Webb are always "managing" you. They sit behind the scenes, touching buttons, pulling wires, making the figures on the stage dance to their rhythms. To their modest table come the great and the powerful to learn their lessons and to be coached up in their facts. Some fear to enter that parlour of incantations, and watch the Webbs with unsleeping hostility. A mere suspicion that they are prompting behind the curtain is enough to make them damn the most perfect play.

And yet it would not be possible to find two more wholly disinterested people in London. They have no axe to grind, no selfish objects to serve. They seek neither honours nor rewards. They work tirelessly, incessantly. They spend their modest income in costly researches which they carry on together, and what they save on their housekeeping goes to employing more clerks—and still more clerks. They have no antipathies, and are indifferent to party labels. If they can score a point here through the Tories, good; there through the Liberals, good also. If they come up against an obstinate Minister, who thinks they want to " manage " him, and means " to have none of their intriguing, sir," they smile across at each other and wait. They are the solvents of party politics. They break them up with the subtle chemistry of ideas. They combine extreme aims with the most moderate and unsensational methods. They do not march round the walls of the capitalist Jericho blowing a trumpet. Anyone can blow a trumpet. They go to the gate like simple travellers, they talk to the citizens, ask questions, suggest that the walls are out of date, that they hinder the traffic, keep out the fresh air, are wasteful and useless—all this with the air of merely curious inquirers, voyagers from a far country, with a philosophic interest in the habits and customs of strange peoples. Mr. Chesterton, who, I think, expects to find Mr. and Mrs. Webb in the last circle of the Inferno, wants to lead us back to the Middle Ages through revolution and rivers of blood. Mr. and Mrs. Webb laugh gently at all revolutionists. The New Jerusalem they hope to build in England's green and pleasant land will be founded, not on broken heads, but on Blue books—it will spring out of a soil watered, not with blood, but with statistics.

They are not humanitarians, or philanthropists, or even idealists. I do not think that their pulse quickens with a tale of wrong. The emotions that surge through us—the joys that thrill us, the fears that depress us, the hopes that raise us—leave them placid and unmoved. They are scientists. " We shall strive," they said in announcing their aims when starting the *New Statesman*—" we shall strive to face and examine social and political issues in the same spirit in which the chemist or the biologist faces and examines his test tubes or his specimens." We are their "specimens." They have taken humanity for their theme as one might take ants or bees. They look with calm, dispassionate eye into the human hive. They find it in a deplorable muddle, the ways at the bottom blocked with struggling masses, trampling on each other, destroying each other, the young crushed and maimed in the confusion, while the honey that is created passes in a golden stream to a few corpulent fellows who occupy the spacious and luxurious chambers above. They do not pity the bees, but they hate disorder, and waste, and ugliness. They see that there is room for all and plenty for all, if only the thing is organised, and with deft and cunning fingers they set themselves to rearrange the structure so as to give air space and a share of the honey to all and to dispossess the fat fellows above. They do not hate the fat fellows any more than they pity the others. But they do hate idleness and luxury. They want a hive run on decent business lines, and they mark with approval the short way the working bees in the hive of nature have with the drones, who are simply dropped out of the hive to die on the ground below. If they won't work, neither shall they eat.

In that world of perfect order to which we move under their guidance even love will obey the Blue book. There are few more romantic scenes than that of Cardigan Bay from Harlech. The Bay sweeps round in one wide curve to the sharp peaks of the Rivals and from the sloping shores with their villages and pastures, the vast mass of Snowdon rises in great surges of cliff and fell to the lonely summit. That noble scene is linked in my mind with eugenics and the laws of love. I had been invited to speak (and be spoken to) at the Fabian School at Llanbedr, and on the Sunday I had gone with a companion to lunch with Mr. and Mrs. Webb at their cottage near Harlech. In the afternoon we walked round the Bay. Going, Mrs. Webb talked with her wonderful lucidity of the morass of destitution and the break-up of the Poor Law; returning, Mr. Webb talked with equal lucidity of the mysteries of local government, and of the chaos of society, and pictured that fascinating future, when we shall each have our dossier in the public archives, when we shall all be numbered and pigeon-holed, and when the State will by a bonus encourage me, who perchance am in the A1 class, to marry you, who are also in the A1 class, rather than the lady I love who has the misfortune to be, let us say, in D2 class. At this point I stopped in the road and laughed aloud, and I fancy I heard an echo of the laughter from the deep caves and great sides of Snowdon.

The clash of the subject and the scene seemed symbolic of the clash between intellect and emotion, between science and nature, between Blue books and the great tidal impulses of humanity. To Mr. and Mrs. Webb we are statistics. We are marshalled in columns, and drilled in tables, and explained in appendices. We do not move to some far-off divine event, but to a miraculous perfection of machinery and a place in decimals.

It is this unemotional view of humanity that makes the Webb philosophy so distasteful to all visionaries, romantics, anarchists, poets, and other unpractical people who are indifferent to dirt and disorder so long as they can have dreams and liberty. And as a scheme of life, it must be confessed, it does not satisfy. In the clear, dogmatic atmosphere of the 'eighties it seemed all-sufficient. Science had deposed man from his place in the universe; but what he had lost in spiritual significance he seemed to have gained in material competence. He was no longer a potential angel, but he was the master of things, and things were the only realities. When Fabianism dawned upon us, it seemed to solve all the conundrums of society, to open out before us a wonderful land of promise, the final goal of all the dim gropings of humanity. The vision has faded. We have become less assured and find our Canaan still some way off. We have come to distrust the merely material solution of things—the "test tubes" and "specimens" solution—and to suspect that we shall not find the ultimate peace we crave in any perfection of analysis and organisation. We have become modest in the estimate of our powers and find humanity too vast and incalculable for our neat systems and formulas. And with the waywardness of intellectual fashions, we turn from the precise structure of Fabianism, with its invulnerable statistics and perfect drains, to Bergson's fascinating vision of humanity as a vast organism reaching out into the darkness upon its eternal and inscrutable adventure.

But because we find the Webb philosophy insufficient it would be foolish to dismiss it as useless. One might as well object to the surgeon because he doesn't paint pictures, or to the plumber because he doesn't write sonnets. They have chosen a vast and fruitful field for their labours, and are content with its limitations. The nation owes no deeper debt than that due to these two great and disinterested public servants, these unrivalled surgeons of the body politic, who have given unostentatiously and without reward the devotion of a lifetime to diagnosing the material ailments of society and prescribing the remedies. They have done more than anyone else to redeem politics from guess-work and to give it an exact and scientific basis. And though their labours have been confined to the material fabric of society, I am not sure that they have not done as much as the poets to cleanse its soul as well.

ARCHDEACON LILLEY

It is one of the vices of an official Church that its great representative positions fall to official minds. In this it shares the tendency of all institutions which are privileged and independent of the popular judgment. In a purely competitive profession like the Bar the highest capacity—the highest, that is, for the purpose of the Bar—never fails of recognition, if once it can secure a hearing. If you have a supreme surgical gift the public will discover you and dictate your professional status. But if you are an artist of great and original powers the Royal Academy will not hasten to make you its head. It may admit you grudgingly and of necessity; but it will reserve its laurels for those who accept its formulas and share its love of authority and its reverence for mediocrity. Millais would never have been President if he had retained the great note of his youth: the Presidency was the reward of his surrender to the commonplace. The same is true of the Church, and never more true than in these days. The fact that the highest appointments are in the gift of the State does not qualify the tendency to exalt the official type, for ultimately promotion comes from official influence within the Church and not from without.

We may put the matter to the test by the case of Canon Barnett. If the Church has had an authentic prophet in these days it was the founder of Toynbee Hall—the man who, more than anyone else, gave impetus and direction to the social movement of the time. There have been others, no doubt, whose passion for humanity was not less than his; but there have been none in whom it was so instructed by wisdom, so free from all pettiness, and in whom it glowed with such an equable fire. To know him, to come under the influence of that large and gracious purpose, was to feel life at its amplest and noblest. It was to pass into "the pure serene." The vision which comes to us fitfully, the hopes which expire in us so easily, were in him constant and abiding. His emotions were deep and tender; but they were never idle, for they were governed by a masculine understanding that gave continuity and design to the energy they generated. Thought and feeling were in just equipoise. You felt the saintliness of his mind: but you felt equally its extraordinary mastery of the worldly facts, its quality of statesmanship and practical wisdom. There has been no one in our time, I think, who seemed so completely free from the limitations of personality, to be so all-embracing, all-comprehending, and yet so near and human. His influence, to use St. Augustine's great image of the power of God, was like a circle whose centre is everywhere and whose circumference is nowhere. He had the large serenity of one who dwelt outside "the shadow of our night," and yet the intimacy of one who brought an understanding sympathy to the meanest life. Wisdom and love have rarely been found in such perfect union, and added to them was an administrative faculty of the first order.

And yet, in a time when the resources of the Church were conspicuously wanting in the qualities of greatness, he remained in an obscure canonry until near the close of his life, and the riches of his powerful mind and enlightened spirit were never allowed to add distinction to the thin stream of episcopal statesmanship in the House of Lords. The beauty of his character, the rareness of his gifts, his genius for affairs, were universally recognised; but the breadth of his view, his entire freedom from all the narrowing influences of clericalism, placed him outside the circle of official success. He be longed to humanity even more than he belonged to the

Church, and the Church is a jealous master. It distrusts prophets and rewards ecclesiastics. Hence its loss of touch with the great movements of thought, its negligible place in the influences that are shaping the future.

It is this distrust that has permitted the withdrawal from London of the chief ornament of the Church's pulpit. That pulpit is to-day admittedly undistinguished. It makes little appeal to the understanding. The amiable and ingenuous spirit of the Bishop of London is its characteristic note, qualified only by the sensationalism of Dean Inge. It was not accident that left the Rev. A. L. Lilley at fifty-two still the obscure vicar of the odd little church on Paddington Green. You ask, reasonably enough, " But who is the Rev. A. L. Lilley? " Probably you have not heard his name. You will not even find it in *Who's Who*, for he has that self-forgetfulness which not so much rejects as is unconscious of the arts of self-advertisement. He plays no part in the politics of the Church, his name is never borne far and wide on the wings of rumour, he dwells apart in a certain cloistered stillness. And yet to many his name is an inspiration. It has a fragrance of its own that, for them, no other contemporary name possesses. It is like a quiet pool in a thirsty land.

If we ask for the secret of his power, we shall find that it is also the secret of his neglect. He is the representative Modernist of the Church. Modernism is a new word, but the thing is not new. It is eternal. Nor is it confined to one Church. Erasmus was a Modernist in the sixteenth century, as Sabatier and Tyrrell were Modernists in the nineteenth. Robertson Smith was a Modernist in Presbyterian Scotland just as Mr. Montefiore is a Modernist among the Jews to-day in his crusade for the inclusion of Jesus among the prophets of Israel. Every soul that is alive is a Modernist soul. How else can it be alive? For the spirit that is vital cannot be imprisoned in the letter which is dead. The spiritual facts are eternal, but the interpretations are human, temporary, and changing.

And it is because the Church seeks to convert these temporary interpretations into final and inexorable statements of revelation, because she forgets that, in Mr. Lilley's phrase, "God's revelation is given *in* us," and that the spiritual experience of the whole Christian society, and not any group of formulas, is the real measure of that revelation—it is because of this that "her net has lost its due sweep in the wide waters of humanity." And it is because of this that she stones the prophets in one age, burns them in another, and leaves them on Paddington Green in our own.

Against this petrifaction of the Church Mr. Lilley's life and teaching is a protest. It is not the protest of the rebel or the bitter controversialist; but of the seer who stands aloof in some spacious solitude of the spirit, catches the vision, and utters it in grave, abstracted speech. There is no note of the popular preacher in his style. The fine sense of accent, the exquisite balance of the sentences, the beauty of the phrasing, remind one that he is a scholar as well as a seer, and that his career at Trinity College, Dublin, was a record of brilliant intellectual triumphs. But these are not the things that make the impression so deep and enduring. Every successful preacher has his own peculiar note of appeal. Dr. Horton seems to come hot into the pulpit under the compulsion of some sudden flash of lightning that has illuminated the whole landscape of life. He is exalted with this vision, desolated with that. He is a harp upon which the winds of heaven seem to blow alternate dirge and song. Dr. Jowett utters his message with a gracious tenderness of spirit that suffuses the sky with a sunset glow. Dr. Campbell Morgan holds his vast congregation by a dramatic realisation of a simple gospel story. All these are speaking consciously and definitely to their hearers.

Archdeacon Lilley

Mr. Lilley seems like one detached from the world, forgetful of his audience, sounding the deeps of his heart in some still sanctuary of the recluse. The mood is unchanging. It is the mood of one who has been through deep waters and has come to a secure haven. When I hear him, I think of that great line of Whitman:

> "No array of terms can say how much I am at peace about God and about death."

Peace has come not through indifference or self-delusion or the anodynes of superstition, but through an emancipated spirit, a sovereign view of life, a large tolerance, a tender sympathy, a splendid faith in humanity and its destiny. The muddy vesture of decay has fallen magically away. "We are free of the oak and the pine scrub: we are out on the rocks and the snow." We have ascended to a high place and a quiet air, from whence we survey all the feverish movement of life, its pageantry and its mourning. We see what is temporary and what is eternal, the false things that men pursue, the true that they reject. There is a great pity, but also a great hope, for beyond is the goal to which through age-long endeavour the soul of humanity moves—the goal of the Kingdom where justice shall prevail and the things of the spirit shall triumph over the things of the flesh, and love, stronger than death, shall make all things plain. It is all strangely impersonal, strangely moving, a voice speaking out of eternity—

> "A voice far up beside the sun,
> Where sound and warmth and glory
> Are melted all in one."

In this spacious air there is no place for the pettiness and acerbities that vex the soul. All is resolved because all is understood, because all is touched with a certain radiance of love. He searches the heart of man with a terrible power, but he searches it with a healing, never with a wounding, touch. He lays bare the dark secret of the soul, but you do not shudder at the revelation, hardly are you ashamed—only it seems that the secret has vanished with the light and that you are whole.

He is a profound student of the theological movement, one of the few Englishmen—if the term may be used in its wide sense to include an Irishman born in Co. Armagh—with a European reputation. His works on *Modernism* and *Good Citizenship* are better known in Germany than in England, better known in France than in either. But in his preaching there is neither dogma nor controversy. He leaves the schools and on broad wings sweeps a larger sky. It is always of the Kingdom that he speaks. The volumes of his sermons might be called the Books of the Kingdom. They are laden with skyey-tinctured grain. And the Kingdom is the Kingdom of the spirit. There are no gates of creed or race to that Kingdom, but all are of it who love justice and mercy, who hear the Word of God and do it. "God is the fulfilment of the good we would do but cannot, of the love we would give but fail to give, of the justice we would establish perfectly but can only partially achieve. We find God alike in the good we can do and in the still greater good towards which we are always ineffectually striving."

And the Church should be as wide as the Kingdom. Let her make her human doors of admission and exclusion if she will, but let her not shut those doors against the soul that truly seeks. If she does she is not the Church of the Kingdom—

"Let her remember that if she is a human society she is also in a very real sense a Divine society, and that it is always her last and worst apostasy to claim a Divine and eternal validity for those conditions of membership which, as a human society, she may think herself compelled to impose. Above all, let her not be satisfied while she finds a single soul on fire with enthusiasm for righteousness, a single life offered in ready sacrifice upon the altar of human service, a single sincerity that follows truth into the wilderness in scorn of consequence, shut out from her pale. All such are most conspicuously of the Kingdom of Heaven, and are most surely making that Kingdom. All such are sons of God, for from whom but from God could such a high quality of life proceed? All such, even when they think they cannot say, 'Lord, Lord,' are sworn brothers of Jesus, since together they are accomplishing the will of their common Father which is in Heaven. If belief separates us from men like these, then let us accept the natural and inevitable conclusion that belief is subordinate to the full reality of Divine Sonship and membership of the real Kingdom of God."

And on that note of challenge the sermon of "The Draw Net" closes. The appeal is never to opinion, never to external authority—always to the individual soul, the God *in* us, for "No man can hear the Word of God for another." And it is in the effort to fulfil that word that satisfaction alone consists. Without that effort, all material success is vain—"The hands are full of things, but the heart is empty." And "The empty heart finds or makes an empty world."

And the sphere for effort is here and now. It is in bringing in the reign of justice on earth that we advance the Kingdom, and win peace. For "the man who is most himself is the man who gives most to society." The emotion of goodness is not enough, may indeed be weakness. For with all his tenderness he is no sentimentalist. He wastes no tears. "Think of all the good feelings that are used up in being felt." They must be translated into action. "There are the people who live with us day by day, who have to endure the actual reality of our character, who shrink before its unbridled temper, or freeze under the icy breath of its reserve, or harden under the stony pressure of its indifference. And if that cannot shame us into self-knowledge, nothing can. It is the one supreme glory of the family that it usually does that for us. For when it fails even to do that, we have reached the perfect tragedy of human life."

But it is not enough that we should learn that lesson in the family; we must learn to learn it more and more in the larger society outside the family. And as we learn it in action we grow in stature. " For our actions react upon ourselves. They form in us a something immeasurable which we call character, a certain type of inward power which transcends action, which is greater than any expression of itself in what we do. . . . And so it is that influence keeps ever ahead of power. Alike for good or evil we are something greater than we know." The Kingdom of God is indeed within. But it would not be within at all if it were not also without, and it is in the social mirror that is held up before us that we see the measure of our inward struggle, our victory or failure:

" There in the world around us, in the ideals by which it lives, in the things it is doing and wants done, is the measure of ourselves. There is the kingdom of the devil which our slackness has allowed to come into being, to which our slackness, if it were to continue, would give a permanent lease. But there also is the potential Kingdom of God calling us to be ourselves, to get back to simplicity, to sincerity, to the healthy joy of unwearied effort in the service of the highest things."

This is the message that has been preached for twenty-one years in London, first at Holy Trinity, Sloane Street, where Mr. Lilley was curate for eleven years, then at St. Mary's, Paddington Green. No loftier or more sustained message has been delivered in our day. It has made the little church on Paddington Green a very well of living water to many to whom the appeal of the churches had grown sterile and unreal. And yet, as I say this, I hear the repudiation of the preacher—" Nay, but blessed is he who hears the Word of God and does it." He will not have the vessel exalted. He cares only for the message, and would have you care for it only also.

For, as I have said, he has that fundamental humility

of mind that seems entirely self-forgetful. It is not the humility of the ascetic who retreats into his cell and flagellates the flesh. He is entirely human and happy, glowing with that steady fire of enthusiasm that never leaps into flame or smoulders into ashes, but burns bright and clear to the last ember. He lives his gospel of service in his own life. No good cause, especially if it be the cause of tolerance or liberty or justice in any form, appeals to him in vain. When Miss Malecka was in peril in Russia, it was he who told the world the truth about the woman who was threatened with a living death in Siberia. He has been one of the chief inspirers of the Christian Social Union, and his passion for citizenship has revealed itself in his enthusiasm for the Progressive cause in London. He is a Liberal in sympathy, but takes no part in politics.

His friends are of all communions and none; but most of all I think his heart goes out to those exiles of the Roman Catholic Church, priests who have fallen under the ban of Modernism, and who earn a precarious living in our midst, some teaching Italian, some even as waiters. For these, as for all who make sacrifices for liberty of conscience, he has not sympathy merely, but reverence. In his talk the impression he gives is of his entire freedom from insularity. His mind dwells in no backwater, but sails the broad currents of the world, and his conversation covers the literature and thought of the Continent with the freedom of one who is unconscious of intellectual or racial barriers.

Withal, he is the ideal parish priest, simple in manners and tastes, happy in the lowliest company, ready to pour out the treasures of his intellect to a young men's debating circle or to read *Mr. Dooley* to a mothers' meeting. He is gentler than his fellow-countryman, Father O'Flynn. He would not "help the lazy ones on wid a stick," but he has "the way wid him," the winning comradeship that makes even a rebuke irresistible.

His sphere is not in affairs, for he is without the genius for statesmanship that characterised Canon Barnett. He is abstracted, and gives the impression of one who might occasionally be uncertain about his own address, and who would accept any change that was offered him with nothing more than a faint feeling of surprise that any should be offered at all. His desk I should expect—and hope—to find extremely untidy. He is, in short, an entirely unworldly person, who seems to have strayed from the infinite into the midst of this eager life. But he brings very precious merchandise with him—that healing touch of the spirit that ministers to the mind diseased by the world, that sense of the larger significance of life which is so easily in the midst of our " getting and spending." The Bishop of Hereford has paid his rare gifts a belated tribute in making him Archdeacon of Ludlow; but his true sphere is not in the countryside. It is in " streaming London's central roar " that that large utterance should be heard. His exclusion from the great pulpits of London is a disservice to the Church and a wrong to the deepest spiritual interests of this great city.

SIR WILFRID LAURIER

THE quality of personal distinction is a rare and elusive gift. It does not depend on intellectual qualities alone. Mr. Asquith's intellectual gifts are at least as conspicuous as those of Mr. Balfour, yet he is without that subtle atmosphere of distinction which makes Mr. Balfour so fascinating a figure in any connection. It is not the result of moral qualities alone, for the moralist often only succeeds in making men see "how awful goodness is" in a sense which Milton did not intend. It does not depend simply on rectitude of public conduct. If it did the position of the two examples I have quoted would be entirely reversed, for few careers of our time have been more free from the falsities of expediency than that of Mr. Asquith, while the career of Mr. Balfour is a record of casuistical surrenders in the interest of ultimate and often obscure purposes. It is not necessarily associated with the external graces of bearing or magnitude of achievement. Lord Roberts is a more amiable man than Lord Kitchener, and his record is more heroic: but his personality excites none of the strange interest which Lord Kitchener's arouses. It would seem, in a word, to be the emanation not of precise qualities, however admirable, but of something incalculable and esoteric—the Oriental magic of a Disraeli or the Sinaitic fervour of a Gladstone.

But however elusive the quality may be, its presence is always indisputable. You felt it on that day of the Jubilee Procession in 1897. The brilliant cortège that moved up Ludgate Hill to St. Paul's Churchyard contained gloriously-apparelled princes and potentates from all lands. It was radiant with gems and cloth of gold and shining helmets and glittering swords. But the figure that, next to the aged Queen herself, was honoured with the most attention and greeted with the most enthusiasm was that of a plainly-dressed gentleman, grey-haired and clean-shaven, seated in an inconspicuous carriage. It was Sir Wilfrid Laurier, the new Premier of Canada, paying his first official visit to England. It would be difficult to give a convincing explanation of that reception. It was not a tribute to the Colonies simply, for all the Colonies were represented. It was not a peculiar compliment to Canada, for the great Canadian boom had not yet begun. It was not gratitude for Sir Wilfrid's initiation of preference to British trade, for the Tariff Reform movement, which was to exploit that preference, was still unborn. Something, no doubt, was due to the interest aroused by the novelty of a French-Canadian—to whom English had been an unfamiliar tongue until he had approached manhood—filling the position of Prime Minister of a British Colony. But mainly the interest was personal and peculiar. For the first time a Colonial statesman—in those days it was not disrespectful to speak of the "Colonies," and the stilted locution "Overseas Dominions" had hardly been invented—had touched the imagination of the British public, and had become something more than a name even to the man in the street. Since those days the political stature of Sir Wilfrid Laurier has steadily increased, and whether in or out of office he is the most considerable figure in Greater Britain.

To some extent, no doubt, he owes this eminence to very unusual personal advantages. Sir Wilfrid Laurier's appearance is alone a handsome fortune. It would assure him success in any sphere of action. There is about it the sense of an antique chivalry and an ancient culture. He carries the mind out of the heat and hurry of the present into a larger atmosphere and a more tranquil mood. "He is a picture gallery all to himself," said one of his political contemporaries. It is a picture gallery that suggests France before the Revolution, but the France of the intellectuals, touched with the great manner of an authentic aristocracy, easy and assured, free alike from boorishness and simulation. His figure, in spite of his seventy-two years, is still lithe and straight as a larch; his face unwrinkled; his glance clear and searching, but a little enigmatic; his mouth full and pursed, with a hint of whimsicalness. The breadth of the brow contrasts curiously with the length and narrowness of the face. His utterance in conversation is precise and a little formal, every word being given its full value, and the phrases being rendered with something of that staccato quality which is characteristic of the United States, of whose intonation also there is more than a suggestion in his speech. He is the most accessible and cordial of men, and talks with great apparent candour—a candour which does not conceal the reserve and astuteness of an extremely wary mind.

Those qualities of reserve are largely the source of the commanding attention he excites. They suggest spacious hinterlands of thought to which you are not admitted in spite of the cordiality of your reception at the front door—hinterlands in which he is carrying out the evolutions preparatory to some stroke of policy which is not yet ripe for disclosure. He has the art of keeping the public mind alert and expectant. You do not know how or where he will strike; but you know that behind that bland and serene exterior he is surveying the field with the swift eye of the strategist, and that the bolt will be sudden and masterful.

This obscurity is not merely superficial. It is inherent in the facts of a career which—in the absence of a key to solve the riddle—might easily be condemned as tortuous and inscrutable. If one were to bring Sir

Wilfrid to the Bar to answer an indictment of opportunism and political levity, one would be sure of a true bill from the grand jury. The *primâ facie* case would be complete and irresistible. Take his record on Free Trade. Under the banner of Mackenzie, he came into politics a Liberal of the English school, "a pupil," as he has said, "of Charles James Fox, Daniel O'Connell, and, greatest of them all, William Ewart Gladstone," a gold medallist of the Cobden Club, and one of the most brilliant exponents of Free Trade. He was supreme in Canada for fifteen years, and in all that time did nothing to redeem the pledges of his party on Free Trade. He opposed the Confederation and became its chief strength. In opposition he was the advocate of unrestricted Reciprocity with the States; when he came into power he dropped that policy; at the end of fifteen years of office he revived it, and fell fighting on its behalf. He assailed the corrupt railway policy of the Macdonald Ministry, and saw his own Government become the instrument of new railway interests. A man of the highest probity himself, he allowed his great reputation to be used as a shield for politicians whose standards were, to say the least, less delicate than his own. A French-Canadian, with unquestioned devotion to that race and its traditions, he has done more than any other politician to shift the centre of gravity of Canadian politics from French Quebec to the English-speaking West. The indictment might be lengthened with other equivocal counts.

And—to cut a long story short—it would be idle to deny that Sir Wilfrid is an opportunist. In that he is true to the genius of Canadian politics, which have never turned on principles, but on material problems—railways, tariffs, and commercial treaties. If he is condemned it will be because, with great endowments, great power, and a true vision, he did not risk all in order to give Canada a higher ideal of statesmanship and to turn the currents of its public life into better channels.

While there would be a certain justice in such a verdict, it would ignore the governing motive of Sir Wilfrid's career and the magnitude of his actual achievement. What is that achievement? It is that he has finally established the understanding between the two races of the Dominion which is the keystone of the arch of Canadian Confederacy. Perhaps no one but a French-Canadian could have done this: certainly no one could have done it who had not Sir Wilfrid's tact and astuteness. He has had to placate his compatriots, while they have seen the power of the West rising and overshadowing them. He has kept them loyal to the British connection, while seeming to yield a little unwillingly to courses which that connection imposed on his country. He showed no enthusiasm, for example, for the Boer War, and seemed to yield to pressure in sending Canadian contingents to South Africa; but the result justified his caution, and when later he defended the despatch of Canadian troops to the war against Mr. Bourassa, the leader of the extreme Nationalists, he did so in one of those speeches which, whether in English or French, have few parallels in the oratory of any British Parliament to-day. The close touched with eloquence the dominant note of his career. He was speaking of the racial conflict that still existed, and said:

"But there is no bond of union so strong as the bond created by common dangers faced in common. To-day there are men in South Africa representing the two branches of the Canadian family, fighting side by side for the honour of Canada. Already some of them have fallen, giving to the country the last full measure of devotion. Their remains have been laid in the same grave, there to rest to the end of time in that last fraternal embrace. Can we not hope, I ask my honourable friend himself, that in that grave should be buried the last vestiges of our former antagonism? If such shall be the result, if we can indulge that hope, if we can believe that in that grave shall be buried the contentions of the past, the sending of the contingents would be the greatest service ever rendered Canada since Confederation."

It is well, when tempted to think that Sir Wilfrid is cold to the imperial connection, to recall this incident, and to remember that Mr. Bourassa is ever on his flank, appealing to extreme French sentiment against him, and always ready to unite with the Conservatives to destroy him, as he did at the last election. But whatever the temporary fluctuations may be, there is no doubt as to the permanent improvement which Sir Wilfrid has effected in the relations of the English and French Canadians. He has taught the French that they have won Canada as well as lost it. He summed up the position of the French under British rule in a very memorable way in one of his French speeches. "En effet," he said, "nous Canadiens français, nous sommes une race conquise. Mais, si nous sommes une race conquise, nous avons aussi fait une conquête—la conquête de la liberté."

And while this work of reconciliation is the chief outward achievement of his career, there has been one motive of which it is the fruit, and to which he has been constant throughout every apparent contradiction. That motive is the exaltation of Canada, and the development of a spirit of Canadian nationalism as opposed to racial antagonisms. He believes in British institutions and in the British connection, but only in so far as that connection is consistent with the unobstructed freedom of Canada. He sees the Empire as a voluntary confederation of free nations. Anything which limits that freedom in the interests of a centralised Imperialism he regards as a menace to Canada as a nation and to the Empire as a free system. It was in that spirit that he opposed Sir Joseph Ward's jejune Imperialism at the last Imperial Conference, and it is in that spirit that he is to-day fighting against the Borden scheme of a contribution to the British Navy. He believes that scheme will be bad for Canada and for England, and that it will involve a mutual interference that will be fatal to the free relations of the two countries. He does not doubt the duty of Canada to relieve England of some of her naval burden; but he insists that the true course is to take over the defence of Canadian shores with a Canadian Navy, built, maintained, and manned by Canada. In this he is making an appeal to the national instinct of his country, and he is defining very definitely and clearly the real spheres of national development and imperial relationship. It is by far the greatest issue that has yet been raised in Canada, and on this issue he is right in so far as he means that Nationalism is the root of the only Imperialism that can endure. If there is to be a centralised navy, it can only come out of the conviction of all the parts of the Empire that a common machine of government is essential not merely in an Imperial but also in a national sense. That conviction may come from events.

LORD HALSBURY

WHEN it was announced that Lord Halsbury was to be the Chairman of the Marconi Committee in the House of Lords there was a not unreasonable lifting of eyebrows. There had been no such *cause célèbre* in the political world since the Parnell divorce brought the Home Rule cause to disaster. The fall of Parnell left the Nationalist party in ruins, and it was hoped or feared that the Marconi affair might visit the Liberal party with similar destruction.

The great conflict that opened with the Budget of 1909 had reached a phase of unprecedented bitterness. The long delayed collision between the two Houses of Parliament, which Gladstone had foreshadowed in his last speech in the House of Commons, had come with a violence that gained in intensity as the struggle proceeded, and was approaching that sinister stage in which there began to be dark hints, and more than hints, about the Army. Twice Mr. Asquith had been driven to appeal to the country against the arrogant claims of the House of Lords and twice the country had supported him. The veto of the Peers was destroyed, the constitutional action of the King had made it clear that there was no hope of relief in that direction, and, driven from one entrenchment to another, the Opposition were beginning to talk of civil war and to look to the disaffection of the Army as their last reserve. The immediate issue had shifted with the course of the struggle from the Budget and the land to the veto of the Lords, and from the veto to Home Rule. Ulster was drilling and arming, German rifles were being surreptitiously brought into the country, and Sir

Edward Carson was openly reviewing his rebel troops and declaring his readiness to break every law in the pursuit of his object.

It was at this moment that the Marconi affair burst on the public. It was welcomed by the Opposition as an intervention of Providence and was exploited by the baser part of the press with incredible ferocity. Essentially, it was an affair of indiscretion and nothing more. The utmost that could be justly said in regard to it was that it revealed a levity and thoughtlessness which the traditions of public life severely discountenanced. At the time that the Government were engaged in making an agreement with the British Marconi Company, Mr. Lloyd George, the Master of Elibank, who was the Chief Whip of the Liberal party, and Sir Rufus Isaacs, had bought shares in the American Marconi Company. Although the two companies had intimate commercial relations it was proved that the American Company could not benefit by any contract of the British Company, and that, therefore, the American shares could not be affected by the action of the British Government. But the incident was sufficient on which to build a mountain of suspicion. It offered the Opposition the supreme prize they sought—the fall of the enemy they most feared and hated. For four years Mr. Lloyd George had been the Hotspur who had carried the war into their camp. It was he who had raised the issue of the land which had led to the thrilling sequence of events that was still unexhausted. Already he was preparing for a new campaign on the land question which was to follow the issue of the Home Rule controversy. So long as he was politically at large, with his fearless enterprise and his incomparable powers of popular appeal, Toryism seemed helpless. Now at last there was a chance of destroying him, of discrediting his character, of driving him out of public life. It was seized with a passion and venom which reflected the fear that his career and his potentialities inspired. Had he been caught picking pockets in Piccadilly he could not have been assailed with more violence. Guilty or innocent, he must be convicted.

And now a Commission—the second to be appointed—was to hold an investigation into the affair. And at the head of the Commission was Lord Halsbury. Whoever was responsible for this daring choice was not without humour and certainly not without insight. On the face of it, it was like handing over the Duke of Monmouth to Judge Jeffreys. There had been no more bitter foe of the Government during the thrilling events of the first few years than Lord Halsbury. It was he who, when his official leaders in the House of Lords had bowed to the storm, headed the revolt against them, was entertained at a famous dinner by the Die-Hards, and in the end very nearly carried the majority of the Peers with him in a defiance that would have plunged the country in revolution. Nor was it the violence of his political prejudice alone which, superficially, seemed to disqualify him for a case in which political prejudice was so largely involved. There was an element of practical satire in associating with a rather fine question of political purity one whose career had been so notorious for its unblushing assertion of the right of the party in power to the enjoyment of the loaves and fishes. In this respect he had won a reputation which had become a cherished possession of the comic stage.

There was a still further quality of piquancy in this unexpected choice. It was a new reminder to the public of the vitality of this indomitable old man, who, on the threshold of his ninetieth year, was still the most pugnacious figure in politics. His memory links the present day with the passing of the great Reform Bill in 1832, but his mental and physical energy are unabated by time. There is a defiant air of immortality about the man which seems to keep the enemy at bay. Old age has left what Oliver Wendell Holmes calls his "visiting cards" on him in profusion, but he treats them with scorn and goes along twirling his cane like a gay young fellow who has all his days before him. He has never yielded to anybody, and he is not going at his time of life to yield to such a thing as old age. He stands like a block of granite, four square to all the winds that blow—a quaint figure with exiguous legs, a powerful body and a mighty head set square and challenging upon the square shoulders. The features are instinct with the spirit of combat. The broad turned-up nose, the grim mouth drooping at the corners, the projecting under lip, the square aggressive lower jaw give him an air, at once humorous and formidable, which is a delight to the caricaturist.

And if his physique is made to last, his temperament is no less virile. It is the temperament of a man who, however much his ideas may belong to the past, always lives in the present. The Bishop of Carlisle once told me that when he sought to get the late Archdeacon Jones of Liverpool to talk about Gladstone, whose tutor he had been sixty years before, he found him singularly uninterested. Finally he cut the subject short by asking how the Philharmonic concert had gone off the previous night, observing by way of explanation, "I like to talk of the present; it keeps me young." That is the secret of Lord Halsbury's vitality of mind. He refuses to be pensioned off by time, and the older he gets the keener becomes his passion for the fight. When, after eighteen years' tenure of the Lord Chancellorship—a tenure only exceeded by those of Eldon and Hardwicke—he was driven from the Woolsack, he began the task of editing *The Laws of England*, and took advantage of the Act he himself had passed which gave him the right to preside in the Appeal Court. At eighty-five he headed the rebellion of the Die-Hards, and very nearly succeeded in overthrowing the official leadership of Lord Lansdowne. And there is no obvious reason why, at ninety-five, he should not still be found barring the way of Sir Robert Finlay to the Woolsack.

His opinions are as obstinate as his temperament. It was said of his father, Stanley Lees Giffard, who was the first editor of *The Standard* when that paper was founded in 1827 to oppose Catholic Emancipation, that "in the obduracy of his sympathies and antipathies in politics he was a man after Dr. Johnson's own heart." That might be said with equal truth of Lord Halsbury. He is one of the few indisputable Tories that are left to remind us of that incredible breed. He stands for everything that is in possession and is the enemy of everyone who is dispossessed. Sir Frederick Banbury himself is not a more uncompromising foe of democracy. He would not even let them have trams across the bridges in order to get to their work, lest such concessions should breed in them a perilous hunger for more luxuries and liberties, and his achievement in that matter is immortalised in a famous cartoon of *Punch.* When he led the Die-Hards he talked of his "solemn duty to God and his country." And no one doubted the sincerity of his utterance, for he is not given to talking humbug. He does really believe that God and his country belong to his own class and that Parliament is a sacred institution only so long as it is in possession of that class and makes laws to preserve its privileges against the heathen without. He distrusts democracy and does not care who knows it, for he is far too candid to wear a disguise, and his opinions are as plain and emphatic as his person.

His philosophy of Government is traceable to his grandfather, that famous Jack Giffard who was one of Pitt's instruments in destroying the liberties of Ireland. He was not the basest of those instruments.

That bad eminence belongs to McNally, the record of whose perfidy is one of the most shocking stories in the literature of any country. Jack only betrayed his country, not his friends. He was a creature of Dublin Castle and never pretended otherwise. He lives in the famous philippic of Grattan made in repudiating a charge which Giffard had levelled against him. Here is a passage from that withering utterance:

"When I observe the quarter whence the objection comes I am not surprised at its being made. It proceeds from the hired traducer of his country, the excommunicated of his fellow citizens, the regal rebel, the unpunished ruffian, the bigoted agitator. In the city a firebrand, in the court a liar, in the streets a bully, in the field a coward. And so obnoxious is he to the very party he wishes to espouse that he is only supportable by doing those dirty acts the less vile refuse to do."

It is not an amiable picture and Lord Halsbury doubtless prefers the more friendly description by Sir Jonah Barrington in his *Personal Sketches and Recollections.* It is not flattering, but it looks singularly lifelike:

"He had a great deal of vulgar talent, a daring impetuosity and was wholly indifferent to opinion. From first to last he fought his way through the world, and finally worked himself up to be the most sturdy partisan I ever recollect in the train of Government. His detestation of the Pope and his adoration of King William he carried to an excess quite ridiculous; in fact on both subjects he seemed occasionally delirious. With all his faults or crimes, if they should be called so, he had several qualities which in social intercourse are highly valuable. He was as warm-hearted and friendly a person as I ever met with, and, on the other hand, a bitterer enemy never existed."

Sir Jonah denied that he was a coward, as Grattan said, and it is difficult to imagine this type of bulldog to be wanting in personal courage: but there stands against him nevertheless the record of his brutal and cowardly assault on Potts, the editor of the rival Dublin paper, *Saunder's Daily News Letter,* for which he was sentenced to five months' imprisonment—a sentence which Dublin Castle promptly cancelled by ordering his release on payment of a fine.

It is not necessary here to go over the familiar story of the astounding corruption that led to the Union. That is all told in Lecky, Fitzpatrick and elsewhere, and the part which Giffard played in the squalid business has been illuminated by the discovery of heaps of the letters of the spies addressed to " J. G.," which are still preserved at Dublin Castle. The story of " The Dog in Office," as the people of Dublin called him, is interesting here only as throwing light on the sources of Lord Halsbury's fierce antagonism to Home Rule, the pugnacity of his character and the strength of his prejudices. Sir Jonah Barrington's description of his grandfather fits him like a glove.

There is about him a force of mind and downrightness of speech that are refreshing in a world of compromise and equivocation. He has the courage to say what he means and do what he wants on all occasions, regardless of consequences or criticisms. It is this bulldog quality which has brought him success. Neither at Oxford nor at the Bar was he specially distinguished, and his early career in Parliament was chiefly remarkable for the trouble his scornful disregard of consequences got his party into. But his grim aggressiveness ploughed through all obstruction, and leaves him to-day, when all his old colleagues of the Disraelian days are dead and forgotten, still one of the most formidable figures in politics.

Within the range of his understanding and sympathies, his mind works with a rough vigour and directness that are shattering to falsities or evasions.

"When I hear a counsel say a thing is practically so and so, then I know it is not so and so," he said on one occasion, and the saying expresses the blunt veracity of his mind where facts and forms of speech are in question. It is reminiscent of that plain-spoken lady in George Eliot's novel, who, when assured that her nephew was to be apprenticed "ultimately," said, "Boys oughtn't to be appointed ultimately: they ought to be apprenticed at fifteen." Sometimes he clothes his roughness with a homely humour that is delightful, as when he told counsel, "You must give me something I can take hold of. You are like the captain of a ship who lays out a chart of the Atlantic and spreads his hand down in the middle of it, and says, 'We are somewhere about here.'"

It is difficult to recall that a man with such a merciless tongue was as famous at the Bar for his appeals to the emotions of the jury as to their prejudices and that in the Tichborne case he won the sobriquet of "the weeping counsel." But on the bench there is no need for disguise, and as a judge Lord Halsbury has been as distinguished by his loyalty to the law as in politics he has been distinguished by his loyalty to party. His judgment in the Dover case, for example, was one of the most memorable triumphs for the temperance party in their claim as to the public control of the liquor trade. It is true that as a politician he promptly helped his Government to blot out the effect of that judgment by giving the brewers a freehold in their licences; but the point here is that as a judge he has a legal conscience of unflinching probity. To him the law, whether it is good or bad, is sacred so long as it is the law. He sees in it the only secure secular bond of society. If that is repudiated, there is no guarantee that can prevail. It is the Ark of the Covenant, and with it his conscience permits him to play no tricks. On the bench his impartiality is as indisputable as the robust sense of his judgments.

As a politician he has no use for such an encumbrance as conscience, and no one in great office ever carried the licence of partisanship farther. During the long period he was on the Woolsack he appointed nearly the whole judiciary, and the character of his appointments brought the Bench down to a level that it had not reached in living memory. Even his own party came to be ashamed of the unblushing jobbery. *Truth* gibbeted him systematically as the Lord High Jobber, and the public suffered incalculable loss and wrong by the notorious incompetence of such judges as Sir William Grantham and Sir John Lawrence, to take only two examples of men who were raised to the Bench simply because of their political connections. Nor did he limit his operations to the High Court. He packed the magistracy of the country with his supporters so carefully that practically the whole administration of justice was in the hands of the Conservative party.

Finally, his affection for his friends was so handsomely shown in the distribution of offices that it was said that when the end of his official career came there was nobody but his footman who was unprovided for. This was an exaggeration, of course; but he *was* generous to those about him. He would enjoy the story Mr. G. W. E. Russell tells of the Irish placemen of long ago who were discussing appointments. "I don't mind confessing," said one, "that, cœteris paribus, I prefer my own relations." "My dear fellow," replied the other, "cœteris paribus be damned." I think I hear Lord Halsbury laughing in joyous agreement. For, as I have said, there is no humbug about the man. He would not job a friend into office and then lay his hand on his heart and talk of his sacred oath, as Lord Westbury did. There is a jolly audacity about him that would scorn a sleek lie.

For himself he has found the union of law and politics

a not unprofitable career. In the last 25 years or so he has received from his country a trifle of £220,000, and with his pension of £5000 a year still running and his health unfailing there is every reason why he should reach a round quarter of a million. As he goes along the streets twirling his cane it is not difficult, indeed, to conceive that he may reappear on the Woolsack. It is not far short of ten years since Mr. Choate, the retiring American Ambassador, referring to him, said:

> "Time, like an ever-rolling stream,
> Bears all its sons away.

But the Lord Chancellor stems the tide of time. Instead of retreating like the rest of us before the advancing waves he is actually working his way up stream." To-day he is pulling up stream as hard as ever.

An indomitable old man, carrying the uncompromising Toryism of his father and the grim pugnacity of his grandfather into the seat of power, giving blows with the heartiness of Friar Tuck, and asking quarter from none, a warm-hearted friend and a bitter political foe, shameless in partisanship, but loyal to his creed and a just judge. Never was that ultimate honesty more clear than when, with every temptation to yield to the hue-and-cry of the Marconi rabble, he blew away the monstrous growth of slander and suspicion and robbed that rabble of its quarry. It was a brilliant inspiration to put the enemy in the seat of justice. It was a tribute to a judicial probity that is never deflected by a partisanship as flagrant and aggressive as any in our political annals.

MR. J. L. GARVIN

"ROMANCE," says Kipling, "brings up the 9.15." I do not know what time the train arrived that brought James Louis Garvin from Newcastle to London some fifteen years ago, but Romance stepped out of it. For Mr. Garvin belongs to the realm of fairy tales. He seems to have wandered out of the *Arabian Nights*, or perhaps he is the Pied Piper of Hamelin come back. The proofs are plentiful. They would leave no doubt in the mind of Sir E. Durning Lawrence and the Baconians. Imprimis, the Piper was, it will be observed, Pied, that is the Piper clad in party-coloured clothes. Then, did he not come magically upon the scene just when the Mayor and the Corporation were at their wits' end? Did he not take control of the whole affair and carry it through like a magician? Did he not pipe so bewitchingly that the children—*i.e.* the Tory party—left their fathers and mothers—*i.e.* their old leaders and the old traditions—and followed him gaily to their doom? Did he not vanish into the mountain? And is it not obvious that he went somewhere from the other side of the mountain? And where so likely as to Newcastle? If you ask, "Why Newcastle?" the answer, as the Baconians will see, clearly is, "Why not?" The more one looks into the facts and their meaning the more convincing do they seem. They explain everything.

You may, of course, prefer the theory of a providential intervention. You may hold that Providence got tired of the Tory party and sent this fascinating Irishman with the wild light in his eye and the frenzied pen in his hand to lure it to destruction. Perhaps so. It is a theory which has its merits. But whatever the explanation, Mr. Garvin may claim that at the end of ten thrilling years he has left Toryism in ruins. Something will emerge from the wreckage, but it will not be Toryism. The old, happy creed that the governance of the world was the divinely-appointed prerogative of a benevolent aristocracy is gone for ever. There is none so poor to do it reverence. And more than any other single person, save Mr. Chamberlain, Mr. Garvin was responsible for banishing it.

It is a great achievement for a man who is still young, who until a few years ago was an unknown journalist in the North of England, and who owes his triumph wholly to his own intrepid spirit and his own torrential pen. He flashed into the field of politics at a time of turmoil and confusion, when the adventurer has his chance. The Tory party was rent with civil war. The leaders were engaged in a duel behind the scenes. One retired, a broken and defeated man; the other was finally driven out by his own followers. Through all this turbulent time the voice of Mr. Garvin was heard above the storm. By sheer energy of mind he became the dictator of the leaderless host. He swept them on from disaster to disaster, and from every disaster he emerged more confident, more assured of victory than before. Liberalism never had such an asset.

It was the triumph of sheer rhetoric, of a sustained frenzy of spirit, ungoverned by any permanent purpose or any considered philosophy. In all the tumultuous output of his feverish pen it is impossible to discover any underlying principle or theory of government. There is no nucleus to this wonderful comet. He is a visionary; but his visions have no coherence. They are as erratic as the lightning, and as intense. He sees life with the wild unreality of Doré. Every day is the day of destruction, every day the crisis of our fate is upon us; every day he rises out of the nightmare of his mind, his eye aflame, his arm outstretched, his placards screaming doom. "He used," said Sir John Simon when to the editorship of the *Observer* Mr. Garvin added the editorship of the *Pall Mall Gazette,* "he used to give us an electric shock once a week, now he gives us an epileptic fit once a day."

In all this he is absolutely sincere. There are those who question his honesty, and point to his amazing record in proof of their opinion. Certainly no man ever touched such extremes with such bewildering velocity. His achievement in the autumn of 1910 has never been equalled and can never be surpassed. The conference on the Parliament Bill was still sitting. It was known that its fate depended largely upon an agreement on Home Rule. Mr. Garvin flung all the resources of his mind into an attempt to stampede his party into conceding Irish freedom. The subject touched perhaps the most enduring enthusiasm of his unstable mind, and discovered in him a grave eloquence far removed from his normal note. He wrote a memorable article in the *Fortnightly Review* of November of 1910 in which he pleaded for Home Rule on four positive grounds—the changed temper in Ireland, where "a wonderful constructive revolution" has brought into being "a propertied majority naturally Conservative in every fibre"; the necessity for a *rapprochement* with America, which was impossible "while the Irish question remains on its present footing"; the demands of our Colonies, where the chief statesmen were "full either of Irish sympathies or of Irish blood or of both," and where our treatment of the Irish question seemed to be "madness"; the needs of England, which with the grant of self-government to Ireland would recover its own self-government. As to the objections, he dismissed the fear of invasion as "fantastic," and declared that Ulster would "hold the balance in any future Irish Assembly." And he concluded with an expression of absolute confidence in Mr. Redmond.

Mr. J. L. Garvin

The ink was not dry on this article when the Conference broke down, and the country was faced with a General Election. A wild delirium descended upon Mr. Garvin. Through half a dozen papers he called upon England to "spew out of its mouth the Dollar Dictator." One example will serve:

> "What is the dominating fact? It is this—that Mr. Redmond landed at Queenstown last night with two hundred thousand dollars in his pocket. . . . He comes . . . he comes . . . he comes . . . with the money of Patrick Ford he comes . . . he lands . . . he arrives . . . above all, he returns . . . in a word, he comes once more . . . he reappears."

Mr. Garvin's career is full of such startling episodes, and yet I repeat that his sincerity is above suspicion. He is always sincere: the trouble is that you never know what he will be sincere about. The typical fanatic is anchored to one idea. Mr. Garvin is a fanatic on the wing. He may be caught in this vortex to-day and in that to-morrow. He is a reed through which everything blows into passion—an improviser at the mercy of his theme.

The governing influence of his mind is personality. Principles are cold abstractions. Their aerial music does not stir his blood. He must have the visible emblems of battle—the shout of command, the beat of the drum, the thunder of hoofs. Give him a hero and he will follow him through fire and flood without asking why or whither. His career is the record of two overwhelming personal passions. He began under the hypnotism of Parnell. His impulsive, generous nature made him, of course, a Home Ruler; but it was the magnetism of Parnell, that cold, silent man, who moulded the hot passions of others to his own purposes, that dominated his youthful enthusiasm. He was even then a prodigy of omniscience. He had been discovered by Joseph Cowen in some modest calling, and at eighteen was writing with a Jovian authority on world-politics.

But his passion was Ireland and Parnell, and when the crash came it was he who with others founded the "Independent National League," which backed Parnell against his late colleagues. And up and down Tyneside the young disciple carried the torch of his devotion.

"I can recall the picture of those days with ease," says Mr. Peter Fanning, of Jarrow-on-Tyne—"the back room of a public-house, a score of Irish working men sitting around, Mr. James Louis Garvin holding forth eloquently, passionately, on the glorious days of Cucullian, or Finn and his Fenians, or pouring out his soul whilst he held up for our example the great deeds and sufferings of Lord Edward, Wolfe Tone, and Emmet, or perhaps reciting for our benefit that splendid composition, 'Who fears to speak of '98?'" When his hero paid his last visit to the North of England it was he who went ahead through the Press with drum and trumpet, and perhaps the greatest achievement of his journalistic career was his tribute to Parnell at the end. He was present at the funeral in Dublin, and wrote practically the whole of the issue of *United Ireland* following that event.

The second great passion of his life was when he came under the influence of Mr. Chamberlain, and was caught in the maelstrom of Tariff "Reform." It was not that he cared for Tariff "Reform," but that the powerful personality of its advocate appealed to his instinct for hero-worship. And once captured, his devotion knows no bounds of reason and recognises no considerations of the past. His attacks on the Irish do not mean that he has changed since the days when he used to appear on the platform with Mr. Egan and Mr. Redmond, when he championed the cause of O'Donovan Rossa, and engineered campaigns for the release of the dynamiters, and when he said:

"The business of Irishmen is simply to watch for the whites of their enemies' eyes and blaze away. The first duty of an

Irishman is to fight. The second duty is to fight. And his third duty is still to fight."

They mean simply that he cannot worship at two shrines at once. As his article in the *Fortnightly* showed, he is as sound a Home Ruler as ever, knows all the arguments for it, can meet all the shallow reasons and prejudices against it. But when he bowed the knee at the Birmingham shrine he had to turn his back on his past and raze out the memory of Parnell. He could not bask in the sunshine of Mr. Chamberlain's smile without mumbling the Chamberlain shibboleth. Hence these fierce collisions between his views. Hence we have him in one phase telling Home Rulers to " blaze away at the whites of their enemies' eyes "; in another, declaring that " hell will be let loose in chaos and bloodshed " unless Ulster has its way.

Since the disappearance of Mr. Chamberlain he has wandered forlorn in quest of a hero. Oh, for a falconer's voice to lure him to the wrist! Vainly he sought to make a hero of Mr. Balfour: no sceptic can be a hero to Valiant Heart. He must have someone who has a faith to give him—someone who will lead him with songs and shouts to the carnage of the battle-field—not a philosopher who stands for ever balancing Yea and Nay. I see him eyeing Mr. Lloyd George with a certain hunger of worship in him. Ah, if only he could circle round that brilliant flame and scorch his wings in that radiant incandescence! Instead, there is Mr. Bonar Law and Mr. Austen Chamberlain, and—ah, there is Sir Edward Carson. May he not be the hero? He talks of blood and barricades, reviews his rebel hosts, and takes his royal salutes. He will " blaze at the whites of his enemies' eyes," and though the enemies are Mr. Garvin's old friends that cannot be helped. It is the " blazing " that is the thing. Oh, for a hero who will " blaze."

It will be seen that, in spite of his sensational success, Mr. Garvin cannot be ranked with the great names of the journalist's craft—thinkers like Thomas Paine, philosophers like Lord Morley, robust warriors like William Cobbett. He fails because he is all "sound and fury, signifying nothing"; heat without light; volition without direction; passion without purpose. He flashes from nowhere to nowhere—a trail of fire that bewilders the night. His words boil over in a flood; but they turn no wheels and grind no corn. Emotion is a splendid animal in the shafts; it is a poor tool on the driving seat. You want a horse with fire, but a coachman with a cool head. Mr. Garvin is an emotion on two legs—generous, lovable, fascinating, but dangerous. Keep him to literature and who so delightful? "Do you know your Francis Thompson well?" he asks, dwelling on that "well" with a note of Celtic awe that suggests translunar things. It is the true note of the man—the man of fine visions and generous impulses, but the man also who is hypnotised by his own visions—a Pied Piper piping through a city of dreams.

LORD MILNER

WHEN Lord Milner advised the Lords to throw out the Budget and "damn the consequences," he gave the world a character study of himself in a phrase. It was a phrase that threw a baleful light on the great tragedy with which history will associate his name. It was a phrase that explained the most dramatic failure of our time.

On the memorable night when men of all parties gathered at the banquet to him to celebrate his departure for South Africa, no career in the land seemed so full of splendid promise. Confidence in his genius had become an article of faith among those who were most competent to judge. His brilliant career at Balliol had marked him out for great things, and his subsequent work on the *Pall Mall*, in Egypt, and as head of the Board of Inland Revenue had confirmed the promise. He had been described as "the finest flower of human culture which the University of Oxford has produced in our time." Lord Rosebery had acclaimed his "unrivalled union of fascination and intellect." He commanded in an extraordinary degree the faith and loyalty of his friends—of none more than Mr. Asquith, who was in the chair that night—and he had no enemies. His personal honour was as conspicuous as his intellectual gifts, and his political purposes were grave and disinterested. He had belonged to the band of young enthusiasts who had gathered round Canon Barnett at Toynbee Hall and had been indoctrinated with the social gospel of that great man. His selection by Mr. Chamberlain for the most difficult and delicate task of statesmanship that the time had to offer was almost universally approved. Here, if anywhere, was the man who could raze out the memory of the Jameson Raid and pour oil on the troubled waters of South Africa. There were, it is true, a few who read the man more profoundly—among them Sir William Harcourt. "You are going out with a war in your pocket," he said to Sir Alfred.

To-day he is the most solitary and negligible figure in our public life—a man whose name is synonymous with failure, with discredited prophecy, with harsh and provocative methods and reactionary views. South Africa, it has been said, is the grave of reputations. The tomb of Lord Milner's reputation towers above all the rest.

There have been other conspicuous failures in our time, but none so overwhelming, so final as his. The fall of Lord Rosebery was like the fall of a sky-rocket, brilliant, many-coloured, and harmless. The fall of Lord Milner was like the fall of Lucifer, ending in "hideous ruin and combustion." Both failed; but they failed for widely different reasons, the one from his weakness, the other from his strength—Lord Rosebery because he had the temperament of the artist, perverse, uncertain, the sport of every wind that blew; Lord Milner because he had the spirit of a Torquemada, ruthless, unbending, fanatical. Lord Rosebery's vessel came to grief through lack of direction. He lost his compass, came to doubt the stars, and left the helm at the mercy of his moods and emotions. Lord Milner's vessel came to grief through pride of will and scorn of consequences. He saw breakers ahead, but he would crash through them; rocks, but he would grind them to powder. Warnings passed by him unheeded, opposition gave new passion and intensity to his purpose. Did General Butler say that not 10,000, but 100,000 men would be needed to conquer the Boers? Did he plead that what South Africa wanted was "rest and not a surgical operation"? Did he throw obstacles in the way of a repetition of the Jameson Raid? Then Butler must be sent home dishonoured. Did Mr. Chamberlain falter in his support of this amazing messenger of peace? Then he must be brought to heel by a public challenge, and there came that astonishing "Helots" despatch couched in the terms of a Yellow journalist. He would have peace, but it should be "peace druv in with bagnets." Did the Boer leaders when he first met them in conference assure him of their loyalty in pressing their claims? Then he would let them know that merely to talk of "loyalty" was an intolerable insolence. What had they to do with loyalty or disloyalty? Their business was to yield to their masters like the rabble they were. What were these little Republics doing, cumbering the earth, impeding the path of Empire? An olive branch for this handful of ignorant farmers with their incredible old chieftain? Nay, a sword and a consuming fire. He could not believe that there was any reality in a foe so primitive, so superficially inefficient, so wanting in all the external splendours of civilisation.

It is here that we touch the true source of his failure. If intellect alone could achieve success in the governance of men, Lord Milner would be among the greatest of statesmen. But intellect alone never made a successful ruler. It can deal with abstractions and the problems of things; but to deal with the problems of humanity it must be fused with sympathy and charged with imaginative insight. It must understand the springs of human action, the weaknesses and the passions of men, their inexplicable enthusiasms and those fierce heroisms that make them "ready to do battle for an egg or die for an idea." And of these qualities of sympathy and imagination Lord Milner is more completely destitute than any public man of his time. He is merely an intellectual machine, and he is too honest to play the demagogue or assume virtues that his mind holds in contempt. Mr.

Chamberlain had a will hardly less despotic than Lord Milner's, and was almost equally deficient in sympathy and imagination. But he did not scorn men. All his calculations were based on their emotions and impulses. He appealed to their lower instincts, humoured their elementary passions, but he did not treat them as though they were a herd to be driven. He treated them as though they were a mob to be led. He infuriated them with a red rag and used the passion he generated to accomplish his purposes. But Lord Milner has always left humanity out of his calculations. The problems of politics are to him wholly material problems, never moral or emotional or spiritual problems, and they are to be solved by material forces. His drama is not a drama of men and women; it is a drama of puppets dancing to the will of a master mind.

This profound mistake—the mistake at the root of all Imperialism—vitiates his calculations on every critical issue. There has probably never been a man of the same unquestioned distinction who has been so unfailingly wrong in his estimate of events. It will always be an open question whether he wanted the war or whether he simply blundered into it. The evidence is overwhelmingly in favour of the former view. It is the view held by the Boers. "We have buried the past," said the man at whose house at Bloemfontein the momentous interview took place, in speaking to me some years ago, "but there is one man we can never forgive. Chamberlain believed he was engaged in a game of bluff; but Milner *knew* we should fight. More, he knew *how* we should fight. He had stayed with us and seen how every boy could ride and shoot. And he misled you. . . . No, I do not want to see Milner." He misled us because, with all his knowledge, his calculations ignored the great human factor in the situation—the passion for liberty that had made this peasant people trek into the wilderness generations before and that was to make them wage a war worthy of their forefathers who broke the power of Spain. "They will go home when it rains," he said. Ten thousand men, a million or two of money, and we should be in Pretoria in three months. And so when President Steyn reached the door after the fateful interview and turned and said, "You understand—if this is your decision it means war," Sir Alfred Milner, standing, hands behind his back, in front of the fire, answered grimly, "War let it be." How his calculations were falsified we know.

It has been so on every great issue. Peace, the settlement on the land, Chinese labour, the concession of self-government—on these as on all other questions he was wrong because he "built his trust on reeking tube and iron shard," and left out of his calculations the invincible soul of man. He resisted peace because he believed that the policy of farm-burnings and concentration camps would break the heart of the foe and bring them to unconditional surrender. He planted "loyal" settlers on the soil as a futile substitute for the only garrison that can endure, the garrison of a free and independent people. He forced Chinese labour on the Transvaal in the teeth of the opposition of the English miners, because his only touchstone of Imperial greatness is material gain. He imposed on the Transvaal an extravagant Civil Service in pursuance of his dreams of a mechanical "efficiency." He attempted to destroy the Constitution of Cape Colony, because he came to distrust democracy in all its expressions. He fought the concession of self-government to the conquered Colonies with a bitterness born of a failure that had taught him nothing. And, returned to England, with all the miserable tale of disaster behind him, he becomes the cold, acid champion of every assault on popular liberty—the rejection of the Budget, the resistance of the Lords to the last ditch, Protection, Conscription.

The policy that he brought to South Africa with sword and fire is gone like the fabric of a nightmare. Not one shred of it remains. It vanished before one brave act of a great man. I have heard from one who was present the story of that scene in the Cabinet when Campbell-Bannerman carried his bold policy of granting constitutional government to the conquered States. "There had been many objections, hesitations, difficulties postulated. The old man rose, and in such a speech as I do not expect to hear again, a speech of only ten minutes' duration, he swept all before him by a fervour and nobility that made all objections seem mean and vain. It was the soul of freedom that spoke. At the end there was more than one moist eye around that table. . . . And remember! There were no reporters present." It is by that splendid act of courage and wisdom that C.-B. will live. It is by that great act and its wonderful fruit that we may judge of Liberalism as the vital influence in the affairs of men, just as it is by the record of Lord Milner that we may judge of Imperialism as the spirit of death in the affairs of men.

And the tragedy of his career is deepened by the purity of his motives. It says much for the loftiness of his personal character that in all that time, when he was the instrument of the meanest, most obvious financial conspiracy, his own honour was never doubted. We all knew, we all know, that however disastrous his policy, it is pursued for no mean end. Again like Torquemada, he is free from personal ambitions and self-interest. But he distrusts freedom as Torquemada distrusted it, or as Pobiedonostseff distrusted it, and he would suppress it with the same fanatical ruthlessness—not in the interests of Pope or Tsar, but in the interest of a vain Imperialism. If we would understand what Imperialism really is, it is to his collection of speeches, *The Nation and the Empire,* that we must turn. The Dominions oversea are not free communities: they are the absolute property of the people of these islands, to be administered as the sovereign people choose. He would have no recognition in the Empire of any language but the English language, of any law but the English law, of any currency but the English currency. Quebec, with its French-speaking population, is an offence to him; the idea that "Afrikanders" of Dutch or Huguenot descent should have equal voting powers with "Britishers" in South Africa fills him with loathing. It is not that he loves the English people, for there is no trace of popular fibre in him. He once, in 1885, stood as Liberal candidate for the Harrow division, and I have been told by one who helped him and still admires his intellect that he never once got in touch with his audience, and the longer the campaign went on the more he was estranged from them. All races must be subject to the sway of these islands; but it is not the English democracy that is to exercise the sway. Government belongs to the Crown and the Ministers responsible to the Crown, helped by a consultative council of the Premiers of the self-governing Dominions. Foreign affairs, Imperial affairs, everything that matters should be taken from the House of Commons. "The people! The people! What have the people to do with the laws except obey them?" To read his speeches is like stepping out of the reign of George V. into the reign of George III.

But though I have spoken of Torquemada and Pobiedonostseff, it is neither to Spain nor to Russia that we have to go for his true political origin. The fundamental fact about Lord Milner is that he is a German—born in Germany, the son of a German professor by an English mother, cradled in Germany, educated in German schools and German ideas and, according to the late Mr. Stead—though this I think must be inaccurate—still a German subject at the time he was High Commissioner in South Africa. When this fact is fully realised, his entire divorce from the English spirit is readily understood. He stands for German, or rather Prussian ideas in English politics. In him we see the Bismarckian policy as well as the Bismarckian spirit in being. It is the policy of a harsh, aggressive paternalism—a paternalism conceived, not as the instrument of freedom, but as its deliberate foe. State Socialism, as Bismarck designed it, was intended to provide material for an efficient army—efficient not only for defending the Fatherland against perils from without, but for resisting subversive movements within. It is the same dual idea which possesses our own Conscriptionists. They do not mention the foe within; but he is in their minds much more than the foe without. A drilled and disciplined proletariat is their hope against an insurgent democracy.

It is a vain hope. If Lord Milner's career proves anything it proves conclusively that Bismarckism cannot be successfully engrafted upon the tree of English liberty. The Germans are a patient race. They are a governable race. It was remarked long ago how amiably by comparison with the Russians they took the invasions of Napoleon. They fought him and when he beat them they made the best of it and received him with honours in the adjacent city. The Russians burned their cities before him and devastated their land. The Germans have worn the harness that Bismarck made for them with surprising docility. They work no revolutions, flame up into no blaze of anger; but they march regimented to the polls—five million Socialists, solemn, formal, dressed in their best black coats, undemonstrative, waiting for the inevitable fall of Kaiserism.

In attempting to transplant Bismarckism to British soil Lord Milner makes a mistake both of time and place. The creed is, one may hope, getting outworn even in Germany. In free England it never could and never will take root. The prison plant will not live in British air. Lord Milner makes the mistake because he is not an Englishman, and does not understand what English freedom is. Intellectual liberty he understands and approves; but popular liberty in any shape is unintelligible to a mind rooted in scorn of the people. He has had many lessons, but he has that intellectual pride which is the most unteachable of material.

And so he stands, a forlorn, solitary figure in our midst, with no thinkable future; separated from that memorable feast by twenty thousand British graves that are the only memorial of his statesmanship. For the Chinese have gone, South Africa is free and at peace, and though Kruger is deposed and dead, Botha reigns in his stead as he would have reigned had there been no war. Was ever so much misery wrought to achieve so little?

MR. JAMES BRYCE

If one were asked to name the greatest living Englishman—in the sense of the variety of his gifts and of his practical genius—I think it would be necessary to admit, regretfully, that he was a Scotsman born in Ireland. Barthélemy St. Hilaire used to say that the English were the finest race in the world, but that the Scotsman was an Englishman and a half. It is a chastening reflection which the facts go far to justify, for wherever we look, in politics, business, journalism, even in the Anglican Church, the Scotsman is in the seat of the mighty. The wall of Hadrian, grass-grown and ruined, no longer holds him back, and in Fleet Street, hard by the place where long ago the head of William Wallace dried in the sun as a warning to his countrymen, the air is thick with the accent of the conquering Scot.

Explain it how we may—by the strength born of the age-long struggle with a niggard soil, by the stern discipline of a sombre faith, by the initiative of John Knox that started Scotland on the path of popular education centuries before its neighbour—the fact is flagrant and indisputable. The Scot is in possession by virtue of a superior command of himself and of circumstance. He has cultivated learning on a little oatmeal and comes armed to the struggle with a practical wisdom, a fine balance of mental and physical qualities, that commands success. Thrift, the child of hard circumstance, lies at the base of his character. When Raeburn as a youth went to dine with Clerk (afterwards Lord Eldin) the landlady set two dishes containing three herrings and three potatoes before them. "Is this a'?" asked Clerk. "Ay, it's a'." "'A'!' Didna I tell ye, woman, that a gentleman was to dine with me and that ye were to get sax herrin' and sax potatoes?"

In that Spartan story there is much of the history of Scotland. Out of its poverty have sprung its riches. There is no more striking contrast between England and Scotland than the origin of the prophets of the two lands. Our peasantry has produced no authentic voice: Scotland's great voices all come direct from the soil. The explanation is simple. The English peasantry has not yet emerged from intellectual serfdom; the Scotch peasantry has enjoyed centuries of intellectual freedom. It might be poor in gear; but in the world of the spirit it had "riches fineless."

There is nothing remarkable, therefore, in the fact that the greatest living Englishman is a Scotsman, or rather an Ulster Scotsman, born—though his father was a distinguished mathematician at Glasgow—of a peasant stock. No doubt, the distinction claimed for James Bryce will be challenged. It is challengeable on many grounds and yet I think it is just. To-day English life is singularly deficient in the quality of indisputable greatness. We have no figures cast in the heroic mould—no Gladstone or Carlyle, no Browning or Ruskin. We seem to have lost temporarily the spark of the divine, and for our first man we must take one less than heroic—one who by an exceptional union of qualities touches a certain ideal of perfection which is a sort of greatness.

Now I know no one who fulfils this ideal so completely as the British ambassador to America. "Bryce," said Sir Henry Campbell-Bannerman on one occasion, "is the most accomplished man in the House of Commons. He has been everywhere, he has read almost everything, and he knows everybody." There is no man living of whom this can be said with less feeling of exaggeration. "Yes, sir," said Johnson, "if a man were to go by chance at the same time with Burke under a shed to shun a shower he would say: 'This is a remarkable man.' If Burke should go into a stable to see his horse dressed the ostler would say: 'We have had an extraordinary man here.' "

No intelligent ostler would fail to make the same remark about Mr. Bryce. To sit beside him at dinner is to pass out spiritually into the universe with the most accomplished of guides. The great spaces of history open out before you as familiar as your own back garden. You traverse the continents with the easy assurance of a citizen of the world, known everywhere and welcome wherever you are known. You pass from ancient Rome to modern America and take Iceland and its literature and laws on the way. The flora of Arran, on which he wrote a book when he was twenty, and the unknown plants of South Africa that he brought home to Kew, become as fascinating as the tribal habits of native races. You trip gaily from the question of fleas in a Spanish hotel to the reason why the supervisors of Pike County, Missouri, pass such and such ordinances concerning the keeping of dogs, or to the relation of the Australian States to the Federal Government. Across the field of vision flit the shadows of the past—warriors, statesmen, sages—and the famous figures of the present. You hail them all confidently, for your guide knows all about them and is of their company. Perhaps you mention, let us say, the "Civis Romanus sum" speech of Palmerston and instantly the whole story of Don Pacifico's bedstead is unfolded with all its bearings on European politics. Happiest of all if you chance to love the rocks, for here is one whose passion for mountaineering has carried him alone to the summits of Ararat, and who knows the austere joys of those who

> "Leave their rags on Pavey Ark,
> Their cards on Pillar grim."

It is done with a delightful and unaffected freshness. No scholar ever wore the graces of learning more lightly or revealed them with less sense of vanity or even of conscious possession. He takes you round the splendours of his mental library without ever reminding you that they are his, or apparently even remembering that they are his. His joy is in the contents, not in the possession. He has taken the world for his province, but he has taken it only to make you a freeman of it. Mr. Alfred Lyttelton once told me that in his opinion Lord Morley was the most attractive talker of our time, and that if he were to be cast away on a desert island with only one companion he would be the companion of his choice. He placed him above Mr. Balfour because, while, in his own excellent phrase, Mr. Balfour would supply the butter of conversation, Lord Morley would supply the bread as well as the butter. There is, it is true, a fragrance about Lord Morley's conversation—a tenderness, a light and shade, a certain gentle pathos of memory—that is unique. It is more sensitive and personal than Mr. Bryce's, more touched with emotion; but it lacks its encyclopædic variety, its detachment, its steady optimism. On the whole the companion of my choice on the desert island would be Mr. Bryce, for with him he would bring the story of the ages and the constant cheerfulness of a mind filled with a radiance of its own. With such a companion the days would pass as unwearyingly as the nights with Scheherazade, and when the sail of the deliverer appeared above the horizon it would be greeted almost like an intrusion upon an unfinished and delightful talk.

The wonder of it all is its unfailing vitality. This quality is due to the fact that Mr. Bryce is that rare combination, a profound scholar who is primarily a man of affairs. It is the common failing of the scholar to make his scholarship his world, and to pass out of the stream of vital human interest into a backwater that he takes for the ocean. There is nothing of the "Scarabee" about Mr. Bryce. History to him is a lamp by which he sees the panorama of to-day and illuminates its meaning. His real interest is not in the dead past but in the living present, in the great humane movement of events towards that liberty of speech and action and that reign of international peace which, as he told the Phi Beta Kappa Society at Harvard, is the true measure of the world's progress. It was this enthusiasm for humanity that first brought him into politics at the time of the Bulgarian atrocities, that later plunged him into the struggle for Irish freedom—a subject in which he had a personal as well as a general interest, for his mother was an Irishwoman—and that has made his residence at Washington memorable not merely by bringing the British and American peoples together but, in the language of the Canadian correspondent of the *Times*, by the extraordinary extent to which, through his activities, "old jealousies and old hostilities between Ottawa and Washington have been overcome."

He represents more than any conspicuous figure to-day, except Lord Morley, that noble and temporarily obscured tradition associated with such great names as those of Fox, Gladstone, Mazzini, and Lincoln—that allegiance to humanity, without regard to colour, creed, or country, which is not the negation of patriotism but its finest flower and fulfilment.

His appointment as ambassador was one of the supreme services which that great and wise man, Campbell-Bannerman, performed as Prime Minister. By that appointment he broke down an evil tradition. The most vital interest of this country is its foreign relationships. Upon these relationships depend not merely our prestige but ultimately all our internal concerns. Yet that interest, by a deplorable tradition, is controlled by a narrow caste wholly divorced from the general current of the nation. Ambassadors are drawn from the diplomatic service. No one can enter that service except by nomination and the possession of a private allowance of at least £400 a year, a condition which would have kept out Mr. Asquith, the Lord Chancellor, the Attorney-General, both Archbishops—indeed, practically every distinguished man of the time. The father who can allow his son £400 a year as pocket-money has an income of not less than £4000 or £5000 a year. He belongs, therefore, to a small class, influenced usually by aristocratic and military interests, Jingo in sympathies and hostile to the democratic movement both at home and abroad. Add the fact that the power of nomination is exercised to exclude any political or social "undesirable" whom the money bar does not keep out, and we see that in the last analysis the destiny of the country rests upon ambassadors drawn from a tiny close corporation of wealth and influence—from men whose distinction is that their fathers have at least £5000 a year and are welcome in the diplomatic set. The system is a grotesque impertinence. Ambassadors should represent peoples, not castes, least of all a moneyed and a professional caste. "The sure way to make a foolish ambassador," said Coleridge, "is to bring him up to it. What can an Englishman abroad really want but an honest and bold heart, a love for his country and the Ten Commandments? Your art diplomatic is stuff—no truly great man would negotiate upon such shallow principles."

By appointing Mr. Bryce to Washington, Sir Henry Campbell-Bannerman made a memorable breach in the pernicious system—a breach especially appreciated by America, whose diplomacy is candid and whose ambassadors are always distinguished citizens who speak the accents of democracy.

But Mr. Bryce's appointment was welcome to America for other reasons. He is a prophet who is more honoured abroad even than at home. Germany knew him nearly fifty years ago by his Arnold Prize essay, *The Holy Roman Empire*, whose erudition and maturity of thought announced a new intellectual force of capital importance. That work indirectly did much to stimulate the movement towards German unity, and it laid the foundation of Mr. Bryce's European reputation. But it is in the United States that he is best known and most warmly appreciated. For a quarter of a century his name has been a household word there as the name of the author of the monumental work on *The American Commonwealth* and of the most generous and discriminating critic of American institutions. His presence at Washington changed the atmosphere of Anglo-American relations into something warmer, more personal, more intimate than had ever existed before. Much of this was due of course to his known sympathy with America. Something was also due to his enthusiasm for Home Rule, which he advocated long before Gladstone took it up—advocated with such conviction as led him to oppose his leader on the coercion policy of 1882. And it must be remembered that the Irish question largely governs Anglo-American relations—it destroyed the great arbitration treaty of 1912—and that there is truth as well as wit in Mr. Dooley's rendering of the President's speech: "Our relations with Gr-reat Britain are most frindly, but not so frindly that anny Irishman need think they are too frindly."

But primarily the American enthusiasm for Mr. Bryce is a tribute to his own vital personality. He carries far into the 'seventies the vivacious mind as well as the bright eye and the high hopes of youth, a love for humanity that knows no boundary of race or creed—he was the first ambassador to address a gathering of negroes—and a radiant sanity of outlook that illuminates the whole field of human activity and finds no place for the hates and fears that divide men and embitter nations. He sees life sanely, and sees it whole, and that sovereign vision gives him a steady faith in the destiny of men. "The barque that carries man and his fortunes," he said in a memorable speech, "traverses an ocean where the winds are variable and the current unknown. He can do little to direct its course, and the mists that shroud the horizon hang as thick and low as they did when the voyage began." But the mystery that surrounds the adventure of life does not depress him, or weaken his faith in the forces that drive humanity to its goal beyond the mists. He has the joy of the journey, the unquenchable spirit of old Ulysses—the grey spirit yearning with desire to seek a newer world:

> "For my purpose holds
> To sail beyond the sunset and the baths
> Of all the western stars, until I die."

PRESIDENT WOODROW WILSON

It was the eve of the Lynde debate, and all Princeton University was alive with anticipation. Not that there was any serious doubt as to who would win the coveted prize, for young Woodrow Wilson had established his reputation as the first debater of the University, and his victory was assured. But the event was new, and the interest in it had something of the attraction of the ring or of a baseball match. Each of the two halls furnished representatives for the competition, the choice being determined by a preliminary debate. The subject of this preliminary debate in Whig Hall was "Free Trade *v.* Protection," and the competitors were given their parts by lot. The hat went round, and Wilson took out a slip. It bore the word "Protection." He tore up the paper and declined to debate. He was a keen Free Trader, and not even as a mere dialectical exercise would he consent to advance arguments in which he did not believe. Robert Bridges therefore became Whig Hall's representative, and in the debate he was beaten by Halsey, the Clio's representative, who attributed his victory to the fact that the man who would have vanquished him was too scrupulous to argue a cause against his own convictions.

The incident is typical of the man whose dramatic emergence from a learned obscurity to the most powerful position in the world of affairs, is not merely an event, but a portent. Dr. Wilson's earliest memory is of two men meeting on that great day fifty-three years ago on which Abraham Lincoln was elected President, and hearing one say to the other, "This means war." Since that day there has been no Presidential election so

Woodrow Wilson

charged with significance as that which made Woodrow Wilson the head of the great Republic. It means that America is "finding itself"—that it is emerging from the squalor into which its politics have fallen. There is hope for a people when it can distinguish true metal from false. And Dr. Wilson is the first great coin struck in the mint of American politics for half a century.

It is one of the ironies of nature—against which he humorously protests—that he should in feature so closely resemble Joseph Chamberlain. Whether in full face or in profile, the suggestion is irresistible. There is the same low broad brow, the same deep fold of the upper eyelid that gives so penetrating an effect to the glance, the same challenging nose—that type of nose on which, as Hazlitt said, the younger Pitt "suspended the House of Commons"—the same full lips of the rhetorician. Only about the mouth is there a difference. Mr. Chamberlain's mouth is relentless. It gives no relief to the combative character of the face. But around Dr. Wilson's mouth there play the lines of gaiety and laughter—the insignia of one who loves a little nonsense now and then, delights in limericks and droll stories, is fond of play and a good song. "Even a reformer," he says, "need not be a fool." Even a professor need not be a dull dog. And the world is never dull when President Wilson bursts into it. For one thing there is sure to be a glee club, for he loves singing as much as debating.

But in spite of many marked differences of temperament and outlook, that likeness to Mr. Chamberlain represents one fundamental affinity. The keynote of both is a certain hard masterfulness. There are many ways of being masterful. Gladstone was masterful with a sort of godlike authority. To oppose him was to break the tables of the law. He was clothed with the thunders of Sinai; the very heavens seemed aflame with sympathetic lightnings. You felt yourself a miserable worm lifting your head against high heaven. Mr. Lloyd George is the most masterful man in English politics to-day; but his masterfulness exhibits itself in an astonishing suppleness. He is what Cobbold used to be on the football field. He gets the ball at his toe, and threads his way amid the crowd of opponents, darting, dashing, turning, twisting, but never losing his mastery of the ball or his vision of the goal—a miracle of coolness and agility. President Wilson's masterfulness is like that of Mr. Chamberlain — hard, combative, direct; no compromise, no concealment, no finesse, but smashing drives straight from the shoulder.

Take that case which first revealed to America that a man was in its midst. He had just emerged defeated from his memorable struggle to convert Princeton University from "the best country club" in the United States into a great instrument of scholarship and democracy. He was defeated by the millionaires. What? Make a gentleman chum with a mucker? Break down the club system which divided the University into gentlemen and rankers? Degrade the old nobility of pork by association with penniless brains? Never, *Never*, NEVER! The millionaires charged in the sacred name of dollars—charged and won. "The country is looking to us as men who prefer ideas to money," said Dr. Wilson, with bitter irony. "After all, we are mistaken: we prefer money to ideas." It was a glorious defeat: its fruit is that to-day, five years later, the victim of the millionaires is President of the United States. They have beaten him in a skirmish, only to find that they have made him their ruler with the legions of American democracy at his back. Life has great as well as little ironies, and the revenges of time are stranger than dreams.

But to return to the episode. The conflict had made him famous in the State, and now just when his career at Princeton seemed ended in failure he received an invitation to become the Democratic candidate for the Governorship of New Jersey. Dr. Wilson was puzzled. Ex-Senator Smith was the boss of the Democratic machine and the synonym of corrupt politics, and against him and all his works Dr. Wilson had waged unceasing war. What did this mean? Was ex-Senator Smith hoping to get back to the United States under cover of Wilson's high reputation? He would see. Yes, he said, he would stand on one condition—that Smith did not. "Were he to do so while I was Governor," he said, "I should have to oppose him. He represents everything repugnant to my convictions." Oh, certainly not—nothing was further from the mind of the bosses. Moreover, Smith was too unwell to be a candidate. Dr. Wilson stood and captured the Governorship, which had been held for years by the Republicans. And on the same day James E. Martine was elected in the "primary" as Senator. The way was clear: enter to the Governor, ex-Senator Smith, a gentleman of fine manners and great cunning. The simple professor would, he felt, be clay in his hands. He spoke discreetly of his past and of the improvement in his health. He thought he was well enough to seek re-election to the Senate. Wilson was stiff. The primary had elected Martine, and there was nothing for the Legislature to do but ratify that election. "The primary was a joke," said Smith. "It was very far from a joke," said the Governor-elect. "But assume that it was. Then the way to save it from being a joke hereafter is to take it seriously now. It is going to be taken seriously, and there will be no more jokes. Unless I hear from you by the last mail delivery on Thursday that you abandon this intention I shall announce my opposition to you on Friday morning."

The letter did not come; instead an appeal for delay. No delay: the denunciation appeared on Friday, and Wilson, not waiting for the meeting of the Legislature, went direct to the people, and in a series of great meetings called on them to see that their representatives carried out the will of the people declared at the primary. It was the first great challenge to the machine of the bosses. The legislators were paralysed between the gay defiance of this political novice and the dread of the machine. "Do not allow yourselves to be dismayed," said the Governor. "You see where the machine is entrenched, and it looks like a real fortress. It looks as if real men were inside, as if they had real guns. Go and touch it. It is a house of cards. Those are imitation generals. Those are playthings that look like guns. Go and put your shoulder against the thing and it collapses." They did put their shoulders against it and it did collapse. The Legislature elected Martine to the Senate by forty voted to Smith's four. And now you know why "Boss" Croker, on being asked during a recent visit to America what he thought of Woodrow Wilson, said, "An ingrate is no good in politics." The machine had adopted the schoolmaster as a tool: it had found him its master.

But the mistake indeed was in supposing that Woodrow Wilson was an amateur politician. He is, on the contrary, the best-equipped politician in America. His whole career, as student, as lawyer, and as professor had been governed by the deliberate purpose of qualifying for public life. And it was an English journalist who gave him his bent. It is true that his origins pointed to affairs. His grandfather Wilson had emigrated from Belfast, his grandfather Woodrow from Scotland. They and their families were all Presbyterians, and those who were not journalists were Presbyterian ministers. Scot—and Irish-Scot—Press and pulpit—is there any more natural or formidable combination for public life? But it was the discovery, in the *Gentleman's Magazine*, when he was an undergraduate at Princeton in the 'seventies, of a series of articles on

English Parliamentary life by the "Member for the Chiltern Hundreds" that determined his career. The writer of those articles that made an American President is still in the gallery of the House of Commons. He is a small man, with white hair that stands on end, as if in perpetual astonishment at an incredible world. In fact, he is Sir Henry Lucy in private life, and "Toby, M.P.," to all the world. Starting from these pictures of Westminster, Woodrow Wilson saturated himself in English political history. He wrote on Burke and Cobden and Bright. He went out into the woods to declaim the great music of Burke. He lost no opportunity of debating, and directed all his college life to the mastery of politics. One of the numerous debating clubs he formed was fashioned on the lines of the British Parliament, for he had come to the conclusion that the swiftly responsive English system was right, and that the divorce of the United States Executive from the people's Chamber was a grave mistake. From all this it followed that when once in the saddle Woodrow Wilson swept through the lists like a tornado. Never had New Jersey or any other State seen such a governor. He passed the Geran Bill and other measures which broke the power of the bosses, restored election to the people, stopped corrupt practices, betting on elections, and treating by candidates, set up a public utilities commission to control all monopolies, provided automatic compensation to injured workmen, reorganised the school system, the penal system, and the control of the food supply.

The bosses were awed; the Legislature stampeded. On the eve of the passing of the Geran Bill, James Nugent, ex-Senator Smith's lieutenant, made one more attempt at parley. He called to talk things over with the terrible Governor, and, finding Wilson adamant, lost his temper. "I know you think you've the votes," he exclaimed: "I don't know how you got them."

"What do you mean?" "I mean it's the talk of the State House that you got them by patronage." "Good afternoon, Mr. Nugent," and the Governor pointed to the door. "You're no gentleman," cried Nugent. "You're no judge," replied Dr. Wilson, still pointing to the door.

And now, having fleshed his sword on the field of New Jersey politics, Woodrow Wilson faces the greatest problem of statesmanship that the world has to offer—the problem of how to rescue government from the tyranny of the machine, which is controlled by the Trusts which in turn express ultimately the will of Rockefeller, J. J. Hill, and a few other gigantic financiers, who are the "invisible power" that controls America. That power is an incident of an outgrown Constitution—one of those Constitutions that, as Woodrow Wilson says, "If you button them over the belly they split up the back." Or rather, it doesn't split: it strangles and suffocates. That Constitution has placed the Legislature at the mercy of the Courts and both at the mercy of wealth—hence high tariffs and the triumphant rule of the millionaire. Can Woodrow Wilson break the giants as he broke ex-Senator Smith? Is he the Perseus of this Western Andromeda? He knows the problem and has stated it with that lucidity which he shares with Mr. Chamberlain:

> "We have been calling our Government a Republic, and we have been living under the delusion that it is a representative Government. That is the theory. But the fact is that we are not living under a representative Government: we are living under a Government of party bosses, who in secret conference determine what we shall have and what we shall not have. The first, the immediate, thing is to restore representative government."

In a word, he starts to break the machine, to secure the direct representation of the people as the first step to reform. It is an heroic declaration of war against the greatest money power on earth.

It is not an idle declaration, for he is no demagogue. Mr. Roosevelt raises clouds of dust; but it is the dust of the circus. It is the dust of a real battlefield that Woodrow Wilson raises. He is not out for dialectical victories or triumphal tours, but for very definite deeds. Mr. Roosevelt clothes the poverty of his thought and the vagueness of his purposes in a tumultuous whirl of words. They sound fierce and formidable, but they are blank cartridge. His messages to Congress were of wondrous length and thundering sound, but they signified nothing. Mr. Wilson does great things with an extreme economy of effort. His speeches have the quality of acts. When the Underwood Tariff Bill, which at one stride brought the United States within sight of Free Trade, was introduced, his speech to Congress occupied eight minutes. It is not that he scorns oratory in its place. It is the instrument through which one touches the general heart to fine issues. But when he comes to business he dismisses rhetoric. He is that rare combination, a thinker who loves action, a scholar and a man of affairs, one who reads Greek and writes shorthand, who combines a luminous idealism with the practicality of a plumber and a sunny smile with a ruthless purpose. His courage mounts to any task; but he has a scrupulous tidiness in small things. When he has finished writing he wipes his pen and puts the cloth back in the drawer. He has great energy; but it is not the boisterous energy of Mr. Roosevelt. It is disciplined. "After all," he says, "life doesn't consist in eternally running to a fire."

He has, what Mr. Chamberlain never had, what Mr. Lloyd George, with all his fine intuitions and democratic sympathies, has not—a considered philosophy of politics. It is a philosophy warmed with a generous humanity and a sincere vision:

"I am accused of being a Radical. If to seek to go to the root is to be a Radical, a Radical I am. After all, everything that flowers in beauty in the air of heaven draws its fairness, its vigour from its roots; nothing living can blossom into fruitage unless through nourishing stalks deep-planted in the common soil. Up from that soil, up from the silent bosom of the earth rise the currents of life and energy. Up from the common soil, up from the great heart of the people, rise joyously to-day streams of hope and determination that are bound to renew the face of the earth in glory. I tell you that the so-called Radicalism of our time is simply the effort of nature to release the generous energies of our people. This great American people is at the bottom just, virtuous, and hopeful; the roots of its being are in the soil of what is lovely, pure, and of good report; and the need of the hour is just that Radicalism that will clear a way for the realisation of the aspirations of a sturdy race."

That is true eloquence and true vision. Mr. Chamberlain once had that note without the poetry. He lost it and lost himself. Perhaps that is why President Wilson dislikes to be reminded of his likeness to the lost leader.

MRS. HUMPHRY WARD

WHEN he was staying at Dollis Hill some years ago Mark Twain sat in the garden one sunny afternoon with a friend of mine, talking of many things, among others of the qualities of women. "Have they humour?" asked my friend. "Well," said Mark Twain, "I don't think they have humour themselves, but they appreciate the quality of humour in others. Now, you see that woman crossing the lawn there." The woman was his wife, and the subject of one of the most beautiful love stories of our time; but he spoke with a grave detachment, as if he were discussing a remote star or an abstract theory. "Now," he said, "I don't suppose that woman ever said a humorous thing in her life; but she always sees the point of my jokes."

It is not my purpose here to discuss the truth or otherwise of Mark Twain's generalisation. If it is true it is obviously subject to conspicuous exceptions. The humour of Jane Austen, for example, belongs to the purest vintage of laughter. It is light as air, swift as a swallow, indisputable as Molière. The eyes of Jane are always demurely downcast, but, like Leeby in *A Window in Thrums*, she notes every fray in the carpet, every kink in the character, every subtlety of the game. I seem to see her sitting immortally in her quiet corner by the fire, knitting with swift fingers, rarely talking, a gentle smile flitting about the corners of her mouth as she watches with spacious understanding the foolish little comedy of life. And George Eliot, too—what summer lightnings of humour play about that formidable brow!

But if, in spite of exceptions, Mark Twain's axiom

is true, Mrs. Humphry Ward is in one respect an entirely representative woman. Like Mrs. Clemens, she probably never said a humorous thing in her life. Her books are as innocent of laughter as they are of impropriety. They are a feast of reason, but they are not a flow of soul. When you approach them you do not feel that you are going to have a rollicking time. You do not light a pipe, and fling yourself into the easiest chair and stick your slippered feet on the mantelshelf. These deplorable manners are suited to the company of Cervantes or Dickens, Fielding or Thackeray. They do not mind them. They even like them. They are people with whom you can be really at home, for they laugh and poke fun and shed tears and run through the whole gamut of the mystery that is within us. But when you take down *Robert Elsmere* or *Marcella* or *Richard Meynell* you behave with decorum. You feel the importance of being earnest. Levity in such company would be like sacrilege. You would as soon think of being gay at a University Extension lecture.

And indeed Mrs. Ward is really an Extension lecturer in disguise. As a novelist she was even born at an Extension lecture. She has told us in the introduction to the Westmoreland edition of her works that *Robert Elsmere* sprang out of revolt against a Bampton lecture which had insisted that disbelief was due to spiritual pride. The revolt first expressed itself in a pamphlet, whose thesis became the text of the novel. It was a happy accident, from the effect of which she has never recovered. It came at a moment of challenge, when thought was breaking new ground, when Gladstone and Huxley were exchanging mighty blows in the reviews, and questions of faith were being brought to the touchstone of the Gadarene swine. It was an incident of a phase that has passed irrevocably. It made Mrs. Ward the most prosperous woman writer since George Eliot, and it revealed to her an incomparable medium for the dissemination of her ideas. And she has been writing pamphlets in the form of novels ever since. It is an unparalleled triumph over natural disadvantages. For Mrs. Ward has every disqualification for the rôle of a successful novelist. She is without the divine gift of humour, lacking which life is tasteless and barren. She is without passion, lacking which imagination cannot sound the depths of experience or scale the heights of vision. She is without the note of individual charm, which makes you love the writer despite his views. And, withal, she is, as I have said, the most successful woman novelist since George Eliot, with—low be it spoken—the possible exception of Miss Marie Corelli.

There are, I take it, two ways of writing novels. You may surrender yourself imaginatively to your characters and let them fight out their battle for themselves. That is the way of the realist. Or you may start from a formula and invent characters to work it out. That is the way of the classicist. It is the way of Mrs. Ward. She labours, it is true, with astonishing industry to make her people live, but they refuse to live. They never extract a laugh or a tear from you, for they cannot laugh or shed a tear themselves. They are abstractions of the mind, that move not at their own volition but at the will of the magician who pulls the strings. They come from the intellect, unfused by the glow of emotion, untried by the fires of pain. And the intellect alone cannot create a character. It is feeling, sympathy, passion which clothe the dry bones with flesh and blood and make them breathe and live. Put Mrs. Ward's novels to a simple test. Name one character from them that moves you with happy memories or even painful memories. You will find it as difficult as it is to quote a line from the poetry of Mr. Alfred Austin.

And so with her landscape. No writer has used the accessories of nature more lavishly than she has done to give atmosphere and reality to her tales. But nature is not won by observation any more than man. It must be felt as Keats felt it sitting in his Hampstead garden—felt so that the song of a nightingale may open up all the windows of heaven and reveal all the wonder and pageantry of the earth. It must be felt as Wordsworth felt it when that "huge peak, black and huge," rose on his vision, or when he saw the dawn break over Lakeland and knew himself "a Dedicated Spirit." It must be felt as it is felt in the Wessex tales, which reek with the breath of the earth, are full of the voice of the woodlands, and are enveloped by the "huge and thoughtful night." Nature, in short, can only be rendered through a delicately sensuous or a deeply spiritual medium. And Mrs. Ward is neither. She is pure intellect. She sits down before a landscape to render it with the same industrious purpose with which she would apply her powerful mind to an ethical theory or a proposition in Euclid. She fills in the picture with extraordinary skill and finish. Everything is there—except the soul of nature. The landscape does not smell of the earth: it smells of the midnight oil.

What, then, is the cause of her unexampled success? Largely, no doubt, it is the result of that happy accident which made her the central figure of the great intellectual conflict of the eighties. It is not a bad name only that is hard to live down. Sometimes a good name is equally obstinate. Mr. Kipling, the artist, died a dozen years ago, about the time of the Boer War; but Mr. Kipling, the writer, still carries on the business, and, in virtue of the work of his famous partner (who is dead), probably receives a higher price per word for anything he writes than anyone else living. He will go on receiving it, and the world will go on buying him, and remarking with unfailing freshness that his latest thing is sadly below his old form. Give an author a good name and he may live on it to a green old age.

It is so, in some measure, with Mrs. Ward. The echoes of that great episode of a quarter of a century ago still reverberate about her name and give her a factitious greatness. Fame is so careless and irrational a thing. Mrs. Oliphant was a much more considerable novelist, a writer of real genius, whose *Salem Chapel* will be read with delight when *Robert Elsmere* and *Richard Meynell* are dusty memories. Yet she never became the lion of the moment, and in her old age was forced to write potboilers to live. But the theme is familiar. Achievement and reward have rarely been adjusted in any sphere of art. Nor is it just to labour the point, for Mrs. Ward has never been false to her artistic conscience. And her success is not the mere reward of a fortuitous hit. It is a tribute to one who has treated her public and her powers with an austere respect, and has made the astonishing discovery that it is possible to use the popular novel as the vehicle of the things of the mind.

Her defect both as a novelist and an influence is a certain chill of the spirit. Her books are the sort of books that one would expect if a Greek statue began to write novels. She is faultily faultless, icily regular, and if not splendidly null, at least splendidly ineffective. She has all the qualities of the Arnold strain—the air of serene, slightly supercilious detachment from the vulgarity of life, the intellectual pride of an aristocracy of culture, the polite scorn of a world that is sensuous, emotional, and lacking a Grecian calm. It is all written in her grave, remote bearing and in the large, placid sculpture of her face, with its high, untroubled eyebrows, its bold, classic nose, the prim, ascetic set of the lips, and the philosophic repose of the eyes. There is about her presence the air of a strayed goddess who has wandered down from Olympus and is rather wondering how she will find her way back again out of this strange rabble of fussy mortals. " I can't help it," said the Lord High-Everything-Else, " I was born sneering." Mrs.

Humphry Ward seems to plead, somewhat in the same spirit, that she was born a little superior.

This divorce from mere humanity leaves her singularly isolated. She is the one conspicuous woman of her time who is definitely and intensely opposed to women's suffrage, again excepting—I am compelled to mention the coincidence—Miss Marie Corelli. Now, I understand women being indifferent to the vote. Most of them are. But I do not understand women being fiercely opposed to the vote. Least of all is it superficially intelligible in the case of Mrs. Humphry Ward, who has always maintained a high standard of social duty, has worked ungrudgingly in the cause of the Children's Play Centres, has founded an organisation for introducing women into local government, and achieved considerable publicity by the enthusiasm with which she chaperoned her son into the representation of West Hertfordshire. Probably the explanation is not that she thinks so meanly of her sex that she would have them kept socially inferior, though this view is not without authority, for the most successful studies of women in her novels are the studies of mean, small-souled women.

The true explanation, I think, is deeper. She thinks meanly of humanity. She is an aristocrat—not a vulgar aristocrat, but an intellectual aristocrat, one whose ideal is of a small governing class of exquisite souls who would behave nicely to the poor, make just laws for them, and generally keep them in their proper station with a firm but gentle hand. In a word, she is against democracy. It is no accident that the heroes of her political novels are usually high-minded Tories with, of course, strong social sympathies, and that Radicals are generally discovered to be fellows of the baser sort. In opposing the extension of the suffrage to her own sex, Mrs. Ward is opposing the widening of the basis of democracy. She is opposing it on a disingenuous plea.

Women should take part in politics, she says, but they should take part in it by "influence"—like that of Marcella over Sir George Tressady, or Mrs. Humphry Ward over the electors of West Herts—but not by the vote. Why should "influence," which is an unpleasant and underhand thing, be permitted to women, and the vote, which is open and honest, be forbidden? The reason is obvious. "Influence" is the weapon of aristocratic ladies. They do not want the vote which they would have to share on equal terms with the schoolmistress and the factory hand, while they can retain the "influence" which is their exclusive property.

And yet may it not be the vote that Mrs. Humphry Ward spiritually needs? She is too remote from humanity. She needs a little of the alloy of our common clay. A visit to the polling booth with her humble neighbour would do her a world of good.

SIR JOHN SIMON

THERE was once a conspirator who when he came to the scaffold made a speech in which he said: "I could never believe it right that some men should be born into the world ready booted and spurred to ride and others ready saddled and bridled to be ridden." And having uttered this protest against the world as he had found it, he took his leave and disappeared through the trapdoor. But the words live, and there could hardly be a better text for a statesman's career. There is one sense, however, in which, no matter how we adjust society or how nearly we approach the ideal of equality of opportunity, there will always be men who come into the world "ready booted and spurred to ride." These do not point to their ancestors or to their acres for their authority. They bring their letters of credit with them from a far country and we honour them at sight. It is not necessary for them to elbow their way through the crowd or to attract attention by insolence or eccentricity. They appear, and the crowd miraculously opens out before them. They prance down a rose-strewn path to a shining goal.

The most conspicuous example of the "booted and spurred" class among the younger public men of the time is Sir John Simon. Macaulay, applying to Byron the fable by which the Duchess of Orleans illustrated the character of her son, the Regent, said that all the fairies, save one, had been bidden to his cradle and had brought their several gifts. But the malignant elf which had been uninvited came last, and being unable to reverse what her sisters had done for their favourite, had mixed up a curse with every blessing. It is difficult to associate fairies with Manchester, but fairies there must have been who revisited the glimpses of the moon about Moss-side forty years ago. And most amiable fairies they were. They crowded round the cradle of John Allsebrook Simon, and showered their gifts upon him. And, best of all, there was no uninvited fairy to turn all the blessings to bitterness—unless, indeed, unqualified Success is a malignant elf in disguise.

There is something to be said for that view. Success in such a measure as Sir John has had it must rob life of much of its adventurous delight. (I speak here only of his public career; in his private life he has known the bitterest sorrow.) To have the sun perpetually shining on one must make one hungry for a rainy day; to find that Apollyon always yields at the first onset must make one yearn for a foe who will not fly. When everything is very easy life must be very hard, and a little dull. It must be what billiards is to an expert. The joy of billiards, like the joy of any other game or business, is in its uncertainty. If you do not know what is going to happen there is delight in the happening. But to the expert, who can go on making cannons and red winners and losers almost in his sleep, billiards must be the last expression of boredom.

Now, to pursue the analogy, it is difficult to imagine that Sir John Simon ever found any problem on the billiard-table that he was not sure of solving. Whatever he wanted he has got. Whatever he wants, one feels that he will get. The prizes of Oxford, the prizes of the Bar, the prizes of Parliament, have fallen to him with a certain inevitableness that causes no surprise. When at thirty-seven he became Solicitor-General no one commented adversely on the appointment of so young a man to so great an office. On the contrary, everyone agreed that there was no other appointment which was thinkable. And yet one has to go back a century—to the days when statesmen ripened early and died young, generally of port wine and free living—to find a parallel to his achievement. Charles Yorke, it is true, was Solicitor-General at thirty-three and grumbled because he had not done better. But Charles Yorke was the son of a Lord Chancellor, and he had a devouring appetite for office which finally led to perhaps the most tragic personal episode in the political life of his time. For when every great and self-respecting lawyer had refused to accept the Lord Chancellorship and become the instrument of George the Third's despotic aims, he took the office, went through an agony of shame and repentance, and died within twenty hours under circumstances which are generally slurred over with a kindly hand by the historian.

It is his freedom from insatiate ambition of this sort which is one of Sir John Simon's chief claims to distinction. His career has been extraordinarily undemonstrative, almost deliberately humdrum. He is like a tradesman—if such there be in these days—who relies absolutely upon the quality of his goods and refuses to advertise or to lavish his arts upon a showy shop window. Montaigne says that when he was a young man without wealth he made a brave show in his attire in order to impress the world; but when he came to his estates he allowed his *châteaux* to speak for him. That is Sir John Simon's way. He leaves his estates to speak for him. He does not advertise. He did not, like his famous contemporary at Wadham, burst upon Parliament with a brilliant display of fireworks. He made his entrance with a plain, unpretentious speech on a practical issue. And as he began so he has continued. He aims neither at epigram nor at wit, and displays a chilly scorn of all rhetorical devices. His appeal is never to the passions, but always to the mind. He treats his audience with respect. He does not offer them an entertainment, but an argument, and his hold upon the great constituency of Walthamstow is a remarkable witness of the power of an intellectual appeal to the democracy when that appeal is based on sound knowledge and just thought. He avoids all exaggeration and over-emphasis. Emotion never breaks through the icy reserve of a temperament naturally under a rigorous discipline, and further restrained by the influence of Oxford, which does not help a man to be expansive. He neither yields to temper, nor betrays it, but goes on his way with an imperturbable gravity and a serene persuasiveness that nothing can disarm. Whether with a jury or a political audience, his method is the same. He weaves no magic spells, indulges in no artifices. Most of the famous pleaders rely largely upon histrionic effects. Sir John Simon is entirely free from them. He has a cultivated urbanity of manner which makes his presence and address pleasing; but his aim is to convince his hearers, never to stampede them. His mind is at once capacious and minute, and it is extraordinarily luminous. There are no dim recesses and no mysteries. The result is a rare atmosphere all light and air, coupled with a certain lack of surprise and of imaginative stimulus. The demesne is wide, but it is all revealed, all radiant, all perfectly laid out. You may wander at large without fear of being lost and without the hope of experiencing any adventure or getting any unexpected vision.

To understand his merits and his limitations, we may contrast him with the two most original minds in the House of Commons—those of Mr. Balfour and Mr. Lloyd George. He has none of the speculative curiosity which makes Mr. Balfour so fascinating and suggestive a personality. Mr. Balfour seems like a voyager in space who strays accidentally into the affairs of our curious little planet and takes an amused interest in them. But it is the sort of interest which Gulliver took in the affairs of the Lilliputians. He hears our lamentations, but he hears them as "a tale of little meaning, though the words are strong." The drama is amusing enough, but it is a drama of marionettes moved by some power that

> " Turns the handle of this idle Show."

It is the realm of ultimate speculation and inquiry that alone truly engages his interest. He himself admitted that the House of Commons did not " extend his mind." Hence his light contact with facts, his apparent levity in handling theories, his perplexing obscurantism. But hence also the refreshing air he brings with him into the narrow realm of dogma and fact; hence his power of stimulating thought and enlarging the horizon of the mind. Sir John Simon has nothing of this quality, and he has as little in common with the empirical genius of Mr. Lloyd George, whose mind works as if there were no such thing as solemn doctrines to be considered and as if the world were a new problem that had to be solved according to the perceived facts and without regard to the operation of theories. No one ever called Mr. Lloyd George a philosophic Radical. Sir John Simon is a philosophic Radical. His thought proceeds on strictly academic lines. In the clear realm of his mind cause and effect follow as the night the day, and political doctrine is an exact science which admits of no question. This formal, unadventurous thinking gives stability to politics. Its value has never been better illustrated than in the co-operation of Mr. Asquith and Mr. Lloyd George—the one giving inspiration and ideas, the other the authority and restraint of a powerful grasp upon first principles.

The admirable clarity of mind of which I have spoken expresses itself in speech equally lucid. The most complex argument " he will unloose, familiar as his garter." He moves through the labyrinths of the law with an easy assurance that communicates itself to the hearer. He has that rare gift of making difficult things seem simple and crooked things seem straight. It is the result first of clear thinking and next of clear speaking. He does not cloud his meaning with words, but exercises that economy which the skilful etcher employs to secure the simplicity of his effect. This does not mean that he always speaks briefly. On the contrary, his speech on the telephone arbitration occupied ten days, and is the longest legal utterance on record. It means simply that he is never verbose or redundant.

In all this it might be supposed that one was describing Mr. Asquith. And in method and habit of mind, clearness of view and of statement, severe restraint of manner, and cold, rather unimaginative processes, there is a strong likeness between the two. Sir John Simon's mind works with something of the same mechanical perfection as the Prime Minister's. "It is as though you put a penny in the slot at one end," said a friend of his, "and the verdict of the jury drops out at the other." But there are differences. Intellectually, Sir John Simon is a slighter man than Mr. Asquith. He gives none of that impression of rude natural force, of elemental power, that his leader conveys, and he will never dominate the House of Commons with the same masculine authority. It would be difficult to explain the wide gulf between the two men in the Parliamentary sense. It certainly does not represent an inferiority of conviction in the younger man. There is probably no one on the Front Bench to-day the quality of whose Liberalism is more universally appraised than Sir John Simon's. It is at once advanced and instructed. It is the product of a Nonconformist origin and Oxford culture, the fruit of whose co-operation is not always so satisfactory.

Sir John Simon's natural foil in the House is Mr. F. E. Smith. The rivalry between these two old foes of the Oxford Union has become the most entertaining problem of personal politics. They are at the poles in temperament and conviction, in their methods of speech, and in the way they pursue their several ambitions. In solid gifts, in the enduring qualities of character, in sincerity of opinion, there can be no doubt that Sir John Simon has the advantage. But in brilliancy and adventurous insolence Mr. Smith is easily first. He is free also from the air of polite weariness that afflicts his rival and gives him an appearance of having found us all rather trivial people and of being bored with our follies.

So far as one can foresee, the career of these two men will be largely bound up with the destinies of the country. Each is in the rare position of having either of the two great offices in the State within his ultimate reach. Sir John Simon has gone farthest, although he has striven least, and in the language that Mr. Smith will best appreciate he looks like the better "stayer." But, on the other hand, he has more rivals in his own stable for the Premiership than Mr. Smith has. For the Lord Chancellorship he has none.

If this sketch seems dull, the fact must be attributed to its true cause. The lives of successful men are dull. If Sir John Simon is to become interesting he must show us that he can fail, he must be discovered in some splendid indiscretion, he must burst through that panoply of restraint with some flame of passion. Then we shall know that he is not only with us, but of us.

A Bonar Law

MR. BONAR LAW

THERE are those who call the House of Commons a dull place. It certainly has its moments of dullness, its somnolent afternoons and its drowsy evenings. It would not be half so interesting a place as it is if the drama never flagged. "You can no more have poetry all gems than a midnight all stars." And a House of Commons that was always brilliant would be intolerable. But there is no stage like it for the variety of its fascination. It is as sensitive as an orchestra. You may know what is happening by the way it sits, by the low breathings that come from it, by the shades of its laughter or its anger, by its significant silences. An ordinary gathering is subject only to the mood of the speaker, and responds with the simplicity of a chorus to the march of the theme; but here, where everyone is an actor, and where the spirit of battle is always present, there are a thousand subtleties of action and emotion which express themselves in their own peculiar voice. At first these nuances are baffling. You do not understand that sudden shout, or that burst of Homeric laughter. Why are all eyes turned into the corner under the gallery? What is the meaning of that momentary gust of anger that is swallowed up in a roar of laughter? After a time the signs become as significant as raised letters to the blind. You are initiate. You follow the swift movement of the play, and know all the notes in the gamut. But even so there will come some day a moment that you cannot translate.

There was one such moment early in the Session of 1912. It was in the midst of the coal crisis, and the House, grave and perplexed, was in a sombre mood.

Suddenly there rolled over the packed benches a thunder of delighted cheering. It swept the Liberal ranks; it swept the Tories. Labour and Irish were caught in the wave. The note was new and perplexing. It was not merely its unanimity; it seemed charged with emotions outside the drama of politics. It was as though the House had suddenly seen a vision. For a moment I was at fault. Then I knew that only one thing could have produced that unusual outburst. I looked down. Mr. Balfour was emerging from behind the Speaker's chair and passing along the Front Opposition Bench to a seat beside—Mr. Bonar Law. It was his first appearance since his abdication of the leadership. And in the shout that welcomed him there was not merely the joy of the House at the return to the stage of the well-graced actor; there was also its comment upon his successor. It was a merciless, a scornful comment on the one side; a comment of humiliation and apology on the other.

Mr. Bonar Law has placed Parliamentary leadership on the level of the Glasgow Debating Society, in which he learned his lessons. It may be that I am unjust to the Glasgow Debating Society. I hope I am. It may be that even there rudeness is resented and the "new style" is not mistaken for the large utterance of statesmanship. But it is inevitable that its reputation should suffer from the association. It is true that great men have been guilty of rudeness in the House in the past. Mr. Chamberlain was often deliberately rude—as when he likened Mr. Gladstone to Herod, called Mr. Dillon a "traitor," or said that Campbell-Bannerman might try to be a gentleman even if he could not be a statesman. But his rudeness had a purpose in it: it might be a mischievous purpose, but at least it was never simply silly or pert. It was a weapon in the hands of a powerful personality. Mr. Bonar Law has mistaken the weapon for the personality.

He has not realised that to be rude with effect you must have the authority of indisputable power. If I am called a fool it depends on who says it whether my feelings are ruffled or serene. A sledge-hammer is a dangerous instrument in the hands of a strong man. In the hands of a child it is only dangerous to the child. And so when Mr. Bonar Law leaps up in the midst of a speech by Mr. Asquith, who had spoken of principles, and says with shrill acerbity, "You haven't got any principles," he does not hurt Mr. Asquith. He only drops the sledge-hammer on his own toes. Mr. Asquith shrugs his shoulders, turns round to his followers, remarks, "We are getting on with the new style," and proceeds unharmed. "The dog it was that died." It is the modern parallel of the Norse legend. Thor takes the hammer and strikes the sleeping Skrymir a blow on the forehead. Skrymir opens his eyes, passes his hand across his forehead, and says, "Did a leaf fall?"

A contest between Mr. Asquith and Mr. Balfour was a contest between two brilliant swordsmen. A contest between Mr. Asquith and Mr. Bonar Law is a contest between a cat and a mouse—an indiscreet mouse. For although Mr. Law is a Scotsman he has not the Scotsman's gift of restraint. When Mr. Asquith tried his familiar King's Counsel arts on Mr. Balfour, his opponent used simply to put his feet on the table and look up at the ceiling with an air of childlike abstraction. His thoughts were beyond the stars. It was not that he did not hear: it was that he did not mean to walk into any interrogatory trap. He seemed to answer those pitiless questions after the manner of the Walrus:

> "'The night is fine,' the Walrus said.
> 'Do you admire the view?'"

But when Mr. Asquith, pursuing the same methods, asked Mr. Bonar Law if he would repeal the Insurance

Act, the new leader said, with the promptitude of a draper's salesman, "Yes, certainly." And then, under the gentle suasion of the panic-stricken Whips, he spent the rest of the evening in drafting a letter to the Press to explain that when he said "Yes, certainly," he meant "Yes, certainly not."

It was an illustration of the working of what one may call the Tariff Reform mind. The Tariff Reform mind is built in water-tight compartments. It looks at one phase of a subject at a time under the firm conviction that there is no other phase. When it passes to another aspect it is equally isolated. It holds mutually destructive ideas without inconvenience and reverences them all with equal fervour—but one at a time. Thus, at Bermondsey it talks about a tax on leather. But at Leicester it forgets that boots are made of leather, and talks about the blessings of Protection to the boot trade. Thus when contesting North-West Manchester, Mr. Law, anxious to placate the people who lived by bread, explained that Tariff Reform would not benefit the English farmer. Then, pained by the dismay he had caused in the agricultural bosom, he issued a statement explaining that what he really said was that while the farmer would not benefit by an import duty on corn which he sells, he would benefit by a tax on what he buys—that is to say, he would not benefit by a tax on his competitor, but he would benefit by a tax on himself. It sounds all very mad; but there it is.

It was as the magician of Tariff Reform that Mr. Bonar Law captured the heart of the Tory party. They were so astonished to find someone who could talk intelligibly on such an unintelligible theme that they flung the mantle of Birmingham over him in a transport of enthusiasm. Mr. Garvin, as the Warwick of the cause, crowned him in pages of delirious prose. He was, according to one, the "bloodless surgeon of debate." He was the man whose head and pockets bulged with death-dealing statistics. They loved his Scotch accent. They extolled him as the hard-headed business man who had made his fortune in Glasgow, where only hard heads make fortunes. (As a mere historical fact it may be well to mention that Mr. Bonar Law's fortune was left to him by a relative—a member of the Kidston family.) And when the "B. M. G." crusade had driven Mr. Balfour into retirement, and it was found that Mr. Austen Chamberlain would not yield to Mr. Walter Long nor Mr. Long to Mr. Chamberlain, the hope of the militant Protectionists was fulfilled, and the Scotch ironmaster became leader.

His leadership shows at once the poverty of the Conservative Party and the change that has come over its outlook. For Mr. Bonar Law is entirely remote from the sentiment and experience of traditional Toryism. His selection is a confession that as a governmental system Toryism is dead. He is neither of the land nor of the aristocracy. He does not represent the public-school system, nor the universities, nor the services. He is not a Churchman and he is a lifelong abstainer. He is more divorced from the old spirit of his party even than Disraeli, who had imagination, the fascination of the inscrutable, and was clothed in a cloak of mystery. Mr. Bonar Law has none of these attractions. He is as unimaginative as the ledger in his counting-house. His speech is dry and colourless, his voice thin and unmusical. He has the intonation and the oratorical method of a Scotch preacher. Close your eyes and your understanding, and you will imagine him in a pulpit, clothed in a black gown, his fingers extended before him and gently tapping each other as he expounds his firstly, secondly, thirdly, and finally. He clips his vocables in the Glasgow fashion, tilts his voice at the end of a sentence, and is fond of the word "the'for'." Unlike Mr. Balfour, whose movements are as flexible as his voice, he stands at the table stiff as a grenadier, his right arm by his side, his left making automatic up-and-down motions from the elbow, his eyes fixed before him and filled with the sadness of incommunicable things. He is as innocent of humour as a dirge and has never made an epigram. But he can sting. His qualities are an unhesitating fluency, an orderly argumentative progression, a certain business-like exactness, and an unaffected sincerity. He is in personal contact a pleasing and modest man. It is only in public that he has adopted methods of controversy which are as new as they are mistaken. He adopted them on a theory. When he opened his career as leader with the declaration "And now I have done with compliments," he felt that he was giving his party a strong fighting lead. They were dispirited and beaten; he would put pluck into them. The intention was good, but the method was wrong. It was reminiscent of the curate in the play when he said, "And now I am going to give you a good hard knock." I do not remember what happened to the curate, but the result to Mr. Bonar Law has been disastrous.

Take the charge of corruption which he levelled against the Government. The Government has made plenty of mistakes. Many of its appointments have been challengeable; but they have not been challengeable on the ground of corruption. They have more often been challengeable on the ground of undue disregard of the party that placed them in power. And the suggestion that public money had been used for the party propaganda on the Insurance Act was an act of gross folly. "Does the right hon. gentleman make a definite charge?" asked the Prime Minister. "No," said Mr. Bonar Law. "I only ask a question." Could futility further go?

For so typical a Scotsman, indeed, his lack of caution is singular. It proceeds from a failure to understand the difference between a platform in the country, where you can say anything you please without much danger, and the floor of the House of Commons, where a hundred keen minds are waiting to swoop down on you; between the licence of a private member whom the Press ignores and the fierce light that beats upon a leader who has equivocal advantage of being reported in the first person. It is largely a consequence of a late arrival in serious politics, a failure to apprehend the atmosphere, and an attempt to live up to a certain theory of leadership rather than to be simply himself. It was because W. H. Smith never tried to " live up " to his position but relied on the intuitions of a plain mind that he was so successful a leader. Mr. Bonar Law does not trust his intuitions. He conceives a part and acts it as he thinks it should be acted. He is naturally amiable and unpretentious, with real democratic leanings and a temperamental distaste for the aristocratic view of society, but circumstances have placed him in a position in which he is not happy and in which he does less than justice to himself by assuming a masterful and bitter manner which is not true to his spirit. Hence the falsity of his note, as in the wild talk about the lynching of Ministers if Home Rule is passed and trouble arises in Ulster. Hence the disastrous brusqueness which invites the crushing retort of swifter and more weighty combatants, and which gives point to the delightful *bon mot* of a member of the Cabinet—" We dig our grave afresh every week, but Mr. Bonar Law fills it up before we can get into it."

He has been swept up on the tide of Tariff Reform. The tide is ebbing. The " two bad winters," which he said would do for the cause what the Irish famine did for the cause of Cobden, have failed him. British commerce, over which he and his colleagues have chanted so many dirges during the past ten years, develops month by month to vast and still more vast dimensions. The tears of the mourners have become the joke of the man in the street, and the parrot cry of yester-year, "Tariff Reform means work for all," has been turned even by the boy in the street into a jingle:

> "Tariff reform means work for all,
> Chopping up wood in the workhouse."

No crusade can survive ridicule. And Mr. Bonar Law himself has turned it to ridicule. He went to the Albert Hall and endorsed Lord Lansdowne's withdrawal of the pledge to submit Tariff Reform to a referendum—a pledge that had been given on the eve of an election in order to influence Lancashire. Immediately, Lancashire Toryism was aflame with revolt. Mr. Bonar Law went to Ashton to face it and quell it. This is not the time, he said bravely, to haul down the flag, and in any case "I am not the man to haul it down." The revolt flamed higher. The electors of Bolton delivered a crushing comment on the new policy. And Mr. Bonar Law went to Edinburgh and hauled down the flag. Food taxes were not to be imposed without a second election. They were, in other words, postponed to the Greek Kalends.

Tariff Reform could not survive such a comedy. It has been laughed out of court, and there is hardly a Tory candidate to-day who does not try to escape its fatal association. Mr. Balfour has won his long battle for the soul of his party. He has lost the leadership in the struggle; but his successor reigns in virtue of a cause that is dead. Such a reign can hardly be long or happy.

MR. H. G. WELLS

" THE best thing that ever happened to me," said Mr. Wells on one occasion, " was to be born." The remark gives the keynote to his personality. A witty young lady has classified literary men as " melancholy blokes " and " cheerful coves." Mr. Wells is the Cheerful Cove. There are some men to whom life is a pilgrimage of pain. Their nerve ends are, as it were, exposed to the brutal contacts of life. Their sensibilities are tortured by everything that happens. They would be unhappy on a bed of rose leaves, for the rose leaves would be crumpled. Genius is often afflicted with this pain of living. Swift cursed the day of his birth. Goethe, who might be assumed to have had a life of singular serenity, told Eckermann in his old age that he had not had a month of real happiness in all his life. Johnson, when pressed to admit that a man was sometimes happy in the moment that was present, answered, " Never but when he is drunk." " There has not been a day in my life," said a distinguished writer of our time, " when I did not wish that I had not been born," and Mr. Watson expresses something of the tragedy of the stranger and the exile in the world in the lines:

" In this house with starry dome,
Floored with gem-like lakes and seas,
Shall I never be at home,
Never wholly at my ease? "

It is the men of action and not the men of reflection who get the joy out of life. Every cricketer knows the meaning of this. He knows the exaltation of that moment when the vague forebodings and terrors which possessed him during all the dread preliminaries of putting on his pads, walking to the wicket, and taking his " middle " vanish at the first true impact of bat and ball. The shock of action steadies him, nerves him, inspires him. He is his own man again. The phantoms of the mind flee with the ball to the boundary.

Perhaps it is because they are so largely men of action that the most conspicuous literary men of to-day are so gay. Mr. Chesterton, Mr. Shaw, and Mr. Wells are engaged less in writing books than in fighting battles. They are concerned not with literature but with life. They do not use words like artists, but like warriors, loving them not for their perfume, but because they hit hard. Each has an enemy and it is the same enemy. It is Things as They Are. Mr. Chesterton takes the world in his vast embrace and tries to heave it back into the Middle Ages. Mr. Shaw and Mr. Wells —flinging jolly gibes at each other, by the way—rush at our poor orb and seek to kick it into centuries unborn. They are all perspiring and they are all happy. Perhaps Mr. Chesterton perspires most, and certainly his laugh submerges those of his rivals beneath its buoyant waves.

But Mr. Chesterton's joy is in repose. Give him an easy-chair and a foeman worthy of his steel, and he will shake the rafters from the dusk of evening to the dawn of day. It is otherwise with Mr. Wells. His joy is not in physical repose, but in motion. He is like a man who runs to keep pace with his thought. The energy of the mind is reflected in the activity of his body. It is as though he is charged with a vitality that is inexhaustible and gives him no rest. It suggests something of that fever of living which characterised Dickens, with whom he has many traits in common, apart from his origin.

A day with him is as brisk as a day at a country fair. He will emerge from his work hot and triumphant, have a thrilling half-hour at the pianola, plunge into those elaborate floor games that he pretends to provide for his children, but which really are for his own amusement; will mystify you with the drolleries of "guyping"—in the creation of which he collaborated with G. K. C.—fling himself into the great war game which he has invented, and which he plays with the fervour of a schoolboy and the intensity of a mathematician, dance you a two-step and sweep you off to dress for charades after dinner. No make-up so inimitable as his, no patter so full of Puck-like fancy. And all the time he is talking. You may imagine you hear the whirr of his mind. He seizes an idea and plays with it as a conjurer plays with the rabbits he extracts from his hat. There seems no end to it and its ramifications. In the soil of that fertile mind the merest suggestion bursts into luxuriant growth. You may make, let us say, a casual allusion to changes in the bookselling business only to find you have embarked upon the causes of the disintegration of society. You may start with soap and end in Sirius. An allusion to chop-sticks will suggest an adventure in a Chinese eating-house off Euston Road, and from that promising hint will spring a fantastic romance that grows before your eyes, with subterranean passages from the Euston Arch to the Marble Arch, dark stairways and secret meetings. "Give me men who steam at the head," said Holmes. Mr. Wells' head is always on the steam.

With all this lavish output of thought and invention he does not forget to garner as he goes. He takes impressions as another man takes snapshots and stores them away for future use. It may be only a trick of the eye you have or a tone of voice: it is recorded in that capacious memory. "Why," said a former comrade of his to me, "since he has given up invention he has lived on photography. I can tell you where such-and-such conversations took place. They are meticulously accurate. So are the descriptions of persons and things. Why, he has this room we are sitting in pictured to the last detail—even to the pattern of the paper on the wall—no, it is the pattern of the last paper." It is only fair to remember that Mr. Wells always denies the charge of individual portraiture, but of the extraordinary exactness of his observation there is no doubt. No one since Dickens has possessed the quality in a higher degree than he does, and such scenes as the opening chapters of *Tono Bungay* show that the child was as observant as the man.

It comes from his intense curiosity about life. If we are curious about things, we have no difficulty in learning about things. It is because we are indifferent that we are dull. Emerson says that if the stars were visible only once in a hundred years, the whole world would await the spectacle with breathless interest. We should know the map of the heavens as we know the map of England. They are visible every other night, and we hardly give them a glance from the cradle to the grave. Mr. Wells has an infinite capacity for being interested. There is nothing in the heavens above or in the earth beneath that he does not want to know about. And once captured the knowledge is no idle trophy, but is woven into the fabric that his restless mind is always weaving. Perhaps it was well for him that he had little formal education. Had he gone through the ordinary machine of culture he would have emerged a learned professor, of whom the great world would probably have heard nothing except once when he revealed his famous theory as to red seaweed to the British Association and once when he died. But he was educated in the sharp school of poverty—his father was a professional bowler for Kent, whose special glory was that he once took four wickets with four balls—graduated in a draper's shop, from which he ran away as Dickens ran away from the blacking factory; and gained his freedom by a hard-won science degree from

London University. And so he emerged an authentic voice from below—a critic of the universe, a challenger of the established, equipped with science and with something of the impish audacity of the swift-witted man who has fought for his own hand from boyhood.

From this unorthodox approach to life comes his untrammelled view of its problems. He sees them freshly and vividly as a child with the understanding of a man might see them. And he sees them with the impatience of an elderly lady who loves tidiness and sees nothing but disorder, fortified by conventions and unexamined formulas. And so he takes his broom to sweep the cobwebs out of the sky and to tidy up the world. It is not that he is a philanthropist or a Marxist or a Fabian. He has sampled all Socialisms and found them vain. Away with the Socialism of condescension! Who is he that he should seek to "raise people," using his own tastes and sympathies as the standard of life? Away with the furtive Socialism, "the benevolent scoundrelism" of the specialist and the expert—this, with a side glance at the Fabians. Who is he that he should regulate the intimate life of others? Away with the Socialism of revolt and class war! Will the substitution of one passion of self-interest for another advance the reign of love? Socialism, as he conceives it, is not primarily a battle against poverty and its train of miseries; poverty is only a symptom of a profounder evil, and is never to be cured by itself. It is a battle against human stupidity and egotism and disorder, a battle fought through all the forests and jungles of the soul of man. Change the economic fabric by all means; it is the outgrown shell of the dead past. But that change is only the incidental aspect of a deeper change, a change in the spirit and method of human intercourse.

The fundamental conflict, in a word, is not between theories, but between emotions—between hate, which is the emotional aspect of antagonism, the expression of the individual's separation from others, and love, which is the synthetic force in human affairs, the expression of the common element and interest. The history of humanity is the history of this conflict—always changing in character and enlarging in scope. The savage loves in gusts one or two about him, and fears and hates all other people. The love of the civilised man widens and embraces his family; widens and embraces his town, his country, humanity. And in widening it changes in character and depth. It becomes less individualised, more an expression of a collective consciousness in humanity, out of which finer individualities may arise for ever in a perpetual series of fresh endeavours and fresh achievements for the race. And in this process hate becomes sublimated, too. For hate in its nature is a good thing. It exists, like love, for the accomplishment of what he calls the Purpose in things. In the ascent of man it is not abolished, but transfigured. It is the active principle in the savage; in the civilised man it is subordinate to love, the instrument of love. We are individuals in order that we may hate the things that have to go, ugliness, baseness, insufficiency, unreality, that we may love and experiment, and strive for the things that collectively we seek—power and beauty. Before our conversion, he says, we did this darkly and with our hate spreading to persons and parties from the things for which they stood. But the believer will hate lovingly and without fear.

Philosophically he suggests Whitman. "My most comprehensive belief about the external and internal and myself is that they make one universe in which I and every part are ultimately important. . . . I see myself in life as part of a great physical being that strains and I believe grows towards beauty, and of a great mental being that strains and I believe grows towards knowledge and power." And to the philosophy of Whitman he joins Whitman's naked candour. Not to communicate one's thoughts without reserve is either cowardice or pride. It is a form of sin. Let us have no privacies or concealments. Wherever he sees a door marked "private" he bursts in and calls all the world to witness the profanation. He will take nothing for granted; however ancient or however respectable it may be, it must stand criticism and pass its test. If it cannot do that it cumbers the ground. And so, with an entire lack of reverence for authority, he goes through society, prodding the splendid apparitions of things to see if they do not contain sawdust after all, and rather pleased if the sawdust falls out. Every question is to him an open question. Even as a boy of fifteen—it was in the drapery days—he gravely discussed with himself the problem of suicide. Ought he to live? Were his dispositions such that he would contribute most to the sum of happiness or the sum of misery? If the judgment had gone against him many things would have slept a little longer; but he entered a verdict for life, and became the disturber of ideas in a time of transition and unrest—himself the most transitory and restless mortal of us all. For though he suggests Whitman in his philosophy and his candour, he has none of that great man's magnanimity and security of faith. Whitman saw all the manifestations of life as the expression of some benignant purpose: Mr. Wells seems only to see in them the material for a new and more perfect floor game. It is the difference between a prophetic vision and a mechanical ingenuity.

He has the defiant spirit of the challenger. "We are going to appeal," he says, "to the young and the hopeful and the curious against the established, the dignified, and the defensive." In such a crusade one must expect rubbers, and Mr. Wells has not been disappointed. But he never takes an attack lying down.

No one is more ready with his fists, or has used them more freely. He has a great facility for making foes, and, though "a cheerful cove," is intellectually "gey ill to live wi'." It is not merely that, with a mind rooted in no sanctities but entirely exploratory and curious, he has no permanent resting-place in any theory or social setting: it is that he is essentially combative and loves

> "To prove his doctrine orthodox
> By apostolic blows and knocks."

His fights with the Fabians are immortal. But in the dialectical battle he was not, I believe, a match for Mr. Bernard Shaw, and the true Fabian remembers the final scenes with triumph.

Mr. Wells, in fact, with his thin voice and restless manner, is not at his best on the platform. Yet it is the platform on which we may see him, for I believe his ambition is to drop all his other activities, to formulate his social doctrines and to preach them from a chair of his own in the midst of London. It seems a mistaken ambition for one who can explore the heavens and the humours of men, create the Kippses and the Pollys and the Popes, and delight a whole world by the children of his fertile invention. But he is, before all else, a preacher and a propagandist, and he will never be happy until he has taken this muddled world thoroughly in hand, cleared up its confusions and its dirt, and set it spinning, neat and clean and orderly, on its old path through space.

MR. LLOYD GEORGE

MR. LLOYD GEORGE tells, with that boyish merriment that makes him so gay a companion, the story of a man who, having saved someone from drowning, was presented with a public testimonial. When, after the eulogies of the mayor, he was called upon to reply, he said, "Really, I have done nothing to deserve this reward. I saw the man struggling in the water, and, as no one else was by, I saw he would be drowned if I didn't save him. So I jumped in, swam to him, turned him over to see that he wasn't Lloyd George, and then pulled him out."

There is nothing unusual in this story except its humour. You will hear the animus without the humour wherever you go. You cannot escape it—in the tram, the train, the 'bus, on the platform, in the Press, even in the pulpit. The amiable doctor who wrote to a certain paper insisting that any member of the faculty who attended Mr. George should be hounded out of the profession was not rebuking his brethren in terms of irony. He was stating what he believed to be the solemn duty of his class. He saw that the pests that afflicted society varied with the ages. Sometimes it was the Black Death, sometimes the small-pox, now it was Mr. Lloyd George. The significant thing is that the more polite the circles in which you move the more bitter is the hostility. I can only dimly imagine what happens when duke meets duke, for I am almost in the same forlorn position as Disraeli when he was writing his youthful novels of the great and the noble. "Your son," said an admirer to old Isaac, "your son must know quite a lot of dukes." "My dear sir," replied Isaac, "I doubt whether my son has ever seen a duke."

But in circles more accessible, hatred of Mr. Lloyd George has become a frame of mind, a freemasonry, a kind of eleventh commandment—unlike most commandments in the constancy with which it is observed. It is doubtful whether any statesman has ever aroused such bitter hostility in " Society." The old lady who, when told at a royal funeral that Gladstone had entered the church, observed that she hoped " he wouldn't make a disturbance," truly reflected the feeling of Society towards that great man. He was denounced as " a Russian spy," he was known to be a kleptomaniac —did not his wife pursue him from jeweller's shop to jeweller's shop and take the silver spoons out of his pocket as fast as he put them in?—even his chivalrous service among the outcasts of the streets was turned to his dishonour, and the music-halls rang with the refrain about letting Ananias and Judas go free " to take in the Grand Old Man." But at least Gladstone had been to Eton; at least he was " one of us "—a traitor, it was true, but still with something of the splendour of the fallen angel about his baleful head. But Mr. George did not go to Eton: he went to a penny village school—worse, a Welsh village school. The uncle who brought him up did not own land; he mended boots—think of it, O Mayfair! He mended boots and preached in a strange tongue in the little tabernacle at the foot of the mountains. And now . . . but words fail Mayfair. It feels that the linchpin has fallen out of the universe. The truth is that someone has turned over a stone in the field, and all the little creatures who have dwelt under it are running about in wild confusion and with wild cries.

And what of the man who has turned the stone? As he sits before you at the breakfast table—for the breakfast hour is his time to talk—he seems the most light-hearted and untroubled of men. Even little Megan does not seem more gay, nor the black pug that snores on the hearthrug more free from care. Perhaps he has been up at an all-night sitting, perhaps he is in the midst of a world crisis. No matter; there is not a care in life, not a cloud in the sky. The sun streams over the broad parade-ground of the Horse Guards outside, it streams in at the window, it streams through the talk. The postman has brought the usual delivery of anonymous vilification (unstamped). The victim is radiant as he reads aloud some new flowers of venom—perhaps some denunciation of his well-known habit of plundering the Treasury. How, if he has not plundered the Treasury, has he built that castle at Criccieth? "Two rooms and a kitchen on the ground floor," interpolates the plunderer gaily. "And I wanted three so badly," says his wife. Mr. George makes no repudiation of the charge; nay, he delights to prove it; he races over the fatal evidence of his misconduct—he owns a motor-car, he is suspected of having a *château* in the South of France, and then there is the Welsh shepherd. You cannot disbelieve the Welsh shepherd, he says. And what did the Welsh shepherd say? "It was when I opened the Tom Ellis memorial. A friend of mine met the shepherd toiling over the mountains to the ceremony. 'Are you going, too?' said my friend. 'Yes, indeed, I'm going to have a look at him. I suppose he's very rich?' 'Well,' said my friend, 'he gets £5000 a year.' 'Yes, indeed,' said the shepherd knowingly, 'but that's not it. *He's near the pile.*'" His eyes dance with mirth at this final and damning proof of his shame. For on his brow, as Mayfair will readily understand, shame is ashamed to sit. No exposure will do him any good—not even the Welsh shepherd's.

Or perhaps one of the letters reveals his secret intention of setting up the guillotine in Whitehall. The idea delights him—he develops it with enthusiasm, he insists that the parade-ground outside was simply designed by Nature and the architect for a place of execution. He discusses who shall go in the first tumbril, and gallops on in sheer revelry of invention. It is the sparkling improvisation of a spirit all fun and fancy. A book arrives by post. "Christina Rossetti." "Yes, sweet meditative verse," he says. "Beautiful—for occasional use. It is like a shelter on the mountain side when you are caught in a storm. You are grateful for it, but you cannot stay in it long. You must get out into the free air and the wind, and even the hail."

And as he puts the book down a little indifferently, you feel for the first time that a chill has come over him. The spirit of that quiet cell of reverie in which Christina Rossetti habitually dwells makes no appeal to the devouring thirst for action which possesses him. He has little use for shelters on mountain sides or elsewhere. He has the fever of motion in the blood, and is always at the gallop. "Rest!" said a famous Frenchman, "shall I not have all eternity to rest in?" And Mr. George, too, is determined to reserve his rest till the great silence falls. He has never learned the gentle art of loafing, never sat on the beach in the sunshine all the morning and flung pebbles at nothing in particular, never felt that intoxicating peace which falls on one when there is literally nothing to do and all the day to do it in. A holiday is splendid for a day, tolerable for two days—the third day you discover that he has flown. He has poetry in him; but it is not the poetry of "wise passiveness." You will never hear him mention Wordsworth. It is the poetry of life and action that moves him—the poetry of sudden and swift emotions, of old romance, with the clash of swords and the hint of battles long ago. He delights to picture those descents from their fastnesses in the mountains of the wild Welshmen upon the towns on the Welsh marches. You may almost catch the thunder of the hoofs and see the flames of the burning towns that they leave in their wake. And at the head of the raiders there rides a slight man with a large head, a gay laugh, and a dancing eye. I think I know him.

For the fundamental fact about Mr. George is that he is a fighter, and, since it is no longer possible to lay waste the towns on the Welsh marches with fire and sword, he is out with other weapons to lay waste English Toryism. He leaps to battle as joyfully as Lord Herbert of Cherbury. "The first words I heard," says that fiery Welshman in his autobiography, "was 'Darest thou come down, Welshman?' which I no sooner heard, but, taking a sword in one hand and a target in the other, I did in my shirt run down the stairs, open the door suddenly, and charged ten or twelve of them with that fury that they ran away."

That is Mr. George's way to the life. A challenge is music in his ears. He is down the stairs and at 'em, and if there are ten or twelve, why, so much the happier. He pinks them all with flashing impartiality, wipes his sword, and goes back to bed. It was so when, as a schoolboy, he roused the young Hampdens of the village school to refuse to repeat the Church Catechism; it was so when, as a young solicitor, he broke the tyranny of the country bench and saw the magistrates file out one after another rather than withstand his onset; it was so in the Boer War, when he took his life in his hand and fought the popular frenzy; it was so in the crisis of the Budget, when he was threatened with disaster if he did not consent to the withdrawal of the land clauses; it was so through the long struggle of the Insurance Act. Even his respect for Gladstone did not mitigate his daring. "What will you do if Mr. Gladstone will not give us Disestablishment?" he was asked in his first campaign. "If I met the King in battle I would fire my pistol at him," came the audacious reply, in the words of his favourite Cromwell. And he did fire his pistol at him later on over the Church Discipline Bill and incurred his Olympian wrath. He will never avoid an issue because it means a fight against great odds. He will attack it the more cheerfully for that fact. He loves to go out against "ten or twelve of them," for he likes to see them run.

And with what gaiety he handles his sword. "There are fanatics in every party," interrupts Mr. "Tim" Healy, sitting lonely in his corner seat. "Yes, even in a party of one," comes the swift retort, and Mr. Healy, who loves a neat stroke, even though it goes through his own body, raises his hat in recognition of the swordsman. "What is the right hon. gentleman's scheme?" he asks Mr. Bonar Law, who has attacked the Government's proposed settlement of the great coal strike. "It is not our business to provide a scheme until we are on the Treasury Bench," says Mr. Law smartly. Mr. George leans forward, smiles, and says winningly, "He wants the strike to last four years." And who that was present can forget the delicious raillery with which, at the Holborn Restaurant, he drove Lord Rothschild out of the fighting line. Never had a Rothschild come into action before. It was the attack on the land that made him forget that the financier is only safe while he is silent. He will not make the mistake again. Mr. George suffers, of course, the disadvantages as well as the advantages of this swift wit. Discretion is never the better part of his valour. It is but a hobbling beldame that cannot keep pace with his wit and his habit of exchanging thrusts with his audience sometimes leads him farther than he means to go. It is natural that one who is so challenging in speech and action should arouse violent hostility. To put him out of the fighting line has become the first article of Conservative policy. Hence the extreme virulence of the Marconi campaign. His rather casual habit in his own affairs had laid him open to attack on a matter of judgment rather than of morals, and, owing to the fury of the storm that broke over him, he came perilously near disaster. He learned then how little mercy he has to expect if ever the battle goes against him.

The intensity of this hostility does not overstate his political significance. So long as he remains effective the struggle will rage around his personality. The problem of the influence of personality in politics is fascinating. When the great adventurer appears the question always arises, Did he make the events or did the events make him? How would the Great Rebellion have fared had there been no Cromwell, with his Ironsides and his Self-denying Ordinance, to sweep away the timidities of the Essexes and Manchesters? What would have happened to the United States had there been no Lincoln, with his pathos and his jest, to keep the soul of the North stable through the dark hour? What would have been the history of France if the great spirit of Danton had not been extinguished on the scaffold? What the history of England if Gladstone had suppressed his distrust of Joseph Chamberlain and made terms with him in 1886?

It may be said that the great uprising in 1906 made Mr. Lloyd George. It certainly gave him his opportunity. It foreshadowed vast changes in the State; but it was formless—a vague revolt against existing conditions. It was for the Government to give direction and shape to that revolt. If it could not do so, then Liberalism had failed, and Protection would be the mould into which the future would run. For three years it seemed that the opportunity had been lost. It is true that great things were accomplished. United South Africa was founded and Old Age Pensions were granted. But we had opened up no new horizons. We were still in the old prison, and the Lords held the key of the gate. The country was turning against the Liberal party in weariness. Men were beginning to calculate when the election would come, and by how much the Liberals would lose. Mr. Chamberlain had made his bid. For the moment he had failed, but if his bid remained without challenge, if Liberalism could offer no alternative policy, then his victory was assured. It was the moment for a great adventure. If the Liberal party was to save its life it must be ready to lose it, and with the instinct of the great strategist Mr. Lloyd George seized on the vulnerable point in the enemy's defences and staked everything on the throw. He attacked the land monopoly. It was a bold stroke. It brought him into conflict with powerful interests in his own party. A formidable cave of Liberal landed magnates threatened him. Journalistic fainthearts appealed to him to withdraw the land clauses of his Budget. Even in the Cabinet I fancy there were hints that the Budget would be better without them—that, in fact, *Hamlet* would be a better play without the Prince of Denmark. "If they go I go," was Mr. George's attitude. "This is a flag worth going into the wilderness with for ten years," he said. But the Prime Minister stood by him immovably, and the triumph was complete. The Liberal cause was rehabilitated, the land monopoly received its first check, and out of the struggle came the defeat of the House of Lords, with all that that defeat implied.

Now in this case personality certainly controlled events. The country was at the parting of the ways; but its direction was doubtful. Already it seemed to be turning, not confidently, but in despair of Liberalism, to Protection, and but for that dramatic stroke of the Budget of 1909 there is small doubt that to-day we should be discussing tariffs instead of social reform. The opportunity was there; but it was personality that seized it and moulded events in this way rather than in that.

It is his union of courage, imagination, and sympathy that makes Mr. George the most formidable figure that has appeared in politics since Gladstone. He has vision touched with a certain humanity, and when he has seen his course he never hesitates or thinks of consequences. He is always out to "win or lose it all." It is the comradeship of high courage that explains Mr. George's well-known admiration for Mr. Chamberlain. "Had he not been driven out of the Liberal party," he said to me once, "there would have been little left for us to-day—he would have settled the land and the lords and social reform." One wonders what in that case would have been the task of this restless, energetic spirit.

But though he shares the adventurous courage of Mr. Chamberlain, his spirit is different. He bears no enmities. If you stand in his way it is true that he brushes you aside ruthlessly, but without malice. He carries himself with a frank gaiety that is irresistible. There is no livelier companion at the table, or on the links, or in the smoking-room. His talk flashes from grave to gay with swift, prismatic changes—now a snatch of a sermon, then a phrase of Welsh poetry, now a joke, then a story—and if you are very lucky he will give you a nigger song that he has learned from little Megan. And his talk all comes straight from life. If he speaks about books it is only as lamps for the present. I found him one day with his mind full of Ferrero's *Greatness and Decline of Rome*, but Cæsar and Brutus, Cicero and Pompey and the rest, only appealed to him as parallels to the men who are on the stage of politics to-day. I will not reveal who in his judgment is the Cæsar, or the Cicero, or the Brutus of to-day. It may serve as an amusing speculation for the fireside.

This intense interest in the actual world is the source of his vivacity and freshness. Whether right or wrong, he is always giving you life at first hand. He does not see things through the spectacles of theorists or the formulas of parties, but with his own eyes. He has no abstractions, and his ideas are flesh and blood. It is as though he has come into the world from another sphere and sees it all anew. No man ever rose to such power with so light an obligation to the past, by so free an action of his own powers of flight, with such an entire reliance upon the immediate teaching of life. All his lessons, like his talk, come straight from the mint of experience. Thus, speaking of the perils of the poor from insolvent friendly societies, he will tell you how, when he was a boy, he used to take his uncle's shilling a week to the friendly society. " And when he fell ill the society had failed." Out of that memory largely came the Insurance Act. The result is that he is the least doctrinaire of men. You will never hear him talk about a theory, and his speeches are brilliant improvisations upon a theme rather than elaborately constructed arguments. They have the quality of vision and swift intuition rather than of the slow processes of thought. He is motived by quick sympathies, not by cold reason, and he is more at home in attacking a visible wrong than in defending an abstract right. His defence of Free Trade, for example, has never been one of his conspicuous achievements. Indeed, he is not happy in defending anything. He prefers to hear the cry, " Wilt thou come down, Welshman ? " and he holds, with the German War Minister, that " the best parry is the lunge." From this reliance upon intuition and impulse comes not merely his strength but his weakness—that light hold of principles, that indifference to doctrine, which he shares with Mr. Chamberlain and which keeps you always a little uneasy. Where will his pragmatism lead him? You rejoice in this splendid breadth of sail that takes the wind so gaily; but you wish you were a little more sure about the sufficiency of the ballast in the hold. And then perhaps your doubts are resolved by remembering how loaded down the ship is with the ballast of old wrongs and present interests, how crushing is the *vis inertiæ* of society, and how priceless and rare is the dynamic energy which Mr. Lloyd George has brought into politics.

And, with all his likeness to Mr. Chamberlain, he has a saving quality that Mr. Chamberlain had not. It is that nearness to the heart of the poor which is, I think, ultimately the motive-power of his life. He came from the people and his heart remains with the people. That, in the absence of a political philosophy, is the compass that may keep his course true—that, and the touch of imagination and poetry that gives wings to his purposes and range to his vision. His peril is that his attachment to democracy is sentimental rather than the product of ideas. He has as little contact with organised labour as he has with the theories of Socialism or philosophic Radicalism, and democratic sympathies alone, unfortified by democratic thought, may in time of stress be strangely perverted. He is the portent of the new time—the man of the people in the seat of power. He has no precedent in our political annals. Our politics have been governed by men who have studied the life of the people as others have studied the life of ants and bees, objectively, remotely. Even Bright, Cobden, Chamberlain were not of the people. They were of the middle-class, and knew the poor as the instruments of the great employer. Mr. George comes out of the great hive itself. In him democracy has found its voice, and to him it will be loyal as long as he remembers.

And he does remember. On the day he became Chancellor he left the House with a friend of his boyhood. As they talked of his advancement he said, "In all my career I do not remember a hand being held out to me from above, and a voice saying 'Dring i fyny yma' (Climb thou up here). But don't misunderstand me," he went on, "there have been thousands of hands which have pushed me up from behind." He does not forget those hands. He does not forget from whence comes his authority and his commission. There have been times when one has feared—times when his light anchorage seemed in danger of yielding to the impact of opportunism. But that memory of his own people, that loyalty to the inspiration of the mountains and the simple traditions of his fathers, has kept his course true. For, however much the glitter of the great world delights him, his heart, untravelled, always turns back to the village between the mountains and the sea. On the day of the memorial service to the late Marquis of Ripon, as he left the Westminster Cathedral with a colleague, he talked of the splendour of the ceremony. And his companion remarked, laughingly: "When you die we'll give you a funeral like that." "No you won't," came the swift, almost passionate reply. "When I die you will lay me in the shadow of the mountains."

MR. G. W. E. RUSSELL

THERE are moods in which there is no companion quite so delightful as Horace Walpole. You may dislike the man with his elegant sneer, his mockery and his heartlessness; but you cannot resist the fascination of his pen. To read his letters is like going a journey into a strange land in company with one who knows everybody, has seen everything, is at home everywhere. The eighteenth century leaps to life at his touch. You take snuff with the great, move in the innermost circle of an exclusive governing society, hear the latest bet and the newest scandal at the club, suffer all the romantic miseries of eighteenth-century travel, share in all the emotions of that wonderful time when the British Empire was being founded east and west, and in the very different emotions of a later time when a foolish king was doing his best to raze the fabric that Chatham had erected. Walpole's Letters, in short, are a stethoscope through which we hear the beating of the heart of the eighteenth century. They do for that time what the Paston Letters do for the fifteenth century and Pepys' Diary does for the seventeenth. They are the secular equivalent of Fox's Journal and Wesley's Journal.

Now there can be no doubt as to the guide who will reveal to posterity the intimate mysteries of our own day. It is, I know, a hazardous thing to predict immortality for one's contemporaries—for those, that is, whose claims rest not upon deeds but upon some forms of artistic achievement. Posterity selects its own favourites, and of one thing only can we be sure: that they will not be the popular favourites of to-day.

They will not be Bernard Shaw or H. G. Wells. "He who browses on his glory while it is green does not garner it when it is ripe." The brilliant journalist and propagandist pays the price of his success by extinction. He belongs to his time and dies with it. But among the men of this generation Mr. G. W. E. Russell is, I think, as sure of immortality as Francis Thompson, though for vastly different reasons. He is sure of it because when posterity wants to gossip about our time it will be to his fireside in Wilton Street that it will go. It is his letters and his causeries that will tell our grandchildren all about us. He is our reporter to posterity. He is the "chiel amang us takin' notes," and, faith, "he prents 'em." He stands a little aloof in spirit from our giddy activities, his pen ever in his hand, his face lit by a kindly but searching cynicism. He writes with the airy detachment of one who is at a puppet show. Our antics delight him, he follows our excursions and alarums with unflagging interest; but he is always outside the play. He is among the Olympians—the onlooker who sees most of the game.

It is not that he is a mere dilettante. He shares the persiflage and irony of Walpole; but behind the mask there is a genuine passion for humanity and for noble causes. He has the temperament of the aristocrat, and cannot help approaching you from an altitude of his own. It is not the pride of a noble ancestry of which he is conscious so much as the pride of a long tradition of culture and high thinking. He is sorry to be a little superior, but he cannot help it. And he takes his revenge on his aristocratic sympathies much as Spurgeon dealt with his Tory sympathies. "You ought to mortify the old man," said one of his friends apropos of Spurgeon's enthusiasm for Liberalism. "I do mortify him," said Spurgeon. "You see, my old man is a Tory. I make him vote Liberal. That mortifies him." In the same way Mr. Russell's old man is an aristocrat. He mortifies him by making him an uncompromising democrat. He calls himself a "Gladstonian," and reveres above all things the memory of the great man under whose auspices he came into politics, but his views far outstrip Gladstone's. "I have always," he might say with the late Lord Ripon, "been in favour of the most advanced thing in the Liberal programme. Just now the most advanced thing is Home Rule; so I'm a Home Ruler." That is Mr. Russell's way. He is always abreast of the band—sometimes ahead of it. He was preaching the gospel of Social Reform while the Liberal party was still eating the husks in the wilderness. He welcomed the Budget, he rejoiced in the attack on the Lords, he was one of the founders of the Progressive cause in London. Home Rule, Welsh Disestablishment, the cause of Labour—all find in him an enthusiastic champion. You cannot be too advanced for him. He does not care who leads so long as he gives a strong lead. And to that lead he will march and sing *Ça ira* with anybody.

In all this there is nothing of the mere perversity of the younger son. Mr. Russell's politics spring not from his class, nor even from revolt against his class, but from his religion. He was once rebuked in the House of Commons by Mr. Jesse Collings for saying they were a part of his religion—as though religion were either a plague that would poison politics or an invalid that, in Holmes' phrase, has to be taken out in a closed carriage with a gentleman in black on the box seat. Mr. Russell does not understand that frame of mind. He is a politician because he is a Christian. From his earliest days religion has been the main interest of his life. "My home," he says, "was Evangelical, and I lived from my earliest days in an atmosphere where the salvation of the individual soul was the supreme and constant concern of life. No form of worldliness entered into it, but it was full of good works, of social service, and of practical labour for the poor. All life was lived, down to its minutest detail, 'as ever in the Great Taskmaster's eye.'" Oxford changed the Evangelical to an Anglo-Catholic; but it only deepened the religious current of his life, and it is upon that current that his political barque has sailed.

It is this fact that has to be remembered in estimating Mr. Russell. The cynic and the satirist is on the surface. Behind Walpole is the hot gospeller of righteousness. Hence his devotion to Gladstone: hence his indignation against Lord Rosebery, under whom he had served with such enthusiasm as an Alderman of the London County Council, and under whom he served also in those miserable days of 1895, when that unstable genius brought the Liberal Party to disaster. "Since then," said Mr. Russell afterwards, "we have had fourteen years of picturesque eloquence about things in general; ill-timed interventions in current politics; speeches which required letters to explain them, and letters which could only be elucidated by speeches." Has Lord Rosebery ever been better summarised?

Perhaps Mr. Russell was a little angry that his own political career was extinguished in that great *débâcle.* He had seemed marked out for distinguished service. It is not difficult for a man of family to make a position in politics. Very modest abilities will carry him swiftly on to the Treasury Bench. But Mr. Russell had quite exceptional abilities—a genial presence, enthusiasm and ideals, and a real gift of eloquence. His speech on the Welsh Disestablishment Bill of 1895 was easily the most memorable delivered on that occasion. I may recall its peroration, because it illustrates not only his oratory, but also his attitude to the Politics of Church and State. "I am persuaded," he said, "that it would be a proud and happy day for the Church when, in reply to the just boast of the Nonconformist communities that they were 'free born,' she was able to say, 'With a great sum obtained I this freedom.' . . . We claim for the Church of which we are members, and just now especially for the Welsh branch of it, freedom from the control of those who do not believe her doctrines or share her worship; freedom alike from the trammels and allurements of a State alliance; freedom to discharge, in the uncorrupted simplicity of a pure devotion, that great spiritual commission which she holds neither from Kings nor Parliament, but from the Church's supreme and invisible Head."

But posterity will gain what Parliament lost. And after all, many can fill an Under-Secretaryship, but no one else has such a glorious gift of gossip as he has. No one has so much to tell or quite such an easy charm in telling it. To live with his books is like living in the best society without the trouble of getting there. It is to have the entrée to all the best clubs without the preliminary of paying the subscription. It is true that he is an incurable Londoner, that he cultivates no Strawberry Hill like Walpole, and that he does not care a row of pins for anything outside the limits of Charing Cross and Kensington Church. But that is the note of the diarist and talker. Johnson hated to leave London. "Yes, sir, I would like to see Giant's Causeway, but I would not like to *go* and see it." In that reply Johnson speaks for all the tribe. There never was a more entirely urban spirit than Mr. Russell's. He himself has described his tastes. It was when he was asked what he would do if he were a millionaire. "If I were a millionaire ten times over," he said, "I could not conveniently eat and drink more than I do. 'If,' as Mr. Pecksniff said, 'we indulge in harmless fluids we get the dropsy; if in exciting liquids, we get drunk. What a soothing reflection is that!' And so about all the main incidents of my life. None of the novel ways of spending money make the slightest appeal to me.

As I live constantly and inveterately in London, I could not buy landed estates. I have never in my life killed anything larger than a wasp, and then in self-defence, so I should not want a deer forest. As to yachting, I say with the late Lord Granville that 'if I was not sick I should be bored.' Music is to me only regulated noise, so a box at the Opera would have no charm. I hold with Miss Pross in *A Tale of Two Cities* that if Providence had intended me to travel, it would not have cast my lot in an island."

And so he dwells delightedly in the midst of what Wordsworth calls this

> " . . . monstrous ant-hill on the plain
> Of a too-busy world,"

and studies the ways of the ants, recording their amusing habits, quaint sayings, and odd tricks. He puts it all down in books and letters and diaries—has been putting it down for half a century, for he has kept a diary since he was twelve, and written myriads of letters on any provocation and none. He is the most instant correspondent I know. You write by one post and have the answer by the next—and not a perfunctory answer, but a jolly letter spreading over page after page with quips and cranks and stories and sly thrusts and ironical comments. And he will go on answering letters for ever and ever, and each one is longer than the one that went before and more subtle and elusive and gay. It is a commonplace to say that the art of letter-writing is dead. " I shall write a penny letter to you next time," said Carlyle to his mother on the eve of the advent of the penny post, and he foretold the end of the old elaborate letter. The prophecy was true. The penny post killed the letter, and any remnant of individuality that remained in it has disappeared before the typewriter. But Mr. Russell — Radical though he is—belongs to the eighteenth century in his love of old ways and long letters. His curiosity is insatiable. An obscure remark in a newspaper will bring from him an inquiry as to its meaning. And from behind the obscurity he drags forth some curious fact of personal history or tradition. And then he is more happy than if he had found the philosopher's stone. I fancy him counting his new treasures at night as the miser counts his money or the nun her beads.

His talk is as fascinating as his writing. Indeed his writing is only his talk written down. It is the talk of one who has both wit and wisdom in such abundance that he has no need to hoard either. He can be sardonic and withering; but the acid of his tongue is always qualified by an essential good nature. His kindliness has taken no pleasanter form than his services to young men. "The youth of a nation are the trustees of posterity," he says, and no one has kept his bachelor's home a more constant refuge for strangers in the great city, especially strangers who have had that "greatest intellectual advantage which a man can enjoy," an Oxford education. Still, he suffers the Cambridge man and "the lesser breeds without the law" quite amiably.

His dreams are of building churches and pulling down slums. If he were rich, he tells us, he would be the greatest church builder in England. He would endow each church he built with money to maintain a body of resident clergy, adequate to the task of celebrating day by day the Divine Liturgy and the auxiliary offices with all the staid splendour of the purely English rite. "And I should rejoice in the conviction that a church so designed and so ordered not only promoted the glory of God and extolled His faith, but also served the social needs of humanity by offering to every child of toil a resting-place, a sanctuary, and a home."

It is a noble dream. Let it rest at that. We are content that Mr. Russell should go on telling us merry stories and correcting our follies with his genial satire.

MR. HILAIRE BELLOC

Some wit has divided society into two classes—dukes and other people. This is a mistake. The true classification should be—the British people and Mr. Belloc. One ought, of course, to put Mr. Belloc first, but perhaps he will forgive the slight for the sake of the cadence. It is not intended to suggest that Mr. Belloc is inferior to the other forty-five millions of us. That would be absurd. No one would recognise its absurdity more readily than Mr. Belloc, for among his many transcendent qualities humility is not conspicuous. He would agree with Hazlitt that it is the least of all virtues. Indeed, he would probably go further than Hazlitt, and say it was no virtue at all—except in other people. In them it would have a certain grace and fragrance; it would be a confession of the ignominy of not being Mr. Belloc. It would almost entitle them to forgiveness.

It was the capital crime of the Liberals when they came into power in 1906 that they forgot Mr. Belloc. They acted as though they were unaware that he was among them—that he, who had served in the French artillery as a conscript and knew more about war than anybody else could possibly know, who had burst upon Oxford like a tornado and swept it with the whiffs of his Gallic grapeshot, who had all the secrets of history in his private keeping and had turned the Froudes, the Freemans, and the Stubbses into discredited back numbers, who had written novels and satires and poetry and biographies and histories, who had discovered the French Revolution and put Carlyle in his place, who had invented a new mediæval Europe after his heart's desire, who had tramped through France and Switzerland to Rome, and from Algiers to Timgad, and had written books about both, with pictures from his own hand, who could instruct you in art and explain to you the philosophy of Classicism as easily as he could sail a boat, mow a meadow, or ride a horse—they forgot, I say, that he was the Liberal member for South Salford. They formed a Ministry without him. They did not offer him even a paltry under-secretaryship when it became vacant. In a word, they passed him by.

It need not be assumed that Mr. Belloc would have taken office. I do not know. So turbulent a spirit could certainly not have run in harness long. But to be ignored, to be passed by for the Aclands and the Macnamaras and the Seelys—that was unforgivable. It revealed the sham of Liberalism, it disclosed the corruption of the party system, it made it clear that England was governed by a nest of rogues, chiefly Jews—probably all of them Jews, or if not Jews, then the friends of Jews. And if not Jews or the friends of Jews, then Puritans. And if there is anything more unspeakable than a Jew, it is a Puritan. For to the abominable fact that he has doubts about the infallibility of the Pope, the Puritan adds an infamy that puts him outside the pale of humanity. He does not drink beer.

Now there are sins which are venial and there are sins which are deadly; but there is one sin before whose scarlet front all other sins pale. It is to refuse good beer. He who would be a man, says Emerson, must be a Nonconformist. Nay, says Mr. Belloc, he who would be a man must drink beer. I think his ideal of a man is the Sussex yeoman of whom he loves to tell, who rode up to a country inn and called for a pot of beer. And having drunk it he called for another and drank that. Then he smacked his lips with approval and got down from his horse. "I'll hev some of that ale," said he. Beer is the soul of gaiety and good comradeship; it is the symbol of a chivalrous spirit. In its amber flood is the rapture of the poet and the passion of the hero. Come, says he to all the world, let us drink beer and be merry and wise.

And so with a flagon for his emblem he sets out on his jehad against Jew and Puritan, routing them out of the holes where they skulk, scorching them with his satire, cursing them by bell, book, and candle. If you cross his path, then sure the trail of Jew or Puritan is over you. It is clear that either you don't eat pork or don't drink beer. Though you have been his bosom friend, yet shall old friendship not save you from scourging. When Charles Masterman, who had shared his dialectical revels in the old *Daily News* days, was given office, he turned and rent him as though he were a heathen or a Turk. He pursued him down to Bethnal Green, he told the electors that he had bartered his principles for £30 a week, and, if I remember aright, even discovered some wholly illusory relationship between his wife and the Rothschilds.

For the gospel of beer, though it may make you merry and wise, does not make you merciful to your enemies. The fact that they are your political enemies is proof that they are capable of any infamy. When he left Parliament he declared in a speech at Worthing that he had left it "perhaps because the bribes were not large enough; but probably because he was getting sick of the vilest and dirtiest society in which he had ever mixed in his life." It is this ferocity of suspicion which is Mr. Belloc's peculiar contribution to political discussion. It is not enough to prove that your opinions are wrong: it is necessary to prove that you are a scoundrel. It is not enough, for example, to prove that the Insurance Act is a hideous mistake: it is necessary to prove that it is a cunning plot on the part of "George"—for when Mr. Belloc disapproves of a man strongly, he drops the civility of a prefix—to destroy the liberty of the working man in the interests of the rich manufacturer. Perhaps this confusion of opinions and morals is due to the Frenchman in Mr. Belloc. In England there is a prejudice in favour of distinguishing between a person's views and his character. It is held that a man may be wrong in his opinions, and yet right in his motive, and honourable in his personal conduct. Most of us, I suppose, have known men whose opinions we shared, and whose personality made us ashamed to share them, and, on the contrary, men whose opinions we hated and whose characters we loved. It is the lack of this discrimination on Mr. Belloc's part that made one of his disciples say to me once, "I share Belloc's opinions about politics; but I hate his opinions about persons."

The truth is that Mr. Belloc had the misfortune to be born in the wrong country, and in the wrong century. It is in the France of the Great Revolution that I always picture him. What a figure he would have made on that tremendous stage! What deeds he would have done! I see him thundering at the Palais Royal and in the Assembly, the square, pugnacious face red with internal storm, his foes redder under the lash of his terrific tongue. I see him at the head of the mob wherever the mob surges, his head bare, his voice rising shrill above the storm. I see him bearding the mighty Danton and hurling hot bolts against the supple Robespierre. I see him at last, standing erect and defiant in the tumbril as it lumbers along the Rue St. Honoré to the Place de la Revolution. He has had his day and is content to pay the price.

For he is made for a world in tumult and disorder, where thrones reel and blood flows and a man can talk at the top of his voice. "The canker of a calm world and a long peace" bores him. It offers no escape for the dynamic fury of the man. He boils with energy. His talk, hard, brilliant, cocksure, thunders along in a ceaseless torrent. He will write an article while you are seeking for a phrase, and books flow from him as fluently as rain from April skies. But what are books and what is talking to a man who heaves with volcanic fires?

It is this energy of mind and body that has won him his greatest success. For in the Roman "triumph" of Mr. Belloc the principal feature will not be himself, but a figure that towers above the rest "like some tall Ammiral," whose girth is Falstaffian and who follows him faithfully wherever he goes. He is a creature of wonderful parts and infinite jest, of an abounding good nature and a chivalrous spirit. He can perform miracles of intellectual jugglery.

> "He'd undertake to prove by force
> Of argument, a man's no horse."

Nay, he would do more: he would prove he was a horse. But his most miraculous quality is his loyalty to Mr. Belloc. Wherever that impetuous Rupert rides he thunders after him with mighty trumpetings and vast perspiration, scattering death and destruction in his laborious path. It was in the days of the war that this great Rabelaisian comradeship began, with laughter and flagons and ballads in the old *Speaker* and thunders in the *Daily News* and jolly battles with the Jingoes and withering blasts for the Jew financiers when

> "Those three hundred fought with Beit,
> And fair young Wernher died,"

as Mr. Belloc sang in immortal strains. It was the hero in Mr. Belloc that captured Mr. Chesterton's heart. For Mr. Chesterton is the boy who refused to grow up. The world is for ever filled with knights and dragons and Dulcineas in horrid dungeons. Spiritually he is with the Rolands and the Amadises of old romance; but Nature has given his chivalrous spirit a vast and unadventurous envelope of flesh, and he cannot chase the dragons himself. But Fortune has provided him with a physical counterpart, and so he watches his volcanic leader flashing into the lists and he winds his mighty horn to cheer him on. There is in him that limitless devotion which Bardolph expressed so touchingly for Falstaff when someone said that that knight was perhaps in hell: "Would I were with him wheresoe'er he be, whether in heaven or in hell."

In the mediævalism that binds them together there is a difference. To Mr. Chesterton the Middle Ages were an Arcadian realm of joyous life. To Mr. Belloc they were something more; they were a realm in which the Church was supreme. It is here that we touch the mainspring of his career. He is out to win England back to Rome. He represents the Oxford Movement of the forties, translated into terms of beer and martial songs. He plays the swash-buckler to Newman's saint. He talks much of democracy, but it is a democracy that goes to Canossa of which he dreams—a democracy that takes Becket and not Bentham for its patron saint. He is, in fact, that rare bird, a French clerical in English politics. His type is familiar across the Channel: it is the type of which Déroulède and François Coppée were representatives: a type which is always crusading against the civil power in the interests of the ecclesiastical power. It is this master motive that runs through all his career. When the conspiracy against Dreyfus was exposed, his voice rose like a hurricane in defence of the anti-Dreyfusards. When the Congo horrors shocked the world, he braved the storm on behalf of the wretched Leopold. When Ferrer was shot after a secret trial for an offence he did not commit, it was he who justified the shooting. It was not that Dreyfus was a traitor to France or Ferrer a traitor to Spain; it was that both were outlawed by the Church. The one was a Jew, the other a rebel against the clericalism of Spain. Rome will tolerate no rival hegemony, whether of Jews, or Freemasons, or Socialists. And Rome never had a more gallant or less scrupulous champion than Mr. Belloc.

His gifts are astonishing, and beyond his gifts is his assurance, which is without parallel. He cultivates an airy omniscience with delicious insolence. He finds it is popular. We like to be reminded that we are mostly fools. We like to hear him say, "Come, good people, gather round and listen. . . . Come, my dear little Anglo-Saxon, Celto-Iberian, and Teutonico-Latin Oddities." It is pleasant to hear this miracle on two legs condescending to poke fun at us. And then how charmingly he dismisses us from lecture or essay, as when, after telling of his marvellous adventures in a crazy boat in the North Sea, he bids us run away and sail too: "You will talk less and think more; I dislike the memory of your faces. I have written for your correction. Read less, good people, and sail more; and, above all, leave us in peace."

And this habit of scornful irony enables him to convey impressions beyond his facts, impressions of unfathomable knowingness, of soaring in altitudes of erudition where you would not dare to follow him. He is the supreme master of the art of "talking through his hat." He will do it with a gay audacity that silences you and leaves you with your head spinning. Authorities, facts, instances, proofs, tumble out in a torrent; they submerge you; they sweep you away; they fling you up a bruised and battered wreck. And all the while you suspect that if you only had time to think, time to turn round, time to stem that torrent, you would find some of his authorities a little shady, some of his facts a little thin. It is the impetus of the man that settles you.

Sometimes, of course, he has his misfortunes. Long experience of the stupidity of the world and of the timidity of men has at times encouraged him to go on ice that will not bear. There was an example not long ago. He had written a work on *Warfare in England*, and the *Times* reviewer, in dealing with it, said he was insufficiently equipped with detailed knowledge of his subject. Mr. Belloc replied in a letter beginning thus: " Your reviewer picks out the campaign of Evesham in 1265 as a proof that I am insufficiently equipped with ' detailed knowledge ' of my subject. I am at a loss, in the light of the original authorities, to seize his meaning." And then, with an air of casual munificence, he runs through his authorities, of which the first is Matthew Paris. To the letter was appended a footnote by the reviewer, who said, " He (Mr. Belloc) tells us that he has perused Matthew Paris on the campaign of Evesham in 1265. Now Matthew Paris' *Chronicle* ends in the year 1259, and he died in that year (see *Dictionary of National Biography*). Mr. Belloc cites as his primary authority a narrative which does not exist, and which he cannot therefore have read." It was an unfortunate slip, and Mr. Belloc was, for one memorable occasion, silenced.

But, after all, it is not facts or politics we want from Mr. Belloc. He has more precious merchandise than these. His novels I find tiresome with their unceasing irony and their obsession about the corruption of English politics; but his books of travel, his essays on anything or nothing, his nonsense verses for children, his poems and his ballads, are priceless. What wit there is, what vitality! What a splendid joy of living sings through his pages! There has been nobody like him since Borrow; nobody so well worth following over the white ribbon of road, or the mountain track; nobody who will give you the same spacious sky, the same jolly breezes, the same sense of the great, happy, enduring world that lies for the asking outside our bickerings and strivings. And when he sings, how can you resist joining in with such gallant stuff as this:

Pillars of Society

" The great hills of the South Country
They stand along the sea;
And it's there walking in the high woods
That I could wish to be,
And the men that were boys when I was a boy
Walking along with me. . . .

If I ever become a rich man,
Or if ever I grow to be old,
I will build a house with deep thatch
To shelter me from the cold,
And there shall the Sussex songs be sung
And the story of Sussex told.

I will hold my house in the high wood
Within a walk of the sea,
And the men that were boys when I was a boy
Shall sit and drink with me."

That strain again, Mr. Belloc, an it please you. Give us that strain and we care not whether you be friend or foe.

THE TEMPLE PRESS LETCHWORTH ENGLAND